VICTIMIZATION
AND THE AGED

VICTIMIZATION AND THE AGED

PETER YIN, Ph.D.

Assistant Professor of Sociology and Social Work
The College of Arts and Sciences
Memphis State University
Memphis, Tennessee

CHARLES C THOMAS • PUBLISHER
Springfield • Illinois • U.S.A.

Published and Distributed Throughout the World by
CHARLES C THOMAS • PUBLISHER
2600 South First Street
Springfield, Illinois 62717

© *1985 by* CHARLES C THOMAS • PUBLISHER

ISBN 0-398-05079-1

Library of Congress Catalog Card Number: 84-16160

With THOMAS BOOKS *careful attention is given to all details of manufacturing and design. It is the Publisher's desire to present books that are satisfactory as to their physical qualities and artistic possibilities and appropriate for their particular use.* THOMAS BOOKS *will be true to those laws of quality that assure a good name and good will.*

Printed in the United States of America

PS-R-3

44493

Library of Congress Cataloging in Publication Data

Yin, Peter.
  Victimization and the aged.

  Bibliography: p.
  Includes index.
  1. Aged—United States—Crimes against. 2. Victims of crimes—United States. I. Title.
HV6250.4.A34Y56   1985   362.8'8'0880565   84-16160
ISBN 0-398-05079-1

TO
SHIRLEY
FOR BEING THERE

ACKNOWLEDGMENT

Several people read earlier drafts of this manuscript and offered insightful suggestions. My thanks go to Graves Enck, Katherine Frank, David Giacopassi, Jerry Michel, Larry Petersen, Paul Reynolds, Marsha Shine, and Karen Wilkinson. However, I especially thank my wife, Shirley, and my daughter, Sara, for their endurance throughout this project.

CONTENTS

Acknowledgement   vii

Chapter
1. Introduction   3
2. Ordinary Crimes   11
3. Fear of Crime   31
4. The Effects of Victimization and Fear of Crime   62
5. Fraud   94
6. Elder Abuse   105
7. The Justice System   129
8. Implications and Suggestions   155
References   175
Appendixes   189
Index   196

VICTIMIZATION
AND THE AGED

INTRODUCTION

Older people as crime victims is a fairly new research focus in gerontology. In the White House Conference on Aging of 1971, for example, no segment of the program was specifically planned for discussion on criminal victimization of older people (Cook, 1981). Instead, a Special Concern Session entitled "Legal Aid and the Urban Aged" was added to the program at the very last minute. It was the activities of this session that provided one of the many final recommendations of the conference, that "police protection of the elderly should become a top priority" (Cook, 1981:129).

The minimal recommendation that emerged out of the special session on crime and the aged is understandable. Very little was known in 1971 about criminal victimization of the aged. Research on this topic had yet to begin, and public attention on the plight of older crime victims was virtually absent. Back then, the prevalence of crimes against older people was not known, nor was the impact of victimization on older victims. People were not aware of the fear of crime among the aged, and the idea that some older people may be abused by their very own adult children was virtually unknown.

The situation, however, was changed in the 1970s. The decade after the White House Conference on Aging of 1971 saw a new literature on victimization of the aged mushroom. Journal articles, scholarly books, in-house reports, research grants, and even mass media attention and congressional hearings had increased substantially. This attention continued into the first half of the 1980s. As of this moment, the study of older people as crime victims has matured into one of the major areas of research in gerontology.

The purpose of this book is to provide a comprehensive overview of the literature on crime victimization and the aged. In addition to an overview, the book will synthesize and integrate works by a diversity of researchers, from gerontologists to criminologists. The book will also interpret and re-interpret published statistics and data on victimization and older people, providing new insights along the way. New theories and typologies will be constructed to further understanding. Suggestions for future research, for example, in terms of research designs and measurements will be recommended.

DEFINING VICTIMIZATION

What is victimization? There are two different approaches to this question. One way is to define victimization broadly, extending beyond legal criteria. For example, inmates of inhumane prisons, subjects of medical experimentation, innocent persons charged with a crime, or even entire groups of people, such as immigrants or ethnic minorities, can all be considered victims (see Galaway and Hudson, 1981). This broad approach to defining and conceptualizing victims has been advocated by several gerontologists. Hacker (1971), for example, considered institutionalization in nursing homes as a form of oppression and social victimization of older people. Along the same approach, Rifai and Ames (1977:47) define victimization as a social condition of oppression and power, "in the broadest sense, social victimization can be considered as occurring when any individual is adversely affected by some aspect of society over which he or she has little or no control." According to Rifai and Ames, the conditions of older people fit this conceptualization of victimization well. Older people enjoy less income, they are discriminated against because of their age, and health care programs for older people, such as Medicare, are inadequate in their coverage. Similarly, Reiman (1976) believed the process of aging itself is a form of social victimization. Because of prejudices toward older people, the implicit message is that it is acceptable to take advantage of and victimize the aged. Crime victimization is but the tip of the iceberg.

The merits of this broad approach are obvious. The interest in studying older people as victims stems from the sentiment that the aged are often wronged in their day-to-day living. Hence, there may appear to be little reason to restrict studying only criminal victimization. After all, crimes are no more than those acts sanctioned by society. Just because an act is not considered a crime does not make the act right. Yet, considering criminal victimization and what may be called unethical actions together lead to many problems. The most obvious one is whose ethical standard should be used. Unlike crimes which are explicitly prohibited in criminal statutes, unethical acts are not. What would be considered an unethical act towards an elderly person by one segment of society may not be by another segment. For example, a pattern of ignoring the requests of elderly patients in a nursing home may be considered unethical by family members of the patients, but in the eyes of nursing home staff, it may be considered perfectly reasonable.

In this book, a more narrow approach will be employed. Victimization specifically refers to crime victimization, an act in violation of the criminal law in which one or more victims are involved. Examples of victimization include burglary, assault, and theft. Acts which are more unethical than criminal in nature will not be considered. The strength of this more narrow approach to the former is that the criminal element of victimization is emphasized. Grouping criminal victimization and social victimization together, as in the broad approach, undermines the seriousness of criminal behaviors and the suffering of victims.

If victim and victimization are defined from the criminal law perspective, who then are the older victims? Without going into an elaborate discussion on the social perception of age and aging, a victim will be considered here as "older" or "old" if he or she is above age 65. There is no apparent reason for using this age other than its common use by both researchers and the lay public. Later on, when statistics on victims and their ages are examined, this definition of old will serve a convenient purpose.

A book devoted to the focus of older victims of crime immediately raised an apparent question: why this particular age category of victims? Does it not presuppose that older victims are somehow different from younger victims? This concern can be addressed in two ways, normatively and empirically. Normatively, one can argue that older victims are, indeed, different from younger ones. While victimization is never perceived as a pleasant event, victimization of older people may be considered particularly despicable (Geis, 1977). Older people are weak and vulnerable, and like children, they should be especially protected and spared from victimization. The fact that victimization of older people violates people's conscience more than victimization of the young is clearly shown in the mass media. Journalists in selectively reporting victimization of older persons simply reflect the fact that such victimizations are more sensational and more capable of arousing people's sympathy, compared to victimization of middle-aged and younger adults.

On the other hand, whether the patterns of victimization of elderly persons are empirically different from those of the young is a more difficult question. This can only be assessed by a careful review of the research on victimization. Although this book is focused on older victims, no assumption is made about differences in victimizations of different age groups. In fact, unless empirical evidence or compelling reasons exist, and these will be discussed when they do, it is safer to assume that victimization of the old is not unlike those of the young. In this book, discussions on research on younger victims may often be used in conjunction with research on older victims.

ORGANIZATION OF THE BOOK

There are many different facets of the study of older victims, and these will be displayed in the organization of the chapters. Chapter 2 discusses ordinary crime victimization. Ordinary crime refers to crimes that people usually think of when the term "crime" is used, such as murder, rape, theft, burglary, and robbery. Lay people (and as a matter of fact, gerontologists up until the early 1970s) often believe that older people are disproportionately victimized in ordinary crimes. Research throughout the 1970s has dispelled this belief. Older people do not have higher victimization rates for ordinary crimes. The type of data required to assess the rates of victimization for the different age groups, as well as how those data are collected, will be discussed. Furthermore, the cautions that are required in interpreting the results of these data will be noted.

Ordinary crime affects not only those who are victimized, it affects almost everybody. The possibility of falling victim to crime arouses some degree of fear in most of us, regardless of our experience with victimization. In other words, even persons who have never been victimized may feel threatened and become intensely fearful by crime. This turns out to be an important consideration for older people. Research has shown that while older people have lower than average victimization rates, they have above average levels of fear. This paradox has created a new interest among gerontologists on fear of crime, independent from victimization per se. The various issues dealt with in this literature are discussed in Chapter 3.

Researchers are interested in crime victimization and fear of crime because they are considered problems in life. If one were to create a utopia, crimelessness would definitely be one of its features. Victimization and its fear are undesirable not only in terms of the actual victimization experience and its fear, but also in terms of their impact on people's lives. Victimization may result in physical injury, financial loss, and may lead to intense levels of fear of crime. Additionally, fear of crime may lead to deterioration of well-being, such as neighborhood dissatisfaction, and avoiding the street and isolation at home. Do older victims suffer more or less from their victimization than younger victims, and does fear of crime affect older people's lives more or less than younger people's? These are but two of several issues discussed in Chapter 4. This chapter concludes with a look at how people cope with crime and its fear.

Ordinary crimes attract the most public attention because they are the most visible and because they are usually committed by strangers. But intimates may also turn into crime perpetrators. The concept of elder abuse is an illustration. Elder abuse refers to victimizations where the offender is one to whom an elderly person has entrusted his care, such as the older person's own children. Research on elder abuse is at an infancy stage at this point, given that the concept itself is rather recent. Hence, most of the discussions in Chapter 5 on elder abuse are devoted to research and theoretical suggestions, rather than the overview of research findings.

If elder abuse is a crime that is hidden from public attention, the same is true of fraud. Fraud is a form of theft and its success lies not on the inattention of the owner but on the deceit of the predator. There are countless ways to defraud people, and the varieties of ways are only limited by the imagination of fraud predators, which should not be underestimated. What are the victimization rates of fraud? Are older people defrauded more often? What types of people are likely victims and why? These questions turn out to be difficult ones given that research on them is almost entirely non-existent. As will be explained in Chapter 6, the lack of research attention to fraud lies in the very nature of the crime.

A book on victimization would not be complete without a discussion of the criminal justice system. The justice system is the institution in society that is charged with the management of crime. Although the system attends far more to the criminals than the victims, victims play the important role of witness. Of course, victims may choose not to evoke the justice system by simply not reporting their victimization. The rate of reporting and its determinants turns out to be a research issue of important standing in criminology. On the other hand, among those victims who do choose to report, what may happen next is a series of interactions with justice system personnel: the police, prosecutors, and judges. How are victims treated? How much influence do victims have on case dispositions? Numerous observers believed that the victim-witness is ill-treated by the system and that the input of the victim on the prosecution of his offender should be expanded. The empirical and normative merits of these positions will be examined in Chapter 7. In addition, a section will be devoted to the recent efforts of the justice system in restoring the victim: restitution, compensation, and social services. Of the various chapters in this book, this is the one where the literature makes the least distinction between older and younger victims. Most of the discussions here assume that little difference exists in the justice system-victim relationship because of the victim's age; an assumption which does not appear to be unreasonable.

The final chapter, Chapter 8, provides suggestions and implications. The focus is not on theoretical and research implications, which are dispersed in all the chapters, but suggestions and implications for individuals, communities, and the society in light of the information contained in this book. In other words, the question is: what can an individual elderly person do to prevent victimization, reduce fear of crime, and lower the chances of being abused and defrauded? The same question is raised at the community or neighborhood level and at the societal level.

RECURRENT ISSUES

Although no one theoretical orientation is used consistently throughout the chapters to discuss older victims, certain conceptual and research issues or concerns reoccur, and a brief note of them at this point may prove to be beneficial. The first of these issues is the definition of concepts. For ordinary crimes, definitions may not be much of a problem; legal definitions are located in numerous Department of Justice publications. However, for other concepts, such as fear of crime and elder abuse, legal definitions do not exist, and researchers are left with the burden and responsibility of defining them. Clear definitions of these key concepts are important not only in terms of measurements, but also in hypothesizing and understanding their causal relationships. Yet, as will be seen in the following chapters, researchers often are all too ready to settle with either murky definitions or no definition at all.

Concepts often may be complex and definitions may not be adequate in clarifying their meanings. In such instances, typologies of a concept may be necessary. An example is elder abuse. Different types of elder abuse have been suggested in the literature, including physical abuse, physical neglect, emotional abuse, financial abuse, and violation of individual rights. Inclusions or exclusions of any particular type have major implications in terms of the prevalence of elder abuse, its significance, causes, and treatments. Another example is the numerous ways people cope with crime and its fear. To understand the similarities and differences among coping methods, such as installing window bars at home, obtaining burglary insurance, purchasing and carrying firearms, and avoiding the street at night, a typology would be essential.

After creating a definition, and maybe a typology, an immediate empirical question is the prevalence of the phenomenon, how frequently does it occur? This same question will be raised with regard to all the different types of victimization that will be discussed: the various ordinary crimes, elder abuse, and fraud, as well as fear of crime. Then comparisons between the age groups will be made; does the older age group fare better or worse than the young? As will be pointed out in the following chapters, the methods to investigate the prevalence of the different victimizations are never easy, and may in fact, be nearly impossible for some types of victimizations.

Finally, much of what is discussed focuses on the patterns of victimization. Causal factors which influence various types of victimization will be examined. The assessment of these causal factors serves two purposes. First, they will identify those who are more likely to fall victims to crime. Second, they should explain why some people are more vulnerable than others. Given that the nature of ordinary crimes, elderly abuse, and fraud are different, their causes may also be different. The same exercise will also be performed on fear of crime, who are most fearful and why are they most fearful? Ultimately, the goal of amassing causal factors for victimization and fear of crime is to create theories for each. A theory is an expedious way of conceptualizing the patterns of a victimization or fear. Its parsimonious nature allows researchers to comprehend a large number of relationships simultaneously. These theories, in turn, account for age groups differences in terms of prevalence of victimization and intensity of fear of crime. In instances where theories do not exist in the literature, they will be suggested.

Chapter 2

ORDINARY CRIMES

O rdinary crime refers to crimes that people usually think of when the term "crime" is used in daily conversation, such as robbery, assault, rape, and burglary. In the early 70s, gerontologists often held the position that older people are over-victimized by criminals in terms of ordinary crimes (e.g., see Brostoff et al., 1972; Butler, 1976; Cunningham, 1975; Goldsmith and Tomas, 1974). In other words, the expectation was that victimization rates of elderly people are higher than the younger population.

The basis of this image of the over-victimized aged is easy to understand. Older people are frequently physically weak and fragile. They are often feeble. They tend to be slow in movement. They do not hear or see as well as younger adults. Their bones are more brittle. In short, elderly people appear to be rather defenseless. When a younger adult confronts a mugger, the adult can flee or fight back. An older person, on the other hand, may have little choice but to succumb to the demands of the mugger. Furthermore, if everybody else recognizes that elderly people are relatively defenseless, so will criminals. Would not one suspect that criminals would single out elderly people as easy targets? A teenage delinquent who is desperate for some quick cash would find it easier to rob an elderly passerby than a younger, stronger male. Similarly, it makes sense that a professional burglar would prefer to burglarize homes of elderly residents than homes of middle-aged or younger adult residents. Yet do facts support this

11

belief that victimization rates against the aged are higher than those of younger age groups?

CRIME STATISTICS AND VICTIMIZATION STUDIES

On the surface, two sources of data exist for comparison of crimes committed against the aged versus the younger population: police records and the Federal Bureau of Investigation's (FBI) annual Uniform Crime Report (UCR). In reality, these two sources of data are identical, and both are of little use for assessing rates of crime against various age groups.

The crime statistics in the UCR are not collected independently on a case-by-case basis by the FBI. The UCR is nothing more than a compilation of police statistics reported by local law enforcement agencies all across the country. As such, the UCR and police records are alike. Since the FBI is a federal agency and local police and sheriffs are employed by local and county governments, the FBI does not have jurisdiction over local agencies and cannot force them to keep their crime records in any specific manner. Although the FBI does suggest a specific format to local law enforcement agencies for keeping crime records and tabulating crime statistics, it is often not followed. In some jurisdictions, the age of the victim is not even recorded. Hence, when the FBI provides national statistics based on these poor police records, they cannot provide any breakdown on crime rates by age of victim.

Although at a national level, police statistics fail to assess age-specific victimization rates, it may still be possible that researchers could use local police records to inspect the prevalence of crimes against the older population, at least in jurisdictions that do record the age of victims. However, even this more limited goal proves futile because of various problems associated with police records.

Conklin (1981) provided a good summary of the problems associated with police statistics, which ultimately makes police records unreliable data in assessing the prevalence of crime. First, different jurisdictions have different ways of recording crimes. Some jurisdictions record crimes as soon as the complaints are received, others require a rather detailed investigation. Some jurisdictions use computers to record crime, while others record crimes manually. These differences have proven to be important factors in artificially inflating or deflating crime rates. Second, some jurisdictions may have political reasons to manipulate crime rates. Sometimes crime rates are inflated to indicate the need for more funds; other times crime rates are deliberately deflated to illustrate the effectiveness of the police force. Finally, and most importantly, many crimes simply never come to the attention of the police, for many victims simply do not report crimes to the police.

Crimes are not reported to the police for a variety of reasons. Some victims consider reporting crimes too troublesome. Other victims think that police cannot do much. Still others do not report because they are afraid of revenge from the criminal. It may even be that some victims feel that exposing the crime may in some way incriminate them. At any rate, because of non-reporting, deliberate manipulation of records, as well as the irregularity in the ways complaints are recorded, criminologists believe that police records are poor indicators of the prevalence of crime (Biderman and Reiss, 1967; Conklin, 1981; Reid, 1982). As a result, little reliable knowledge exists from police data on crime rates against the aged and the younger population.

Although the accuracy of police statistics has long been debated among criminologists, it was not until the mid-60s that empirical research was conducted to assess the prevalence of crime independent of police records and FBI reports. This new research method for establishing the prevalence of crime is called the victimization survey. Victimization surveys are not surveys of victims as the name may imply. Actually, they are surveys of representative samples of the general population. Based on findings from the samples, the pattern of victimization among the entire population is inferred.

Three pilot victimization studies were conducted by the Bureau of the Census in the mid-sixties. All three research projects were sponsored by the first President's Commission on Law Enforcement and Administration of Justice. Biderman, et al. (1967) surveyed Washington, D.C.; Reiss (1967) surveyed several major metropolitan areas; Ennis (1967) used a national representative sample. Because Ennis used a national sample, his study drew the most attention. Based on interviews conducted in 10,000 households, Ennis found the issue of non-reporting to the police was indeed problematic; only half of all crimes were reported to the police.

More pilot studies were conducted between 1970 and 1972. This series of pilot studies was designed to address numerous methodological problems raised by earlier research. A couple of methodological issues illustrate the complexities involved in victimization studies.

First, contrary to expectation, victimization experiences often slip from many people's consciousness (Biderman, 1967). For example, one study showed that when victims (those who had reported their victimization to the police) were interviewed, a sizable portion failed to report their experience to the interviewer (Law Enforcement Assistance Administration, 1977a). To compensate for this factor, the interview guide eventually adopted for victimization studies is rather lengthy. Two generic questions on victimization experience in general as well as eighteen specific questions on personal and household victimizations are used as screening questions. A series of stem questions on victimization experiences are then used only for the victims (see Law Enforcement Assistance Administration, 1977a, for a complete version of the questionnaire).

A second problem facing researchers is that while some victims forget the victimization event itself, others forget the date of the victimization. For example, did the event happen four or six months ago? This issue of timing is extremely important since the estimation of rates for a given period could be confounded. To compensate for this, the current victimization studies use a semi-panel design. Randomly selected households are visited every six months for a period of three years. Victimizations that were previously reported by the respondents were used as a reference frame to detect the occurrence of any "new" victimizations.

In short, despite various methodological problems involved in victimization studies, attempts have been made to solve them. Though clearly not all issues are treated satisfactorily (see Johnson and Wasielewski, 1982; Levine, 1976), victimization survey data are usually considered better data than are police records (O'Brien, 1983).

In 1973, after years of preliminary research, the National Crime Survey (NCS) commenced. The National Crime Survey is a series of victimization studies conducted jointly by the Law Enforcement Assistance Administration (LEAA) and the Census Bureau. This project has been in progress ever since. The NCS consists of a randomly selected sample of 60,000 households (Law Enforcement Assistance Administration, 1977a). Within each household, all residents aged 12 and over are personally interviewed. This yields approximately 136,000 total respondents. As indicated above, a selected household is revisited every six months for three years, after which time the household is dropped from the sample and a new one added.

National statistics inform us of the status of the nation as a whole, and, by definition, local differences are ignored. In addressing this need, LEAA in the first half of the 1970s conducted a series of victimization surveys of specific cities, a total of twenty-six cities in all. Half of these cities were surveyed once in 1974. This group includes Boston, Buffalo, Cincinnati, Houston, Miami, Milwaukee, Minneapolis, New Orleans, Oakland, Pittsburgh, San Diego, San Francisco and Washington, D.C. (Law Enforcement Assistance Administration, 1975). The other thirteen cities were surveyed twice between 1972 and 1975. This second group included Atlanta, Baltimore, Chicago, Cleveland, Dallas, Denver, Detroit, Los Angeles, New York, Newark, Philadelphia, Portland, and St. Louis (Law Enforcement Assistance Administration, 1976a, 1976b). The victimization surveys in the city samples were cross-sectional in design, unlike the national sample surveys which were panel studies. Within each city, a sample of 10,000 households were randomly selected; residents aged 12 and over within the selected households were interviewed. On the average, this yielded 22,000 respondents in each city (Law Enforcement Assistance Administration, 1977a). The value of this data set and its findings will also be briefly discussed.

Respondents of the cities sampled responded to a victimization questionnaire equivalent to that used in the national studies. Half of the respondents from each city were also given an additional questionnaire asking about their beliefs, attitudes, and behaviors regarding crime and the criminal justice system. Results from this survey constitute a major data source for studies on fear of crime (see Chapters 4 and 5). Refer to Gaquin (1979) or Law Enforcement Assistance Administration (1977a) for a complete version of this latter questionnaire.

VICTIMIZATION STATISTICS:
1981 NATIONAL AND OTHER DATA

One of the most unexpected findings which emerged very early in the National Crime Survey is that the 65 and older age group was not the most victimized age category (first reported in Law Enforcement Assistance Administration, 1976c). In fact, elderly people are the least victimized age group for most crimes; in general, those who are in their late teens and early twenties are the most victimized. In short, the likelihood that an aged person will become a victim of crime is actually lower than that for other age groups.

Data from the 1981 National Crime Survey (Bureau of Justice Statistics, 1983), the latest available at the time of this writing, will be presented here. The NCS divides crimes into two broad categories: personal crime and household crime. Personal crimes are further sub-divided into violent crimes and crimes of theft. Violent crimes include rape, robbery, aggravated assault, and simple assault. Crimes of theft include personal larceny with contact and personal larceny without contact. On the other hand, household crime consists of burglary, household larceny, and motor vehicle theft. The meaning of these crimes as defined in the NCS is provided in Figure 2.1

As shown in Figure 2.2, the 1981 statistics for rape indicate that the 65 and older age group has the lowest victimization rates. In fact, the estimation for the aged is so low that it is statistically unreliable. This is not surprising given that older women are not socially defined as sexually attractive. However, the same pattern persists for the other three types of violent crimes. For robbery, aggravated assault, and simple assault, the 65-plus age group was persistently the least victimized. Not only were the victimization rates for elderly people the lowest, the large differences in rates were also sizable. Victimization rates for the 16-24 age groups, those most victimized, were three times that of the aged for robbery, twenty-five times for aggravated assault, and eleven times for simple assault. (According to the data presented by Wilbanks, 1982, the age-specific homicide rate for the 65-plus age group is also the lowest among all age groups.)

For personal theft, the findings are mixed. For personal larceny with contact (purse-snatching and pick-pocketing) elderly

DEFINITIONS OF CRIME CATEGORIES IN THE NATIONAL CRIME SURVEY

Personal Victimization

(Violent Crimes)

Rape = Carnal knowledge through the use of force or the threat of force, including attempts. Statutory rape (without force) is excluded. Includes both heterosexual and homosexual rape.

Robbery = Theft with a weapon resulting in any injury and attack without a weapon resulting either in serious injury (e.g., broken bones, loss of teeth, internal injuries, loss of consciousness) or an undetermined injury requiring 2 or more days of hospitalization. Also includes attempted assault with a weapon.

Simple assault = Attack without a weapon resulting either in minor injury (e.g., bruises, black eyes, cuts, scratches, swelling) or an undetermined injury requiring less than 2 days of hospitalization. Also includes attempted assault without a weapon.

(Crimes or theft)

Personal larceny = Theft of purse, wallet or cash by stealth directly from
with contact   the person of the victim, but without force or the threat of force. Also includes attempted purse snatching.

Personal larceny = Theft or attempted theft, without direct contact between victim and offender, of property or cash from any place other than the victim's home or its immediate vicinity. In rare cases, the victim sees the offender during the commission of the act.

Household Victimization

Burglary = Unlawful or forcible entry of a residence, but not necessarily attended by theft. Includes attempted forcible entry.

Household larceny = Theft or attempted theft of property or cash from a residence or its immediate vicinity. Forcible entry, attempted forcible entry, or unlawful entry is not involved.

Motor Vehicle theft = Stealing or unauthorized taking of a motor vehicle, including attempts at such acts.

Source: Bureau of Justice Statistics (1982)

Figure 2.1. Definitions of crime categories in the national crime survey. Source: Bureau of Justice Statistics (1982).

people did not have the lowest victimization rates. Yet their rate is still low compared to other age groups. It is also interesting to note that personal larceny with contact is a crime that is distributed rather evenly among the age groups. Comparing the victimization rate for the most victimized age group (those between ages 20-24) with the group that suffers the lowest rate (those

Victimization and the Aged

	12-15	16-19	20-24	25-34	35-49	50-64	65+
PERSONAL CRIMES (rate per 1,000 persons)							
Crimes of Violence							
rape	1.4	2.4	2.0	1.4	0.4[a]	0.2[a]	0.1[a]
robbery	11.8	12.3	12.3	7.6	5.5	4.6	4.0
aggravated assault	13.9	20.4	20.4	12.0	7.1	2.5	0.8
simple assault	31.8	32.6	33.6	22.7	10.3	5.8	2.9
Crimes of Theft							
personal larceny with contact	2.5	3.7	4.4	3.8	2.7	2.9	2.9
personal larceny without contact	125.5	128.3	128.4	97.0	75.1	48.1	19.4
HOUSEHOLD CRIMES (rate per 1,000 households)							
Burglary	217.9		114.7		94.6	67.9	54.2
Household larceny	184.0		155.7		137.5	104.1	63.4
Motor vehicle theft	28.7		25.0		20.3	11.7	6.6

[a] Estimate, based on 10 or fewer sample cases, is statistically unreliable

Source: Bureau of Justice Statistics (1983)

Figure 2.2. Victimization rates by type of crime and age of victim: 1981. Source: Bureau of Justice Statistics (1983).

between ages 12-15), the victimization rate for the former is less than twice as high as the latter. Among all types of crimes, personal larceny with contact is the only one that has such a small variance in age-specific victimization rates.

For the other type of theft, personal larceny without contact, the reverse was found. Like violent crime, the victimization rate for this second type of theft was lowest among elderly individuals. Older people suffer only one-sixth the rate of the two most victimized age groups (those between ages 16-24).

In general, the pattern for household crime was identical to that for personal crime. For burglary, household larceny, and motor vehicle theft, older people enjoy the lowest victimization rates, and these rates were only a fraction of what the teenagers were suffering.

In short, one can generalize that irrespective of whether the type of crime is violent crime, theft, or household, older people are the least victimized age group in 1981. The only qualification is personal larceny with contact, for in this type of crime, older people's rate is not the lowest, but is still below the average.

The National Crime Surveys have been in existence continu-
ously since 1973. In addition, between 1972 and 1974, twenty-six
cities were surveyed independently. Therefore additional data
exist that can provide further verification or disconfirmation of
the above generalization. Is the 1981 finding true of other years
surveyed, and is it true across the twenty-six cities as well? Data
from these two sources are provided in two appendices. Appendices 1.1 to 1.3 provide a comparison of the trends in victimization rates for elderly people and the aged 12 and older population
between 1973 and 1980 for the various crimes. Except for personal
larceny with contact, the pattern is this: Victimization rates for
the aged were consistently lower than for that of the general
population, and for most crimes this difference is large. For
personal larceny with contact, the pattern is somewhat mixed. In
1977, 1978, and 1981 victimization rates of elderly people for this
type of crime were lower than for the general population. However, for every other year between 1973 and 1981, the reverse was
true; rates for the aged were higher. Nonetheless, the differences
for this comparison were small, supporting an observation made
earlier that larceny with contact is a crime that is rather evenly
distributed among the age groups. In sum, national data throughout the 1970s continued to support the conclusion made by Cook
and Cook (1976) based on the 1973 national NCS data: elderly
people are less victimized (and often the least victimized), compared to younger age groups for all crimes, except for personal
larceny with contact.

Appendices 2.1 and 2.2 provide further data to support this
conclusion. National data may mask local differences, and it is
entirely possible that in certain areas older people suffered higher
victimization rates than the younger population. This may be
especially true for large cities where crime rates are often believed
to be substantially higher than the national average. However,
the victimization statistics unveiled by the city samples of the
National Crime Survey showed that the national pattern continues
for all of the twenty-six cities studied. Except in a few instances,
older people are less likely to be victimized for all types of crime
when compared with the general population. The discrepancies
in rates between the old and the young may be smaller in the
cities than the national samples, and elderly people may not
always be the least victimized age group. Nonetheless, in none of
the twenty-six cities did the NCS find the aged to be victimized

more often than the younger population. Personal larceny with contact once again is the exception—older people tend to be victimized more often than the young. Although only twenty-six cities were studied and their findings may not be generalized to other cities, nor, as a matter of fact, to the same cities in other years, available evidence overwhelmingly supports the notion that conclusions drawn from the national studies are applicable to most urban areas.

A VICTIMIZATION THEORY AND THE AGED

When the first wave of results from the NCS became available, gerontologists were, in general, rather surprised by the findings. Throughout the 1960s and early 1970s, the belief had been that rates of victimization against the aged were higher than for the population as a whole (e.g., see Butler, 1976). Hence, the NCS findings on older people's low victimization rates raised as many questions as they answered. Why do old people have such low victimization rates when they are physically feeble and appear to be vulnerable to victimization? Does the NCS data indicate that older people are not selectively preyed on by criminals? To address these questions, attention must be turned to theories of victimization. At the individual level, a victimization theory would identify the characteristics of those who are, regardless of age, most likely to be victimized; at the aggregate level, such a theory would account for the uneven distribution of victimization among the young and the old.

Hindelang, et al. (1978) proposed a theory of victimization which will be used here to explain older people's low victimization rates. Traces of their theory can also be found in discussions by Balkin (1979), Cohen et al. (1981), and Lindquist and Duke (1982). Although the theory by Hindelang and his associates is intended for personal victimization only, not household victimization, their arguments will be extended to the latter as well.

The theory by Hindelang and his associates focuses on the variable of life style. In essence, Hindelang, et al.'s belief is that certain people lead life styles that make them more vulnerable to victimization. Any personal victimization carries with it at least three different components: the setting of the incident, the time of occurrence, and the offender. According to various studies which use police records as well as NCS data, most personal crimes occur in public places: the street, public buildings, parking lots, and so forth. For example, data from the 1981 NCS showed that about 64% of rapes, 69% of robberies, 63% of assault, and 85% of personal larceny with contact occurred in public places (Bureau of Justice Statistics, 1983). The rest of the personal crimes are divided among three settings: "inside own home," "near own home," and "elsewhere." Hence, those whose life style includes frequent visits to public places are more exposed to crime.

These same studies also concluded that victimizations do not take place equally around the clock. Crimes disproportionately occur during the evening hours. According to the 1981 NCS, approximately 35% of rapes, 40% of robberies, and 36% of assaults occur within the six hour period between 6 p.m. and midnight (Bureau of Justice Statistics, 1983). Hence, a second hypothesis was developed by Hindelang and his associates: those who frequent public places during the evening hours are more likely to be victimized.

Besides knowing that personal victimization occurs more frequently in public settings and during the evening hours, it is also important to learn the characteristics of criminals. Based on the Uniform Crime Report (the characteristics of those who were arrested for personal offenses), and the National Crime Survey (the characteristics of offenders as described by victims), the portrait of the typical criminal can be generalized. Most offenders are males between the ages of fourteen and twenty-four—from lower socio-economic groups. Compared to the general population, blacks and unmarried men are also overrepresented among offenders. Hence, those who associate with others who have these characteristics are more exposed to crime; they are convenient targets for offenders.

In short, the typical victim of personal crime is one who frequents public places that attract younger age groups, especially during the evening. Applying this model to elderly people, it becomes clearer why the aged have lower victimization rates. First, the aged tend to go out less often and spend less time in public places. Second, during the evening hours, the aged tend to stay home. Finally, following the principle of homophily, the aged tend to associate with other persons of similar age, thereby reducing their contacts with the typical offenders: young, lower-class males. So, given their life style, older people are less exposed to crime, and therefore, have relatively low victimization rates. Likewise, those between the ages of 16 and 24 have the highest victimization rates because they go to public places frequently, especially at night, and they associate more with persons of their own age groups.

Hindelang, et al.'s (1978) life-style theory of personal victimization may also be extended to account for older people's low victimization rates for household crime. Unlike personal crime, household crime does not involve face-to-face confrontation between the offender and the victim. Hence, explanations for personal victimization may not at first appear to be applicable to household victimization. However, note that part of the argument by Hindelang and his associates relies on the fact that elderly people do not frequent public places as often as younger persons. Conversely, what this means is that the aged stay home more frequently.

In a unique study, Reppetto (1974) interviewed ninety-seven burglars on what factors would prevent them from attempting unlawful entry of a home. The most frequent response was "full-time occupant," 67% said "would prevent" and another 21% responded "might prevent." Not only is this deterrent the most often cited, it is far more frequent than the second most cited factor, "evidence of alarm," where only 36% and 37% responded "would prevent" and "might prevent." The idea that a full-time occupant deters burglars is easily understood. Burglary, unlike robbery which usually results in cash gains for the perpetrator, usually nets only valuable goods which need to be "fenced." Yet, despite this disadvantage, burglars enjoy a sense of anonymity since face-to-face confrontation with the victim is avoided (Conklin, 1981). This in turn makes burglary a safer crime for the offender; neither will he be recognized by the victim later, nor does he need to worry about resistence from the victim. Hence, elderly people, by being home more, avoid both personal and household victimizations.

Hindelang, et al.'s theory of personal victimization as well as its application to household crime point to one conclusion; the aged are less exposed to all types of crimes. Hence, it is not at all surprising to find that the aged, in general, have lower victimization rates than other age groups. On the other hand, the finding that the aged have a higher victimization rate for personal larceny with contact, despite their lower exposure, becomes more of an enigma. Furthermore, the generally low victimization rates of the aged cannot be interpreted as indicating that the aged are not selectively victimized by certain offenders, such as youth gangs, as is believed by some (e.g., see Morello, 1982). If the low exposure of the aged and the high exposure of the young were statistically controlled, it is not known whether the aged would still have lower victimization rates than the rest of the population. To date, no study has incorporated the factor of exposure into considerations of victimization rates.

A related issue concerning exposure also requires attention, although it will be dealt with in more detail in Chapter 5. Hindelang, et al. (1978) suggested that since victimization surveys discovered that fear of crime is higher among elderly people, and that fear led to avoidance of the street, might not fear among the aged be an additional factor in lowering the exposure of the aged to criminals? Since the relationship between fear of crime and avoidance of the street will be discussed in more detail later, I will simply point out here that this relationship is far weaker than is generally believed. While it is true that elderly people go out less often than the younger population, it is not because of crime or its fear that their activities are restricted. Rather, older people have less social activities mainly because of reductions in social roles and ties. In short, the reasoning that high fear among elderly people leads to fewer activities in public places, which in turn leads to lower victimization rates, finds little empirical support.

In an interesting study, Antune, et al. (1977) examined the patterns of personal crime against the aged based on the 1973-74 national sample of the National Crime Survey. What Antune and his associates found may be of use here in further assessing whether young crime offenders selectively prey on the aged. Analysis of the victimization survey data shows that compared to younger victims, elderly victims were more likely to be personally attacked by strangers, youths, acting alone, and without weapons. This finding, of course, should not be interpreted to mean that actual victimization rates against the aged by this type of offender are higher than in the younger age group. Instead it means that the proportion of elderly victims who are involved with this type of offender is higher than that of younger victims. With this in mind, one can infer that youthful offenders who are alone and without weapon, are less reluctant to victimize an elderly passer-by than a younger one. Such an offender, who may be afraid to attack a younger victim for fear of effective resistance, may feel more confident in attacking an elderly victim who has less physical strength.

Published data from the 1981 National Crime Survey provided additional evidence supporting the belief that teenage offenders selectively prey on older victims. In Figure 2.3, the percentage of robberies and assaults committed by teenage offenders in 1980 and 1981 are broken down by the age of the victims. Separate tabulations are shown for victimizations with a single offender and with multiple offenders. Not unexpectedly, teenage victims were the most vulnerable to teenage offenders. This fits Hindelang and his associates' life-style theory of victimization. Through the principle of homophily, teenagers associate with each other and become convenient targets for teenage offenders. Given this, the data on older victims become an anomaly. Besides teenage victims, the percentage of robbery and assaults perpetrated by teenage offenders is either the highest or the second highest (except in one instance) for older victims. If teenage offenders are not seeking out older people to victimize, then the principle of homophily would suggest a relatively low proportion of crimes against the aged committed by teenagers.

In sum, despite the findings of the National Crime Survey that victimization rates against the aged are the lowest among all age groups, some indications remain that older people are selectively victimized. First, older people have life styles that lower their exposure to both personal and household victimizations. If the life-style differences between age groups are somehow controlled for, allowing both the young and the old to have similar exposure to crime, it is uncertain whether the age discrepancies in victimization rates would be reduced, eliminated, or even reversed. Second, for one type of crime, personal larceny with contact, older people have relatively high victimization rates. This is so despite the aged's sedentary life style. Third, besides the teenage group, the proportion of violent victimizations perpetrated by teenage offenders is highest among elderly people. All these considerations point to the conclusion that the "real" victimization risk for the aged is not as low as the NCS data may indicate. Hence, Cook and Cook's (1976) contention that the image of the

| | Multiple offenders victimization | | Single offender victimization | |
| | Perceived age of offender: Percent teenagers (age 20 or under) | | Perceived age of offender: Percent teenagers (age 20 or under) | |
Robbery	1980	1981	1980	1981
12-19	66	69	64	60
20-34	24	28	19	26
35-49	29	30	34	30
50-64	28	30	28	24
65 & over	38	40	43	28
Assault				
12-19	68	69	64	64
20-34	22	24	18	15
35-49	26	35	16	17
50-64	30	43	19	14
65 & over	31	41	27	9

Source: Bureau of Justice Statistics (1982)(1983)

Figure 2.3. Personal crimes of violence, 1980 and 1981: Teenage offenders. Source: Bureau of Justice Statistics (1982), (1983).

overvictimized aged is a myth may be premature. More careful studies with the proper controls are required.

ISSUES IN VICTIMIZATION

In this section, the NCS data will be re-examined to explore several issues in victimization of the aged: characteristics of older victims, the relative prevalence of various crimes, and victimizations in urban areas. Finally, the qualitative experience of victimization will be discussed.

Although victimizations of the aged are relatively infrequent, it is still interesting to observe the characteristics of older victims. That is, who among older people are more likely to be victimized? Figure 2.4 shows comparisons for personal victimizations in 1981 along two dimensions: sex and race. In general, except for rape and personal larceny with contact, older men were more likely to be victims of personal crimes than older women for all types of personal crimes. Personal larceny with contact is higher for elderly women simply because purse-snatching is easier than pocket-picking, and therefore more common. Notice that the pattern for the aged is true for the general population as well. Hindelang, et al. (1978) accounted for this gender difference also by his victimization theory on life style. Men suffered higher victimizations because of their life style. Due to work and other reasons, men are in public places more often, and most crimes occurred in such settings. Men also go out at night more often, again putting them at a higher risk. Finally, men tend to be in places where men frequent, such as bars; there they become convenient targets for criminals, who are predominantly male. In the NCS cities samples Hindelang and his associates analyzed, this gender difference diminished among the sixty-five and older age group. Hindelang and his associates believed that this was due to the reduction in activity levels of males as they grow old, drawing their life style closer to that of older women. This sex-age interaction may be an artifact of the cities samples, however, since it was not observed in the 1981 national data.

Also shown in Figure 2.4 is the comparison for blacks and whites. Other than robbery, elderly blacks suffered higher victimization rates than elderly whites. Other demographic factors may prove to be better characterizations of older victims; however, they are not available from published statistics on the NCS.

	Sex				Race			
	65+		12+		65+		12+	
	males	females	males	females	white	black	white	black
Personal Victimization								
rape	0.0[a]	0.2[a]	0.1[a]	1.8	0.1	0.6	0.9	1.6
robbery	4.8	3.4	9.8	5.2	3.2	9.0	6.2	16.9
aggravated assault	0.8[a]	0.8[a]	14.4	5.3	0.6[a]	3.2	9.1	14.4
simple assault	4.3	2.0	21.9	13.1	2.5	5.9	17.3	16.8
Personal larceny w/contact	2.3	3.3	2.7	3.7	2.5	6.6	2.9	5.4
Personal larceny w/o contact	24.5	15.8	88.0	76.3	18.8	25.5	82.3	79.4

[a]Estimate, based on 10 or fewer sample cases, is statistically unreliable.

Source: Bureau of Justice Statistics (1983)

Figure 2.4. Victimization rates for personal crimes by sex, race, and age: 1981. Source: Bureau of Justice Statistics (1983).

In an interesting study, Liang and Sengstock (1981) analyzed National Crime Survey data between 1973 and 1976. With multi-variate analyses, personal victimization rates among the aged for these four years were expressed as a function of several demographic variables. Their results show that size of community, age, marital status, race, and sex are important determinants of personal victimization rates for the aged. Those aged who live in large urban areas, who are older, who are not currently married, who are non-whites, and who are females have higher victimization rates than their counterparts. Socio-economic status of the aged, however, was not found to be related to personal victimization rates.

A second issue on victimization that can be addressed with NCS data is the relative prevalence of various victimizations. To which types of crime are older people more vulnerable? According to the victimization rates of 1981 shown in Figure 2.2, household crimes are, in general, more common than personal crimes. Victimization rates for the two household crimes of burglary and household larceny were higher than any other crimes. For households headed by elderly persons, one out of every nineteen was burglarized, and one out of sixteen had properties stolen from its proximity in 1981. Personal larceny without contact ranked third in prevalence; about one out of every fifty older persons had belongings stolen when they were not attending them. For crimes with offender contact, such as any of the violent crimes and personal larceny with contact, the chances of their occurrence are considerably lower. The likelihood of an older person being victimized in a given year for each of these crimes is all under one in 200. For motor vehicle theft, a household crime, the probability is also around one in 200.

Notice this pattern of victimization is not unique to the aged. The same applies to the younger population as well. Like elderly people, the younger population suffers from household crimes far more frequently than personal crime. Finally, other data, such as the FBI's Uniform Crime Report, also support this generalization.

Data from the cities samples of the NCS also addressed a couple of issues on urban crime and the aged (see Appendices 2.1 and 2.2). First, among the twenty-six cities studied, victimization rates for the aged were uniformly or almost uniformly higher than the national rates for three types of crimes: robbery, larceny with contact, and motor vehicle theft. Although elderly people were more likely to be victimized for these three crimes in the cities, the issue lies in the urban nature of these crimes and is not related to age. In other words, in the cities, victimization rates for these three crimes are also higher for the general population, not just elderly people. Notice that the nature of the two personal crimes of robbery and larceny with contact are rather similar. Both involve face-to-face confrontation between the offender and the victim, and both offenses are committed for property gains.

Another observation that can be made from the cities samples is the large variances in victimization rates among the cities. It is not unusual to find a city with victimization rates several times those of another city for the same types of offenses. Hence, whenever possible, findings from the cities samples should be used in addition to the national studies. For example, if a researcher were studying fear of crime in Philadelphia, one of the twenty-six cities studied, the NCS data for that city should not be neglected. As the Law Enforcement Assistance Administration (1977b) pointed out, since victimizations are rare occurrences, the samples of victimization studies need to be large, and therefore, the cost of doing a victimization study, even a local one, is extremely high. Researchers in the twenty-six cities of the NCS cities samples are indeed fortunate to have these data available despite their methodological problems (O'Brien, 1983) and the fact that they are now somewhat outdated.

The contributions made by the National Crime Surveys to the understanding of victimization and the aged are illustrated throughout this chapter. In fact, in later chapters other findings from the NCS will also be noted. Hence, the significance of the NCS cannot be over-stated. However, one of the drawbacks of the NCS is that the statistics do not and cannot illustrate the actual experience of victimization. What exactly is it like for older people to become a victim? Are they shellshocked when it happens or do they experience it with a sense of control? Immediately after it happens, do they feel relief or anger? Unfortunately, the NCS did not obtain these qualitative data and, in fact, no such study of older victims has ever been reported.

What is available, instead, is a study of how a small group of New York City victims, of diverse ages, experienced one type of victimization: mugging, or robbery (Lejeune and Alex, 1973). Surprisingly, despite New York City's reputation for crime, many of the interviewed victims were still "caught off-guard" when the victimization occurred. Three factors appear to have contributed to this. First, although most people expected to be mugged some day, the thought is not a conscious one in their daily routine. This is especially true for the middle class who usually define mugging as a crime that only occurs "elsewhere." Second, muggings are rare occurrences. Few people have the actual experience of being mugged. Hence, when they are mugged, the situation is a novel one for them. Finally, the cues available during a mugging may be misleading and ambiguous to the point where the victim would have difficulty defining them properly. For example, a grab on the shoulder by the aggressor or the statement "Can you spare some change?" may not be immediately defined as part of the act of mugging. Though Lejeune and Alex's sample were New York City residents, it is reasonable to assume that their reaction of being caught off-guard could be generalized to residents of other locales as well.

After the mugging was completed, Lejeune and Alex noticed that some victims, especially the males, felt a need to justify their lack of resistance. It is as if their masculinity had been challenged. For example, some pointed to the potential danger involved in mugging to account for their not resisting. At any rate, the researchers noticed the victims' anger. This phenomenon would probably not be too common among older male victims since the norm of masculinity probably declines in significance with age and older men may be spared the humiliation of not resisting muggers.

Curiously enough, mugging victims also reported a sense of enjoyment of their experience. In recounting their mugging to others, they received more attention from friends and acquaintances than usual. Suddenly, victims attained a "star" quality within their social circle. In turn, they also became more aware of other people's victimization experiences.

In sum, based on Lejeune and Alex's research, it may be speculated that elderly people would be caught off-guard when victimized, older men would not feel anger for not resisting muggers, and victimization would become a frequent conversation topic of at least a brief duration after the event.

SUMMARY

Perhaps because of older people's physical vulnerability, gerontologists in the 1960s and early 1970s believed that victimization rates against the aged were relatively high. However, neither
police records nor the Uniform Crime Report offered data to test
this belief because of their numerous methodological problems,
the most important of which is the failure of many victims to
report their crime to the police. To counter this and other methodological problems, the method of victimization surveys was
created. The National Crime Survey (NCS), which utilized this
method, began during the early 1970s, and this data clarified
many issues regarding crimes against the aged. Over the years,
the consistent findings of the NCS, both national and local
studies, have been this: victimization rates against elderly people
are among the lowest compared to other age groups. The only
exception is larceny with contact where older people suffered a
slightly higher rate than the rest of the population.

Yet, the "real" victimization risk of the aged may have been
understated by the National Crime Survey for two reasons. First,
it is entirely possible that life-style differences between the old
and the young account for older people's low victimization rates.
Older people lead sedentary life styles that makes them less exposed to crime. They stay home more often, rarely go out at
night, and tend to associate with young people less. If older
people's life styles were changed to be more like younger people's,
it is not known whether the discrepancy in victimization rates
between the two groups would disappear. A second factor which
suggests that the "real" victimization risk of the aged may be
higher than their victimization rates is that data from NCS indicate that teenage criminals, both individually and in groups,
may selectively victimize older people.

Data from the NCS also suggest that victimization rates of the
aged vary by size of community, age, marital status, race, and
sex, but not socio-economic status. In addition, the same data
from the NCS indicate that crime that does not involve contacts
between victims and criminals is usually more prevalent.

Finally, a qualitative study showed that mugging victims were
caught off-guard when they were victimized, and they spent time
to recount their experience to others afterwards.

Chapter 3

FEAR OF CRIME

Victimization refers to concrete events where individuals are actually involved in crimes as victims, as in a home burglary or a personal robbery. Fear of crime refers to psychological reactions to possible crime victimizations. A victimization experience does not necessarily have to precede the fear of crime; a person can be fearful without any previous experience of victimization. In recent years, the fear of crime literature has grown immensely. More and more studies on fear of crime among older people, as well as the general population, can be found. Yet, despite this increase in research attention, fear of crime as a concept is seldom defined precisely. What exactly is fear of crime?

DEFINITION AND MEASUREMENT

According to Merry (1981), there are three dimensions to fear of crime: a cognitive, an emotive, and a behavioral dimension. The cognitive is the perception that one is exposed and vulnerable to victimization, and that victimization has serious consequences for oneself. The emotive is the sensation of fright in relation to the threat of crime. The last of these three, the behavioral, refers to activities such as purchasing firearms, avoiding streets at night, installing security doors, and not trusting neighbors. Like most other researchers in this area, the behavioral aspect of fear will be treated here as the consequence of fear (see Chapter 4), and not as fear of crime itself. In other words, fear of crime and these coping behaviors are two separate concepts. This leaves the two dimensions of cognitive and emotive.

Skogan and Maxfield's (1981) definition of fear of crime best illustrates the emotive dimension. They defined fear of crime as: "...a psychological state provoked by an immediate sense of personal risk." Using the psychological approach, Skogan and Maxfield argued that the fear is provoked by danger stimuli such as the approach of a gang of youth, a poorly-lighted alley, a run-down street, and so forth. The fear response, in turn, leads to physical manifestations such as "...a rapid heart rate, narrowed field of vision, high blood pressure, enhanced reaction time, an increased flow of blood to the large muscles, and endrocrinal changes such as the release of adrenalin into the blood stream."

Although Skogan and Maxfield's definition is well grounded in the psychological literature (see Gubrium, 1973) and highlights the element of "fear" as an emotional response to danger stimuli, the definition, nonetheless, may not reflect the usual conceptions of the term. If an individual, for example, is never involved in situations with danger stimuli, the emotional response of fear would, therefore, not be triggered. Hence, by definition, this individual would not be considered fearful of crime. Yet is this valid? Consider an elderly woman living in an upper-middle class suburb with low crime rates. Her chances of confronting any danger stimuli are extremely low. She has rarely heard strange noises in her house at night, has seldom been confronted with any "suspicious looking" characters in her neighborhood, and all the surrounding streets are pleasant and well-kept. As such, within the recent past, her emotional/physiological response of fear has not been roused in relation to crime victimization. Yet, this woman still considers her neighborhood unsafe and sees herself as a likely victim. She goes out with a guard dog, installs special locks on her windows, and even keeps a gun next to her bed. Using Skogan and Maxfield's definition, this elderly woman will not be considered fearful of crime since she has not experienced the physiological manifestation of fear. On the other hand, most researchers and laymen alike would consider her to be a fearful individual. Hence, like the behavioral approach to defining fear of crime, the emotive approach creates certain problems. Whereas the former focuses on the consequences of fear of crime rather than on the fear itself, the latter confuses fear of crime with reactions to danger stimuli. Fear of crime is not a situational response to specific stimuli; rather fear is a generalized response to victimization, and physiological responses such as those described by Skogan and Maxfield are not relevant here.

Among the three dimensions of fear of crime identified by Merry, the cognitive appears to be the most appropriate in defining the fear. In this instance, fear of crime becomes an attitude. There are two components to this attitude (see Yin, 1980; Warr and Stafford, 1983). First, fear of crime is an assessment of the risk of being victimized. A fearful person is one who perceives his risk of victimization as high and a non-fearful person is one who perceives otherwise. The second component of fear of crime is an appraisal of the seriousness of being victimized. That is, aside from perceived risk, a fearful person is one who thinks that much harm or damage would result from a victimization, and a non-fearful person is one who believes that he would suffer little harm when victimized. Warr and Stafford (1983) noted that both perceived risk and seriousness are necessary conditions of fear of crime. These two components of fear are multiplicative in nature. Fear of crime is high only when both perceived risk or seriousness are high; fear of crime is low if either perceived risk or seriousness (or both) is low. For example, even when murder is perceived to be an extremely serious victimization, if its perceived likelihood of occurrence is low, fear of murder would also be low. Warr and Stafford measured perceived risk, perceived seriousness, and fear of crime independently for sixteen different crimes. Their analysis showed that the multiplicative model between perceived risk and perceived seriousness explained virtually all (93%) of the variance of fear of crime. Returning to the case of the elderly woman living in the suburb, she would be considered highly fearful, according to this definition, since she perceives her neighborhood as unsafe and the seriousness of victimization high enough to warrant taking extreme precautions.

Notice that this definition of fear of crime may be tied to Skogan and Maxfield's emotive definition in that fear is one's assessment of the chances of confronting danger stimuli as well as one's reaction to such stimuli if confronted. Fear of crime is the assessment that one's likelihood is high and, one's reaction would be fright. The individual does not have to actually be in an emotional state of fear.

One of the merits of this cognitive approach for defining fear of crime is that it reflects the way researchers have been studying this concept. Although defining fear of crime is an often over- looked step in research, as will be shown later, the operationali- zation of that fear is surprisingly consistent. This paradox may be explained by tracing the history of the literature. Fear of crime as a phenomenon was largely uncovered around the mid-1960s by the pollsters (Furstenberg, 1971). At a time of social upheaval, public polls noticed that increasingly crime was emerging as a major social issue in the country, and people were feeling less safe on the street. Social researchers were then alerted to the issue. As recent reviews of the literature (Lawton, 1981; Yin, 1980) show, almost all of the studies were conducted in the 1970s, after the poll results had caught public attention. In doing these studies, researchers often simply borrowed the survey items from the pollsters. The result is a set of rather uniform indicators to the often undefined concept of fear of crime.

Figure 3.1 summarizes three popular ways in which fear of crime has been measured in research. By far, the most popular way is to assess the feeling of safety around the neighborhood street at night: "How safe do you feel being out alone in your neighborhood at night: very safe, somewhat safe, somewhat unsafe, or very unsafe?" The origin of this item may be traced to a National Opinion Research Center (NORC) poll conducted in 1967 (see Erskine, 1974).

At least thirteen different studies use this item, although the exact wording varies slightly in a few instances. Furthermore, in most of these studies this item is the only indicator of fear used. The consensus appears to be that the perception of safety is the inverse of fear of crime and is, therefore, a good way to measure the fear.

Another related and very popular way to measure fear of crime is to assess whether certain areas around the neighborhood are perceived as dangerous at night: "Is there any area around here, that is within a mile, where you would be afraid to walk alone at night?"

At least eight studies have used this item and, in almost all instances, it was the only indicator used. Furthermore, almost all studies used the same data source, NORC's General Social Sur- vey. The Survey is part of a social indicator movement where the national population was sampled periodically between 1973-82.

(1) Feeling of safety around the neighborhood street at night

"How safe do you feel being out alone in your neighborhood at night: very safe, reasonably safe, somewhat unsafe, or very unsafe?"

Conklin (1971)
Garafalo (1979)
Gordon et al., (1980)
Hartnagel (1979)
Kennedy & Silverman 1983
Liska et al. (1982)

Ollenburger (1981)
Riger, et al., (1978)
Sherman et al., (1976)
Skogan & Maxfield (1981)
Sundeen & Mathier (1976,1977)
Yin (1982)

(2) Afraid to walk in certain areas in the neighborhood at night

"Is there any area right around here--that is within a mile--where you would be afraid to walk alone at night?"

Braungart et al., (1980)
Clemente and Kleiman (1976, 1977)
Cutler (1979)
Gerbner et al., (1978)

Lebowitz (1975)
Lizotte and Bordua (1980)
Newman and Franck (1982)

(3) Estimation of risk to specific types of crime

"How likely is it that a person walking around here at night might get held up or attacked--very likely, somewhat likely, somewhat unlikely, or very likely?"

Block (1971)
Conklin (1971)

Furstenburg (1971)
Lewis and Maxfield (1980)

Figure 3.1. Measurements of fear of crime.

Given that this data set is widely available, it is not surprising that it has been used repeatedly to study fear of crime. Like the previous item, the origin of this item can also be traced to a public poll, a Gallup Poll in 1965 (see Erskine, 1974).

Finally in another set of studies using a third approach, survey respondents were asked to estimate their risk of being victimized for specific types of crime. Block (1971), for example, asked respondents, "How likely is it that a person walking around here at night might get held up or attacked: very likely, somewhat likely, somewhat unlikely, or very unlikely?" Furstenburg (1971) and Lewis and Maxfield (1980) are among those who used this approach to measure the perceived risk to a few types of crime. These estimates were then averaged into an index. This third type of measurement of fear may be also traced to a 1966 NORC survey (see Erskine, 1974).

Besides these three major approaches, there are others that are less common. Lawton and Yaffe (1981), Patterson (1977), and Pollack and Patterson (1980) all used Likert scales consisting of more than ten items. The exact items, however, were not reported. Others like Kleinman and David (1973), Lee (1982a), Ragan (1977), Rafai (1977), Shotland et al. (1979), Thomas and Hyman (1977), and Warr and Stafford (1983) used still other unique approaches. Finally, Lee (1982b) and Norton and Courlander (1982) utilized factor analysis to construct scales on fear of crime.

Notice that the first two measures of fear in Figure 3.1 are alike in that both are global measures of fear of crime. Besides not distinguishing differences in fear of the various crimes, the major weakness of these two items is that both measure fear only in one locale, the neighborhood street. Both items, despite their popularity among researchers, fail to consider fear of crime in other locales, such as in one's home, in other neighborhoods in one's community, while using public transport, at concerts, or in bars. The two items also fail to measure fear for one's belongings at home while unattended.

The third measure in Figure 3.1, on the other hand, appears to be superior to the former two in that it allows for a more precise indication of the specific crimes feared. As Warr and Stafford's (1983) data suggest, people's fear of various crimes are not uniform. People seem to be most fearful of burglary (when no one is home) and rape, and least fearful of assault by a non-stranger. However, this approach to measuring fear of crime only captures the perceived risk dimension and leaves out the perceived seriousness dimension. At any rate, it must be pointed out that the two global measures of fear of crime are far more utilized in research at this point. In other words, most of the known relationships of fear of crime, to be discussed, are based on the two global measures. Whether the same relationships hold true with the third or other approach to measuring fear is not known. As Lee's (1982a) research suggests, there are good reasons to be cautious with such an assumption.

THE PERSON-ENVIRONMENT THEORY OF FEAR OF CRIME

Who among elderly people are fearful of crime? Which elderly persons would perceive themselves as likely victims? Why is it that some aged feel unsafe on the neighborhood street, while others feel safe walking around the same neighborhood? To address these questions, a theory of fear of crime is needed. At present, there is a body of literature on the determinants of that fear. However, what is noticeably missing is a theoretical framework (see Garafalo, 1981, for his fear of crime model). Research in this area has generated, instead, a set of empirical generalizations. For example, females are more fearful than males, blacks more fearful than whites, and so forth. Yet, these empirical generalizations, while contributing to knowledge on the topic, do not really increase an understanding of fear. Why are females and blacks more fearful? Is there a common logic behind the relationships between sex and race, and fear, or are these two relationships different from one another? To make sense of the empirical generalizations that research has provided, it is necessary to construct a theory of fear of crime. In other words, a fear of crime theory should provide an intuitive understanding of fear of crime relationships. In addition, such a theory should also be able to suggest new hypotheses.

Although the interest here is in fear of crime among elderly people, a good fear of crime theory should be one that is applicable to the young as well as the old. Hence, studies on fear among the younger population, as well as the older population, will be reviewed in constructing a fear of crime theory.

The fear of crime theory to be presented here includes a personal dimension and an environmental dimension. This person-environment dichotomy is based on Kurt Lewin's (1951) social psychological theory with the equation $B = f (P, E)$: "Behavior is a function of both the person and the environment." Although Lewin's statement is clearly vague and abstract, it has proved to be surprisingly useful as groundwork for a number of theories including Lawton and Nahemow's (1973) ecological theory of aging. Here, rather than focus on behavior, the interest is on fear of crime and how that fear is a function of the person and the environment. This will be called a person-environment theory of fear of crime.

Personal factors are important in understanding fear of crime because that fear usually refers to fear for oneself. It does not matter if an individual believes that crime rate is skyrocketing in the country or even in the neighborhood. As long as he does not consider himself a likely target or that victimizations would seriously harm him, the individual is not fearful of crime. This is the distinction between fear of crime and concern for crime that Furstenburg (1971) made. Furstenburg measured *concern for crime* as the estimation of the seriousness of the crime situation for the country and *fear of crime* as the perception of one's own chances of victimization. He found the two to be unrelated. As such, given the centrality of the personal elements in fear of crime, a theory on fear of crime should include the group of personal factors by which a person may be considered vulnerable, such as physical disability, hearing loss, and lack of physical strength. Personal vulnerability may be defined as any individual characteristics that are associated with weakness, liability to injury, or general unguarded exposures.

A second dimension of actual victimization besides the element of self is that the event occurs within a locale, an environment. Therefore, the risk of victimization is assessed within an environmental context. According to the measurements reviewed earlier, this environment is one's neighborhood. For example, a Minnesota farmer would not assess his chances of victimization in New York City unless he planned to move or visit there. Rather, this farmer would assess his chances of victimization within his own community. Hence, the environmental contexts which the individual frequents, that of the home, the neighborhood, and other parts of the community, become important considerations in understanding fear of crime. Certain features of the community, environmental perils, such as run-down neighborhoods, or suspicious-looking neighbors are often associated with crime and in turn they would lead to higher levels of fear of crime. Environmental peril may be defined as any characteristics of the environment that signify crime and danger.

Note that personal vulnerability and environmental peril independently affects fear of crime. This is demonstrated in Figure 3.2. In situation "a," an individual who is vulnerable but lives in an environment without peril may still be fearful of crime. For example, consider a wealthy widow living in a security highrise in a low crime suburb. She may be fearful of crime despite her environment because of her personal characteristics—the need to walk with a cane, poor eye-sight, widowhood, and so on. Alternately in situation "c," an individual who is not very vulnerable may still be fearful of crime due to the presence of environmental perils, for instance, a young college football player who lives in a

PERSONAL VULNERABILITY, ENVIRONMENTAL PERIL, AND

FEAR OF CRIME

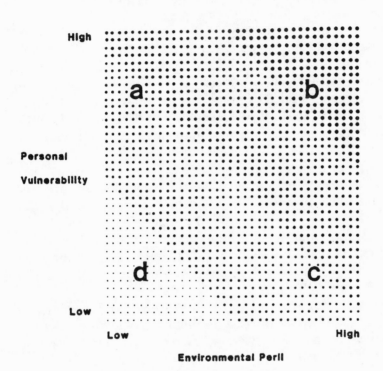

Figure 3.2. Personal vulnerability, environmental peril, and fear of crime.

ghetto neighborhood. Despite his physical build, this young man may still feel threatened by the neighborhood in which he lives. The worst scenario would be where both personal vulnerability and neighborhood peril are present (situation b), e.g., an elderly person living in a slum neighborhood. Such an individual would have an intense level of fear. Finally, in situation "d," where an individual does not live in a perilous environment and does not have vulnerable characteristics, e.g., the young football player living in a low crime suburb, the level of fear of crime would be extremely low.

PERSONAL VULNERABILITIES

There are three variables, all known predictors of fear of crime, that indicate personal vulnerability: sex, age, and perceived health.

The pattern that females are more fearful of victimization than males has been revealed in numerous national surveys (Erskine, 1974; Braungart, et al., 1980; Clemente and Kleiman, 1976, 1977) as well as regional surveys (Law Enforcement Assistance Administration, 1977c, in eight different cities; Lee, 1982a, in Washington state; Norton and Courlander, 1982, in an unidentified metropolitan area; Ollenburger, 1981, in Nebraska; Pollack and Patterson, 1980, in central Pennsylvania). In addition, the same relationship has been found in London (Clarke and Lewis, 1982). The fact that this finding is discovered everywhere attests to the strength of the relationship. In fact, closer inspections reveal that this is the strongest known relationship of fear of crime (Baumer, 1979).

The reason for women's fear may best be explained by personal vulnerability. Through a combination of genuine physical weaknesses, relative to men, as well as to the socialization process, women in this society come to define themselves as more vulnerable. Gorden, et al. (1980), for example, reported that women felt that they are slow and weak in physical ability and believe they could not successfully defend themselves against attack. Another reason for women's level of fear is that women are also vulnerable to rape (Riger, et al., 1979; Warr and Stafford, 1983). In short, sex should be conceptualized as a crude measure of physical vulnerability.

If sex is a crude measure of physical vulnerability, the same is true of age (Goldsmith and Goldsmith, 1976). As Butler (1976) pointed out, ". . . poor vision, hearing loss, slowed motor and mental response, decreased coordination, and a host of other physical and mental impairments increase the elderly's vulnerability to victimization." Younger persons with more strength, faster speed, and shorter reaction time are far more capable of defending themselves. The same environmental perils which may not threaten a younger person would threaten an aged person. Furthermore, like the sex differences in socialization, elderly people are also socialized into accepting their physical weaknesses and are sensitive to them in their daily activities. Many older people are probably reminded daily by others of their reduced physical ability and the need to be more careful with everything they do.

The relationship between fear of crime and age has also been found by numerous researchers. However, this difference is much less pronounced when compared to the sex differences. This is true for several national samples (Braungart, et al., 1980; Clemente and Kleiman, 1976, 1977; Erskine, 1974; Lebowitz, 1975) as well as several regional samples (Garafalo, 1979; Ollenburger, 1981; Pollack and Patterson, 1980). One factor which has been reported to accentuate the age difference in fear of crime is community size. Lebowitz (1975) reported that among urban areas, the relationship between age and fear is significant but becomes insignificant in smaller communities.

Finally, a third determinant of personal physical vulnerability is perceived health. Braungart, et al. (1980) reported that perceived health is related to fear of crime for the aged population, but not among the younger population. Ollenburger (1981) found that health status is weakly related to fear among her all-age sample. Common sense tells us that those who have health problems, or perceived themselves as such also consider themselves to be less able to defend against attackers. The fact that the strength of this relationship is not strong should not be surprising given that perceived health distinguishes those who are healthy from those who are ill. If measurements of the physical body or disability were introduced, the relationships may be stronger.

In short, sex, age, and perceived health all are treated as crude measures of physical vulnerability. All three share objective physical weaknesses, and, in turn, socialization also contributes to perceiving these factors as such.

Besides these variables of physical vulnerability, it is also reasonable to expect that certain psychological traits of the person may be associated with weakness and vulnerability. Lawton et al. (1976) suggested that fear of crime may be related to locus of control, either internal or external (Rotter, 1966), or mastery of the environment (Neugarten, 1966). Internal control refers to the feeling that one controls and determines what happens in one's life; external control refers to the perception that one's life is controlled by others. The former is equivalent to mastery of the environment, the latter to the lack of such mastery. Lawton and his associates hypothesized that high levels of fear of crime are related to external control and a lack of mastery of the environment.

Although Lawton's suggestion appears reasonable, little research has been done to test this relationship. Patterson (1977) found a relationship between manipulation of one's environment on crime prevention and fear of crime and noted that the manipulation measures may indicate locus of control. Those who are internally controlled tend to manipulate their environment for crime prevention, and this leads to lowered fear of crime. A related study (Pollack and Patterson, 1980), however, shows little support for the assumed link between locus of control and manipulation of environment. At any rate, a direct measure of locus of control was never used to assess whether it is related to fear. This relationship still awaits empirical testing.

ENVIRONMENTAL PERIL

The second dimension of the person-environment theory of fear of crime is environmental peril. The environment in which individuals reside contains signs which people usually associate with crime; the presence of these signs in turn leads to high fear of crime.

Two demographic variables, socio-economic status (SES) and race, which are often found to be related to high fear (Erskine, 1974; Braungart, et al., 1980; Clemente and Kleiman, 1977), may best illustrate how environmental peril operates through other factors. Race and SES are two strong predictors of the types of neighborhood in which one lives. Blacks and the poor often live in neighborhoods that are less than desirable. Skogan and Maxfield (1981) documented this vividly when they show that race and SES are related to their measures of "incivility" within the neighborhood: teenagers hanging around, abandoned buildings, signs of illegal drug use in streets, and vandalism. All four indicators of incivility are illustrative of the concept of environmental peril. Those who live in such neighborhoods, blacks and the poor, come to the conclusion that their neighborhood is crime-ridden, and in turn they become more fearful of crime. Notice that the often reported relationship between fear of crime and the four demographic variables of sex, age, race, and SES, are explained differently here. Females and elderly people are fearful because of their physical vulnerability, and blacks and the poor are fearful because they live in neighborhoods which carry perilous signs.

The four items in Skogan and Maxfield's scale of incivility may be further sub-divided into two dimensions. The first dimension emphasizes the physical nature of the environment: abandoned buildings and indications of vandalism. The second dimension emphasizes the social dimension of the environment: teenagers hanging around, and illegal drug use in streets. Other variables along physical and social dimensions may also be suggested.

One such example of physical perilous signs from the environment may be the quality of housing in a neighborhood. People usually associate a high prevalence of crime with lower class neighborhoods. Hence, physical neighborhood signs such as houses that are unkept and lawns that are unattended may generate fear and unease among residents and passers-by, whereas neighborhoods that have well-kept houses and meticulous front yards may induce a sense of safety.

On the other hand, the literature has provided ample illustrations of how the social environment of neighborhoods may also be interpreted by people as perilous. The racial composition of the residents of a neighborhood is one such example (Garafalo and Laub, 1979). This is certainly supported at the city level when Liska, et al. (1982) analyzed results of victimization surveys from twenty-six cities and found that both white's and non-white's fear levels were dependent on the non-white composition of the city. Those cities with a higher racial mix show a higher level of fear among the residents. The explanation for this is clear: a high proportion of non-white residents in the city are perceived as a perilous sign. This perception is not entirely inaccurate. Criminologists and, in fact, lay persons in general know that offense rates among non-white populations are considerably higher than white. Thus despite the more reasonable explanation behind this racial difference, i.e., non-whites are more likely to commit crimes because of their lower social-economic status, the presence of non-whites may be seized by the public as a convenient indicator of environmental peril. (Note that the percentage of non-whites in a city is a powerful predictor of non-white's fear as well as white's.) Unfortunately, Liska and his associates found this relationship only at the city level, not the neighborhood level, which would have given far more support to the explanation here.

This shortcoming, however, is remedied by two other studies. First, in an Illinois sample of the general population, Lizotte and Bordua (1980) found fear of crime to be higher among those individuals who have black neighbors compared to those who do not. Second, a participant observation of a housing project by Merry (1981) also suggests that people use race of neighbors as indications of environmental peril. Merry studied a housing project in an Eastern city. The project was dominated by Blacks and Chinese. Social activities that mingle these two populations are extremely rare. As such, racial stereotypes between Chinese and Blacks are strong. Black teenagers are perceived by Chinese residents as trouble-makers and burglars; Chinese teenagers are perceived by Black residents as Chinatown gang thugs. Merry concludes that fear of crime among the residents of this housing project can be attributed to the fear of the other racial group.

A related dimension of the composition of neighboring residents may also serve as a social indicator of environmental peril. This is the proportion of neighbors who are strangers. As the President's Commission on Crime (1967) noted long ago, the fear of crime victimization is "ultimately" a fear of strangers (see also Garafalo and Laub, 1979). Hence, if the neighborhood is filled with strangers, especially "suspicious-looking" ones, the level of fear may increase. Merry (1981) in her participant observation study also argued that fear of crime among the Chinese in the housing project is largely due to their failure to physically recognize Black neighbors, even though they may have been neighbors a long time. On the other hand, among those Chinese who have social ties with their Black neighbors, fear is lowered. Indirect support for the hypothesis that strangers cause fear can also be drawn from Cohn et al.'s (1979) finding that those who participated in neighborhood crime control programs are less fearful of crime. Because of the participation, knowledge of neighbors increased, and they ceased to be strangers. In turn, fear of crime was lowered. Similarly, Newman and Franck's (1982) finding that the building size of federally-assisted moderate income housing is positively related to fear of crime of its residents may also be interpreted as the influence of strangers on fear. In large buildings, the number of unrecognized neighbors increase, and their presence within the building lead to fear of crime. Finally, Skogan and Maxfield (1981) also reported that low levels of fear of crime are related to their index of social ties in the neighborhood: feeling part of the neighborhood, identifying strangers easily, and knowing many children in the neighborhood.

Besides the presence of minorities and strangers, a third dimension of neighborhood residential composition especially applicable to elderly people may actually reduce fear of crime. Older people are seldom perceived by the public as criminals. Crime statistics support this general belief—arrest rates among the aged are extremely low compared to other age groups, and most elderly criminals are property offenders, such as shoplifters. Hence, the presence of older neighbors is less of a threat to one's sense of personal safety than is the presence of younger neighbors. This is especially true if the comparison is made with teenagers. In short, it is reasonable to expect that any environment with an age-homogeneous elderly population would create a sense of safety among its residents. An environment of this sort may be a senior citizen housing project, a neighborhood with a predominance of elderly residents, or a retirement community. In such an environment, any young outsider is infrequent and could be easily spotted. The perceived threat of confronting an aggressor is, hence, reduced. Through the somewhat different approach of social support Gubrium (1974) also argued that fear of crime should be lower in age homogeneous environments.

Two studies support the relationships between fear of crime and age homogeneity for elderly persons. In a national study of fifty-three housing sites, Lawton and Yaffe (1981) found that fear of crime among older residents is higher among age heterogeneous housing projects than among age homogeneous projects. In a smaller scale study in California, Sundeen and Mathieu (1976) found the same effects of age-homogeneity at the community level. Fear is highest among elderly residents of a central city, with medium fear in the urban municipality, and the lowest fear in a retirement community.

The sheer size of a community may also be an indicator of environmental peril along the social dimension. The idea that large cities have higher crime rates than smaller communities is not only verified repeatedly in research but is also well ingrained in the culture. Cities are usually perceived as decadent and small towns the place where all virtues lie (Poveda, 1972). Thence, it is not at all surprising to find that much research reports fear to be higher in urban areas than smaller communities (Clemente and Kleiman, 1976, 1977; Lawton and Yaffe, 1981; Erskine, 1974). Surprisingly, Lee (1982b) reported that if fear of crime is measured by a scale designed to tap a general and pervasive anxiety about crime, then the level of fear among farm residents is comparable to that of urbanities.

Finally, the reputation of neighborhoods may also have an effect on fear of crime. The basis of this hypothesis is drawn from numerous studies which found fear of crime higher in neighborhoods with high crime rates (Furstenburg, 1971; Janson and Ryder, 1983; Jaycox, 1979; McPherson, 1979; Skogan and Maxfield, 1981). Other researchers have also discovered the same relationship at a city level (Garafalo, 1979; Liska, et al., 1982; Skogan, 1977; note that all three studies used the same data). This relationship is harder to explain than is at first obvious. The crime rate of a neighborhood, whether based on official statistics or victimization surveys, is not information that the public would necessarily have. As such, why would living in neighborhoods or cities with high crime rates lead to higher fear if these rates are unknown to the residents?

One way is that cities as well as neighborhoods within a community usually carry reputations and images. A newcomer to a city will find out in no time which parts of the community are considered "good" neighborhoods and which are "bad" ones; which neighborhoods have crime problems and which do not. These public images are not necessarily based exclusively on police records. The physical and other social indicators of environmental peril discussed earlier could certainly contribute to these images, but police records do play a large part. Through police personnel, the mass media, and daily conversation official crime rates of neighborhoods indirectly lead to images people have of specific neighborhoods. These images and reputations in turn affect the level of fear. One way to assess the validity of this explanation of the neighborhood crime rate/fear of crime relaship would be to ask people to rank-order neighborhoods within the community from "good" to "bad." This rank-ordering by impression should closely approximate the rank-ordering according to neighborhood crime rate. The same argument presented here may be applied at the city level.

In sum, two sets of determinants of fear of crime have been discussed so far. Personal vulnerability, the first set, includes age, sex, and health. Environmental peril, the second set, is further divided into physical and social environmental perilous signs. The former includes boarded buildings, low-quality housing, and unkempt front yards, and may be crudely indexed by SES of the neighborhood. The latter includes racial mix of residents, familarity with neighbors, age-homogeneity for elderly people, size of the community, and reputation of the neighborhood. Both physical and social environmental perils can be used to account for the predictive power of race and SES on fear of crime. The instances in which all these determinants lead to high and low fear is shown in Figure 3.3.

Given these variables in the person-environment theory, three modes of analyses appear necessary. First, the intercorrelation among variables of the same categories should be determined. This is particularly necessary for environmental peril variables where intercorrelation may be high. For example, in poor neighborhoods physical signs of environmental peril may go hand in

		High levels of fear of crime	Low levels of fear of crime
Personal Vulnerability	Physical	old	young
		female	male
		poor health	good health
Environmental Peril	Physical	poor neighborhoods	rich neighborhoods
	Social	high percentage of non-whites	low percentage of non-whites
		unfamiliar neighbors	familiar neighbors
		age mixed/age segregated (non-aged)	aged segregated (aged)
		urban areas	suburban/rural areas
		high crime rates	low crime rates

Figure 3.3. Factors associated with high and low fear of crime.

hand with the social signs. Alternately, for personal vulnerability, sex and physical size certainly are related.

A second research issue is the relative predictive power of the variables within and between the categories. Which, for example, has the most predictive power among the several social indicators of environmental peril? And do social indicators have stronger or weaker predictive power when compared to physical images of the environment? Eventually, it may be interesting to compare the explanatory power of personal vulnerability and environmental peril.

Finally, a third research interest is to see if the predictive power of personal vulnerability and environmental peril are additive or interactive in nature. In other words, under the condition of intense environmental peril does the relationship between fear of crime and personal vulnerability intensify or remain the same, compared to the condition of weak environmental peril?

Victimization Experience: Person × Environment

Besides personal vulnerability and environmental peril, a third set of known determinants of fear of crime, that of experience with victimization, has yet to be discussed. Such experiences may be conceptualized as the interaction between people and their environment. Personal and vicarious are the two types of victimization experiences. Personal experience refers to the actual involvement in crime incidents as victims; vicarious experience refers to knowledge of others who have been victimized.

Victimization experience has been deliberately not discussed until now to highlight the other sources of people's fear. Although it is intuitively easy to think that people are fearful because they have been victimized, the predictive power of personal victimization is weak according to research. Thus, the sources of people's fear lie mostly elsewhere. The person-environment theory was constructed with this in mind. People are fearful of crime not necessarily because of personal (or vicarious) experiences. The proportion of people, especially elderly people, who have been victimized in recent years is too small to contribute much to the level of fear of crime. Rather, people are fearful mostly because of their evaluation of their own personal vulnerabilities and the neighborhood in wnich they live.

There have been many more studies on personal experiences than vicarious ones. As Lawton (1981) pointed out, little doubt exists that a personal victimization experience induces fear and anxiety in the victim immediately after the event. A burglary threatens the sanctity of the home; an assault heightens one's recognition of personal vulnerability. The issue is, however, whether personal victimization has any long-term effects. After their in-depth interviews of mugging victims, Lejeune and Alex (1973) suggested, for example, that the effects of mugging on fear of crime may have only a temporary effect. Using larger samples of the general population, at least one study reported that no relationship exists between personal victimization and fear of crime (Biderman et al., 1967), while a few others reported that though the relationship exists, it is a weak one at best (Ennis, 1967; Law Enforcement Assistance Administration, 1977c; Garafalo, 1979; Lotz, 1979; Ollenburger, 1981; Skogan and Maxfield, 1981). However, among the aged, the relationship appears to be somewhat stronger. Lawton and Yaffe (1980), Lee (1983), and Norton and Courlander (1982) all reported appreciable relationships between personal victimization and fear in their studies of older people. Nonetheless, whether this difference between the old and the young is statistically significant remains to be tested.

While personal victimization has great intuitive appeal as a predictor of fear of crime, its salience not only declines due to its generally weak predictive power. As Skogan and Maxfield (1981) pointed out, the percentage of the population who are victimized each year is extremely low; most of the fearful individuals have not had recent victimization experiences.

The significance of the second type of victimization experience, vicarious victimization, may best be understood through the symbolic interactionist's concept of role-taking and empathy in interaction. When one learns of another's victimization experience, the person essentially takes the role of the victim and mentally re-lives the experience as told. Although the proportion of victims in the general population is limited, the proportion of those who know of someone who has been victimized is considerably larger. Baumer (1979) described this as a "rippling effect": one victim recounts the experience to several persons who in turn communicate it to others. Lejeune and Alex (1973) noticed that mugging victims take pride in telling others they have been mugged and, in fact, experience a star status in so doing. Hence, if a relationship between vicarious victimization and fear of crime exists, the impact would be stronger than personal victimization since vicarious victimization touches more people. For example, in a survey of three cities, Skogan and Maxfield (1981) found that 57% of their sample knew a victim of a recent burglary while only 10% had been burglarized the previous year.

Lotz (1979) reported a modest association between fear of crime and vicarious victimization in his sample of the general population of Washington state. Likewise, Skogan and Maxfield (1981) reported the same relationship in their sample of several U.S. cities. Those who knew a victim were more fearful of crime than those who did not. According to Skogan and Maxfield, this relationship is stronger if the victim was involved in a personal crime than in a property crime. Two additional conditions that make this relationship stronger are: if the victim lives in the same neighborhood as the subject and if the victim is of identical sex, and similar age (Skogan and Maxfield, 1981). (These two relationships illustrate the salience of the environment and the person components of the fear of crime theory well.) In a study of exclusively older people in the state of Washington, Lee (1983) also reported finding vicarious victimization to have an impact on fear of crime.

A third factor which could also be part of this group of variables is the influence of the mass media. Lawton (1981) and Yin (1981) both described this as a labeling process where the mass media portrays an exaggerated picture of crime. Hence, would not exposure to the mass media be related to fear of crime? Gerbner and Gross (1976) focused on the television and proposed a cultivation hypothesis. According to Gerbner and his associates, television programming presents a distorted view of violence in society and cultivates the perception of a dangerous world. In turn, viewers internalize this view and become anomic and fearful of crime. In two studies Gerbner et al. (1977, 1979) presented various data to support their thesis.

However, in recent years, the cultivation hypothesis has been heavily criticized Replications of Gerbner and his associates' study failed to uncover the fear of crime/television viewing relationship. In a general population sample in Alberta, Sacco (1982) found, for example, no relationship between hours of television viewing (and hours of newspaper reading) and fear of crime, perception of safety in the city, or attention to the crime problem. Doob and Macdonald (1979) also reported an absence of relationship between amount of television viewing and fear of crime in four neighborhoods in Toronto, except in the one neighborhood with a high crime rate. Similarly, Skogan and Maxfield (1981) reported no relationship between fear of crime and television viewing or newspaper reading based on surveys of a few American cities. They also failed to find the interaction effect between neighborhood crime rates and television viewing that Doob and Macdonald reported: the relationship between fear of crime and mass media consumption does not exist even in neighborhoods with high crime rates. Finally, the most damaging evidence against the cultivation hypothesis was presented by Hirsch (1980) when he reanalysed the data Gerbner and his associates used to support their thesis. According to Hirsch, when the proper controls, selection of variables, and comparisons between viewing groups were made, the data clearly did not support the cultivation hypothesis. Furthermore, the small segment of the population who do not watch television actually have rather high levels of fear of crime. The explanation for this lack of relationship between exposure to the mass media and fear of crime may be found in the works of Warr (1980, 1982) who contends that the public is not as naive as researchers often seem to believe they are. The public does not accept information and messages from mass media without close scrutiny.

In sum, there is evidence to support the hypotheses that both personal and vicarious victimizations lead to higher fear. On the other hand, research does not support the hypothesis that exposure to the mass media contributes to fear of crime.

THE THEORY AND RELATED ISSUES

Three different sets of variables have been considered as determinants of fear of crime in the person-environment theory: personal vulnerability, environmental peril, and victimization experience. All three factors have independent effects on fear of crime. Victimization experience appears to have the weakest predictive power, although this may be partially because it contains only two variables while the other two factors have more.

When the two victimization variables are conceptualized as intervening variables between personal vulnerability and fear of crime and between environmental peril and fear of crime, the nature of their causal paths is different, and these paths offer additional insights in addressing two salient issues on fear of crime. This is shown in Figure 3.4.

The first issue is the indirect paths through which personal vulnerability and environmental peril affect fear of crime. The most unusual of these paths is that personal vulnerability and personal victimization are negatively related. Those who are vulnerable, such as females and the aged, are actually less likely to be victimized (see Chapter 2), although they are also more likely to be fearful of crime. The implication is that the relationship between fear of crime and victimization experiences may be suppressed or weakened if sex and age are not controlled. On the other hand, personal vulnerability, vicarious victimization, and fear of crime are all positively related. Those who are physically vulnerable are more likely to talk to others about crimes and learn of other's victimization experiences. The rationale for this untested hypothesis is that those who are physically weak, such as females and the aged, actually seek out or start conversations on crime because of their general concern for personal safety. Having learned of other people's victimization experiences in turn increases their perception that they are vulnerable to crime.

Alternately, personal victimization and vicarious victimization are both positively related to environmental peril. Hence, parts of the environment's impact on fear of crime may be channeled through these two victimization variables. Those who live in perilous neighborhoods are more likely to have been victimized personally and to know of other's victimization. Consequently, residents of such neighborhoods hold higher fear.

The final path that is hypothesized here is that personal victimization leads to increased vicarious victimization. Those who have been victimized, in relating their own experience, will in turn learn of other people's similar experiences. The study by Lejeune and Alex (1973) indicated that some mugging victims noticed this phenomenon and were surprised by the presence of friends who also had experienced similar ordeals.

The second issue that may be addressed by the causal paths of the person-environment theory is whether fear of crime is rational (see Janson and Ryder, 1983; Jaycox, 1979) or irrational (see Henig and Maxfield, 1979; President's Commission on Law Enforcement and Administration of Justice, 1967). The enigma becomes clearer when one considers why some claim fear to be irrational while others hold that fear of crime is rational. Those researchers who believe that fear of crime is irrational use the elderly persons' and females' intense fear and its inconsistency with the low victimization rates as support. Those researchers who hold that fear of crime is rational base their argument, instead, on the environmental context of the fear. That is, those who live in high crime neighborhoods are more likely to be victimized and are also more fearful. Both positions are illustrated in Figure 3.4.

Although the elderly persons' and females' levels of fear may appear to be paradoxically high given their low victimization rates, closer examination should reveal that their fear is indeed "rational." According to previous discussion, those who are physically vulnerable, such as females and the elderly individuals, are also more fearful of crime. Furthermore, as Yin (1980) pointed out, information on age-specific (and sex-specific) victimization rates are not usually known by the public. Until victimization studies were first conducted in the mid-1970s, even gerontologists had no knowledge of age-specific victimization

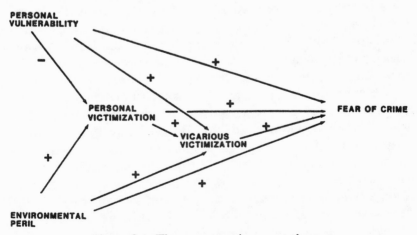

Figure 3.4. The person-environment theory.

rates, and they frequently thought that elderly people were over-victimized. Finally, as pointed out in Chapter 2, victimization rates for females and elderly people may be low because their life styles lead them to less exposure to crime. If elderly people and females are in public places more often, especially at night, whether their victimization rates will increase, and by how much, is not known. Hence, it is not surprising to find that females and the aged think that their probability of victimization is high, and this should not be considered irrational.

Besides considering fear of crime among females and the aged irrational, some researchers further argue that fear of crime among the entire population is irrational because its level is excessively high. For example, Skogan and Maxfield (1981) noted that since only six percent of their sample had been victimized in a personal crime the previous year, there was no reason for almost half the respondents to report feeling unsafe while walking in their neighborhoods. Actually there is little logic to Skogan and Maxfield's argument. There is no basis for using an *annual* victimization rate to compare the aggregate level of fear of crime. Annual victimization rates are compiled for the purpose of keeping statistics on crime, and they do not necessarily reflect the way people think about the totality of their victimization experiences. Although research has shown that people have problems during an interview recalling exactly when, where, and how their victimization experiences took place (Biderman, 1967), it is still reasonable to expect that victimizations from previous years have some bearing on people's current perception of safety. For example, if victimization rates were allowed to accumulate for three years, and then were compared to the level of fear, the discrepancy between objective and perceived risk would decrease substantially. In addition, as the previous discussions on measurements of fear of crime indicate, people's fears are usually not assessed within a given period of time. When people say that they are fearful to walk in their neighborhood, they do not mean that they think they will be attacked on their neighborhood street at least once every year, which is the basis for the comparison with the annual victimization rates. Hence, like the claim that fear is irrational among females and the aged, the position that all people's fears are exaggerated is also unfounded. In short, there is little reason to believe that fear of crime is irrational in nature.

FEAR OF CRIME AND THE AGED

In Chapter 2, various victimization studies were reviewed. The conclusion was that except for personal larceny with contact, the aged have lower victimization rates than most age groups. In this chapter, it is shown that elderly people suffer the highest level of fear of crime. Hence, a discrepancy between the elderly's objective likelihood of victimization and their perception of risk is created. This discrepancy has often been considered to be the most paradoxical issue in the study of crime and the aged (Yin, 1980). This paradox has been treated briefly earlier but it will be discussed in more depth here.

Upon closer inspection, the discrepancy between elderly people's victimization rate and their fear is not as serious as first meets the eye. Two factors point to this conclusion. First, while it is true that older people are more fearful than younger ones, the difference is not large. For example, in an analysis of a national data set, Clemente and Kleiman (1976) reported that 51% of those aged 65 or over, compared to 41% of those under age 65, responded that they were afraid to walk alone in certain parts of the neighborhood at night, a difference of only 10%. Furthermore, in a multivariate analysis of the same data, Clemente and Kleiman (1977) reported a weak relationship between age and fear of crime. On the other hand, the weakness of this relationship may be confounded by the variable of community size. Lebowitz (1975) noted an interaction effect between community size and age in predicting fear of crime. In rural areas, those who are under age 40 actually have slightly higher levels of fear than those who are over age 60. In small cities, there is virtually no difference between the age groups. However, in suburbs, medium cities, and large cities, the elderly group exhibits more fear than younger groups. For example, in large cities, Lebowitz reported that 53% of those under age 40 compared to 60% of those aged 40-59, and 71% of those aged 60 plus were fearful of crime. Similarly, data from eight city samples of the National Crime Survey also indicate a noticeable difference between the old and the young (Law Enforcement Assistance Administration, 1977c). Forty-five percent of the general population felt unsafe when out alone on neighborhood streets at night compared with 61% of the elderly population. In sum, the aged are only moderately more fearful of crime than younger persons, and this difference occurs only in urban areas.

A second factor that needs to be considered in viewing the paradoxically high level of fear among the aged despite their low victimization rate is a point that was raised in Chapter 2. Since elderly people have a life style that keeps them away from settings typical of crime victimization, their low victimization rates are expected. In other words, given the reduced amount of exposure the aged have to victimization, compared to younger persons, the aged should have a lower likelihood of victimization. In turn, if the exposure factor is adjusted between the age groups, whether the aged still continue to enjoy a lower victimization rate or not is not certain.

Two factors, one pointing out the not-so-high level of fear of crime among the aged, the other their not-so-low victimization rates, already reduce the intensity of the paradox at hand. If attention is turned to the person-environment theory of fear of crime and its three determinants, why the aged are more fearful than the younger population can be further clarified.

The most obvious determinant of fear of crime which works against the aged is personal vulnerability. Earlier discussion in this chapter points out how the feebleness of some elderly people may reduce their capacity to resist or escape from offenders. In recognition of this, the aged become more fearful. The fact that elderly people have lower victimization does little to alleviate this sense of vulnerability. As noted earlier, few people would have knowledge of age-specific victimization rates. And if people were to guess, most, like gerontologists of the 60s, would probably suspect that older people have higher victimization rates.

The aged are also more exposed to the second determinant in the person-environment theory, environmental peril. Older people are more likely than younger ones to live in central cities (Ward, 1979) where crime rates are higher and neighborhoods are more deteriorated.

Finally, victimization experience, the last determinant, has a mixed effect on older people's fear. While the aged are less likely to have been recently victimized, earlier discussions showed that a stronger relationship was found between fear of crime and personal victimization among studies of the aged than among those of the general population. Vicarious victimization, on the other hand, may also affect older people more. The aged, because of their physical vulnerability, may be more likely to hold conversations about another person's victimization. In turn, this inflates their level of fear. In sum, the three sets of variables in the person-environment theory, personal vulnerability, environmental peril, and victimization experience, all adversely affect the elderly more than the young.

Before leaving this subject, a new line of thought will be introduced here to further understand older people's level of fear of crime. When Riley et al. (1972) proposed the age stratification theory, one of their objectives was to introduce a way of thinking about observed differences between older and younger populations at one point in time, such as differences in levels of fear of crime. Why are elderly people more fearful of crime than the young? Riley and her associates believed that there are two ways to address this, with an age effect approach or with a cohort effect approach. Age effect refers to the differences in points of human development between old and young; cohort effect refers to the differences in biographies or experiences within specific historical eras. (Note that this conception of the cohort effect has also been characterized as the interaction effect between age and period.) In other words, the issue is this: are the aged more fearful because they are old and younger people less fearful because they are young (an age effect)? Or, are the aged fearful because of some life experiences they all share and younger people less fearful because of the lack of such experiences (a cohort effect)? The relationship between fear of crime and personal vulnerability, for example, utilizes the age effect approach. Given that older people are at a later stage of human development, they are weaker, more feeble, and more defenseless. As a result they are fearful of crime.

On the other hand, the cohort effect approach refers to the fact that not only do the old and the young differ in stages in their life span, they also differ in terms of their birth years and the historical periods they have experienced at various stages in their life. The question that the cohort effect approach suggests is this: are there any experiences in the biographies of the current older cohort making them more fearful of crime, and are these same experiences missing in the younger cohort? Further investigation into this question may help illuminate the reason for the elderly's level of fear of crime.

The present cohort of elderly people were born around the time of or prior to World War I. During their youthful years, transportation as well as the mass media were far less developed than today. People's awareness of events surrounding them (such as crime) was rather low. News of robberies and burglaries and rape travelled mostly by newsprint and word of mouth. Thus, although the thirties were filled with legendary gangsters, such as Al Capone, and crime rates were higher at the beginning of this century than nowadays (e.g., see Younker, 1982, for trends in murder rates), criminals and crimes remained distant images. The reality of crime victimization was not clearly comprehended by many people. Hence, it is not surprising that when most older people think of the past, they remember a more tranquil and peaceful life; crimes appeared far less prevalent in the "good old days." This is not only a process of romanticizing the past, it is also a reflection of the weak communication network of the past and the lack of awareness of events beyond one's immediate experience.

After World War II, the mass media developed and grew at geometric rates, especially with the introduction and proliferation of news films, first shown in cinemas, then on television. The cruelty of crimes and their aftermath were depicted visually, not just described in words. In general, news travelled faster, increasing the awareness of crime. This process was particularly intensified when the Federal Bureau of Investigation (FBI) started collecting and reporting national crime statistics. According to the FBI's annual report, the *Uniform Crime Report*, crime rates increased dramatically over the years since the Bureau first compiled statistics in the 1950s. Since the mass media reports on findings of the Uniform Crime Report regularly, the message communicated to the public is that crime is a growing social problem in this country.

When considering the life history of the older cohort, one can easily see how this cohort becomes increasingly aware of crime as a possible threat as they age. Such awareness is not related to the aging process, the age effect. It is, instead, tied to the life experience of one particular generation, the cohort effect. The elderly

cohort's high level of fear may be a result of this increased awareness of crime over their life history. This is in sharp contrast to
the cohort experience of the 20 year old cohort, for example, who
were born around 1960. Early in life, this younger cohort was
exposed to the urban unrest of the late '60s, the endless rise in
official crime rates, and the reporting of crime news. Unlike the
elderly cohort, crime and its threat were part of the early socialization of this younger cohort. Hence, if future innovations in the
mass communication process do not bring additional awareness
of news events and crime, and the official crime rates do not
continue to increase indefinitely into the future, then a set of
cohort experiences will develop in which the perception of the
crime problem does not intensify over one's life history. This
leads to a possible scenario in which the current younger generation might be saved from becoming more fearful as they grow
older.

Needless to say, the suggestion here is not that personal vulnerability or an age effect have no impact on elderly people's
fear, nor that the cohort effect can solely account for that fear.
Rather, the age stratification theory by Riley and her associates
suggests a cohort effect explanation of observed differences between age groups which may also contribute to older people's
fear of crime. Like other determinants of fear of crime in this
chapter, older people are also adversely affected by this cohort
effect.

SUMMARY

Fear of crime is not an emotion nor a set of behaviors. Rather,
fear of crime is an attitude. The two dimensions of this attitude
are the perceived risk of victimization and the perceived seriousness of victimization. These two dimensions are multiplicative
in nature. The implication is that fear of crime is high only if
victimization is perceived as both likely and serious. Common
measures of fear of crime are typically global measures and they
measure fear in relation to only one context, the neighborhood
street.

The person-environment theory of fear of crime is constructed to explain variations in fear. There are three components to the theory: personal vulnerability, environmental peril, and the interaction between the person and the environment, victimization experience. Personal vulnerability refers to individual characteristics that are associated with weakness, liability to injury, or general unguarded exposures. For example, females, the aged, and those who perceive their health as poor are more fearful of crime. Environmental peril refers to characteristics of the environment that signify crime and danger. Environmental peril may be further sub-divided into physical indicators and social indicators. Indicators of physical peril include abandoned buildings and indications of vandalism. Indicators of social peril include a high percentage of non-white, unfamiliar neighbors, age-integrated neighbors, urban areas, and high crime neighborhood. Finally, there are two different victimization experiences: personal and vicarious. The former refers to self experiences; the latter refers to experiences of one's social group.

Several issues related to this theory require attention. First, personal vulnerability, environmental peril, and victimization all have direct effects on fear of crime. In addition personal vulnerability and environmental peril also affect fear through personal and vicarious victimization. In turn, personal victimization is also hypothesized to have indirect effect on fear through vicarious victimization. Second, considerations of this theory point to the conclusion that fear of crime is not irrational. The public's level of fear of crime should not be considered disproportionately high compared to their general victimization rates.

Finally, the paradoxically high level of fear of crime among the aged in light of their low victimization rate is considered. Though the level of victimization rates among the aged is low, discussions in Chapter 2 conclude that this may be a reflection of their sedentary life style. On the other hand, older people's fear is only slightly higher than that of the young, and only in urban areas. In smaller communities, this difference is negligible. In addition, all three factors within the person-environment theory adversely affect older people. The aged generally are physically weak and vulnerable, they tend to live in central cities; they may be more likely to hear about other people's victimization experience. Furthermore, the cohort experience of the aged also contributes to their fear. The current cohort of older people experienced an increased awareness of crime through the mass media as well as a steady increase in official crime rate.

Chapter 4

THE EFFECTS OF VICTIMIZATION
AND FEAR OF CRIME

In this chapter, the two issues of victimization and fear of crime among the elderly will be re-visited. (Refer to Chapters 2 and 3 for earlier discussions.) Rather than focusing on the determinants, as in previous chapters, the consequences will be examined here instead: the impact of a victimization event on an elderly victim and the effects on the aged of being fearful of crime.

Crime and its fear are generally believed to be problems for the older population. In order to understand why they are problem areas for older people, one has to uncover the exact ways in which victimization and fear of crime adversely influence older people's lives. In the case of victimization, it is important to know how an elderly person suffers from such an event: the kind of harm that would typically be incurred upon an elderly victim, such as, physical injuries, financial losses, and emotional strains. Compared to younger victims, do elderly victims generally suffer more or less from these ill-effects of victimization? In the case of fear of crime, it is important to focus on the effects of fear of crime for elderly people. In other words, what exactly does fear of crime do to the elderly? How does that fear alter their life style? Does it make the elderly avoid the street, reduce their social activities, and feel imprisoned in their homes? Does fear of crime make the elderly less satisfied with their living environments, their neighbors, and their neighborhood? Does fear have adverse effects on the elderly's morale? Only by addressing these questions will the problematic nature of victimization and fear of crime among the aged be better understood.

The final section of this chapter looks at another consequence of fear of crime. In this instance, the impact of fear is assessed by how elderly people prevent victimization. What strategies do older people use to lower their chances or reduce the impact of victimizations? Whether these tactics and strategies are effective or not will be considered in a later chapter. Instead, the focus here will be on what people actually do about the threat of crime.

THE IMPACT OF VICTIMIZATION ON THE AGED

Knowledge of victimization rates is important to illuminate the prevalence of victimization, i.e., how often victimizations occur. A second dimension of victimization also needs to be considered, namely the adverse impact of victimization on the victim. Focusing only on those who are victimized, impact of victimization refers to the severity of victims' suffering. Both prevalence and impact can be considered problematic natures of victimization. If victimization occurs infrequently and/or the impact of victimization is mild, the problematic nature of the crime is reduced. In previous chapters, it was noted that rates of victimization against the aged are actually lower than those of the younger population. In other words, in terms of prevalence, crime is a more frequent problem for younger people than for the aged.

When this finding from the first wave of the National Crime Survey became public, gerontologists were indeed surprised. The myth of the overvictimized aged, which was popular in the early 1970s (e.g., see Brostoff et al., 1972; Butler, 1976; Cunningham, 1975; Goldsmith and Tomas, 1974), was debunked. As such, proponents of the view that crime is a major problem for elderly people shifted their focus from prevalence to impact (e.g., Goldsmith, 1976). They argue, instead, that even though the aged are less likely to be victimized, elderly victims suffer more than younger ones.

There are three different types of impact of victimization—financial loss, physical injury, and diminution of well-being. Financial loss refers to loss of properties (including cash) during victimization. Not all types of crimes have associated financial losses. Murder, rape, and assault do not necessarily result in financial loss unless committed in conjunction with other property crimes such as larceny, burglary, auto-theft, or robbery. Physical injury refers to bodily harm suffered as a result of confrontation between aggressor and victim. As such, victimizations that do not involve contacts with an aggressor, such as larceny without contact, auto-theft, and most burglaries, would not involve bodily injury. Finally, diminution of well-being refers to reductions in general happiness, welfare and prosperity of the victim. There are different facets of well-being and they may be divided into two components, subjective and behavioral. Unlike financial loss and physical injury which are not applicable to all types of crimes, diminution of well-being can result from all types of victimizations.

Common sense suggests that elderly victims suffer more than younger victims in all of the three major areas of impacts (National Council on the Aging, 1978). The aged are more frail and feeble, and less agile than the young. Hence, older victims in confronting an aggressor would be more likely to be physically injured. Elderly people are also poorer than the younger age groups. Hence, when financial losses are incurred, they may hurt older people more than the young. Finally, because of more serious injuries and losses, elderly people also seem to suffer greater reduction of well-being.

Only two empirical studies have reported the impact of victimization on the aged. Cook et al. (1978) studied the financial and physical impacts of victimization on the aged; Lawton and Yaffe (1980) focused on the inverse relationship between well-being and fear of crime. These two studies are explained below in some detail.

Cook et al. used the 1973 and 1974 National Crime Surveys data. In those two years, as in every year since, survey respondents who had been victimized were questioned closely regarding their financial losses and physical injuries. On financial losses, Cook compared elderly victims with younger victims along three dimensions: loss in actual dollars, loss as a percentage of monthly income, and percentage of victims whose loss was above the average income of their age group. For the first of these criteria, actual dollars lost, the elderly group lost less than other age groups. For the other two criteria of loss in relation to one's own income and that of one's age group, older victims lost less than teenagers but more than adults in all other age groups. Nonetheless, it is important to point out that these differences between age groups are small and, given that Cook and her associates did not perform statistical tests, it is not certain that the differences are significant.

For physical injuries, Cook and her associates used a series of hierarchical indicators: (a) Among the victims, what proportion were attacked? (b) Among those who were attacked, what proportion were injured? (c) How serious were the injuries? (d) Among those who were injured, what proportion were serious enough to require medical care? (e) How large were the amounts of related medical expenses? Cook et al.'s data indicate that older victims are less likely to be attacked but more likely to be injured if attacked. Older victims suffer gun and knife wounds and broken bones and teeth less often than younger victims. However, elderly victims are more likely to suffer internal injuries, loss of consciousness, and cuts and bruises. Finally, older victims are more likely to require medical care, and the size of their medical bills are larger than younger victims.

After these findings, Cook et al. (1978:346) conclude:

> The data reported here offer scant systematic support to persons who believe that, when elderly Americans are victimized by criminals, they suffer more severe financial or physical hardship than younger persons. We saw, for instance, that the elderly experience relatively small absolute financial losses and that their loss relative to their income was not so high as for adolescents and persons in their 20s. Moreover, when the elderly were attacked, they were no more likely than other age groups to be injured.... Such findings suggest the inappropriateness and incompleteness of the current consensus that older Americans suffer more than others from crime. The consensus is inappropriate because it is not correct for most crimes, and it is incomplete because it fails to differentiate between age trends for different types of crimes.

To better clarify the complexity of the issues on the impact of victimization on the aged and to resolve the contradictory data and conclusions derived, two concepts will be differentiated, that of seriousness of the victimization and sufferings of the victim. Seriousness of the victimization refers to the severity of harm that is caused or imposed on the victim by the aggressor. Seriousness of victimization measures harm without any regard to the victim. In other words, whether the victim is male or female, young or old, is not considered. In Cook et al.'s study, measures of seriousness of victimization include actual dollars lost, whether the aggressor attacked the victim, and the use of gun and knife by the crime predator. All three variables measure what the criminal did to the victim, without attention to the resulting suffering of the victim.

The suffering of the victim, on the other hand, refers to harms and damages experienced by the victim. In this instance, the capability of the victim to absorb, withstand, and recuperate from the harm is considered. For example, imagine that a criminal attacks the victim bare-handed and stole $100. If the victim were a young, rich male, he would probably suffer less than an old, poor woman. In Cook et al.'s data, measures of suffering of the victim include financial loss as a percentage of monthly income, loss above the average income of one's age group, injuries upon attack, seriousness and types of injury, medical care needed, and median medical expense. All of these measures consider the degree of suffering experienced by the victim given the victim's circumstances.

The seriousness of the victimization, i.e., amount of dollars lost, whether attacked by aggressors, and whether knife/gun wound is inflicted, poorly measure the adverse impacts of victimization. The financial resources and physical status of the victim are not taken into account. Furthermore, the findings that older victims suffer less in terms of these three measures can be explained. The actual number of dollars lost is usually a function of what the victim has at the time of the victimization. There is little reason to believe that when faced with similar amounts of property, criminals would take less from elderly victims than younger victims. Likewise, the chance of being attacked and receiving knife/gun wounds depends on the resistance the victim offers and whether the resistance threatens the aggressor. Elderly victims are poor (Cook, et al., 1978), physically weak, and not likely to resist aggressors (Bureau of Justice Statistics, 1982).

Hence, it is indeed not surprising to find that elderly people lost relatively few actual dollars and that they were the least likely to be attacked, nor is it surprising that crime predators do not tend to attack older victims with guns and knives. In sum, because of these considerations, seriousness of the victimization should not be considered at all in assessing the adverse impacts of victimization.

The level of suffering on the part of the victim, on the other hand, is a far superior concept since it measures the ability of the victim to return to "normal" life. When indicators of victims' suffering were used, Cook and her associates found that, indeed, the elderly suffer more serious impact from victimization. Since elderly victims are poorer it is not surprising to find that they lost larger percentages of their monthly incomes per victimization and that more of them sustained losses above the median income of their age group. In the frail condition of the elderly victim, they are more prone to injury if attacked, to require medical attention more often, and to have more expensive medical bills. All of this points to a conclusion that differs from Cook and her associates: elderly victims suffer more financial loss as well as physical injury compared to younger victims.

Nevertheless, for both financial and physical impacts, the differences between age groups are not drastic. This is especially so with financial loss, where there is only a shade of difference between older and younger victims, Finally, note that Cook, et al.'s study could be replicated with more recent National Crime Survey data. The National Crime Survey has been providing the same data annually since Cook's 1973 and 1974 data. A replication of their study can be easily conducted.

Besides financial loss and physical injury, the third and final adverse impact of victimization is diminution of well-being. There are several differences between well-being and financial and physical impacts that should be noted immediately. First, unlike the other consequences of victimization, well-being is a multi-dimensional concept. Hence, it is entirely possible that victimization may affect some dimensions of well-being but not others. It is necessary to specify which are and which are not influenced. Second, unlike financial loss and physical injury, well-being may not be diminished by victimization at all. There is a need to first establish the presence of this influence before

comparisons between age groups can be made. Third, the effect
of victimization on the fear resulting from it was treated exclusively in Chapter 3. To briefly recapitulate, this relationship is a
weak one, at best. Those who have been recently victimized have
a higher level of fear than do those who were not victimized
recently, but the difference is not large.

With these three points in mind, readers can now turn to
Lawton and Yaffe's (1980) study of a national sample of elderly
residents in public housing, the only one to date which inspected
the often hypothesized inverse relationship between well-being
and victimization. Given that Lawton and Yaffe studied public
housing residents, their findings may not be representative of
older people in other housing environments. Two sets of measures of well-being were examined: behavioral and subjective.
Measures of behavioral well-being include frequency of off-site
activities, on-site activities, contact with friends, social space,
aggregate walking time, and usage of resources that are closest to
the housing site. Measures of psychological well-being include
housing satisfaction, neighborhood satisfaction and morale. Together with other crime-related and personal/demographic predictors, the effects of victimization experience on these measures
of well-being were assessed independently at the multivariate
level.

Surprisingly enough, Lawton and Yaffe found that whether
elderly tenants of public housing sites had been victimized in
recent years or not had no significant effect on any of the behavioral indicators of well-being. In other words, having been victimized did not decrease older people's social activities as expected.
For the three subjective measures of well-being, only one was
related to victimization. Morale was adversely influenced by victimization, while neighborhood and housing satisfaction were
not. Even then, the relationship discovered was rather weak.
Furthermore, the credibility of this relationship was weakened
when Lawton and Yaffe analyzed it longitudinally. The researchers had two panels of data on morale, 1971 and 1974, and when
they analyzed the change in morale between these two years, they
found that it was not related to victimization experiences between
the two time periods.

In sum, Lawton and Yaffe conclude that victimization had no
long-term effect on well-being. There is little doubt that if a

person is burglarized, his immediate reactions include decreased satisfaction with his housing and neighborhood. However, what Lawton and Yaffe demonstrated was that such decrease in satisfaction, even if it does occur, does not last long enough to be detected with their research design.

Earlier, it was pointed out that victimization is weakly related to fear of crime. If that is the case, could victimization lead to a lower sense of well-being indirectly through fear of crime? Lawton and Yaffe acknowledge this possibility. How this happens will be discussed in a later section when the relationship between well-being and fear of crime is discussed.

The conclusion is this: victimization has no long-term effect on well-being, except perhaps on morale. Because of this absence of effect, comparison with younger victims becomes unnecessary. The adverse impact of victimization on older victims is seen in their financial losses and physical injuries.

THE IMPACTS OF FEAR OF CRIME

The study of fear of crime among the aged is rooted in the study of victimization of elderly people. Given this connection, fear of crime among the aged is, therefore, often approached with a social problems orientation. In other words, the view is that fear of crime deserves research attention because that fear creates problems in the lives of older people.

There are numerous indications of this contention: (a) The mass media has reflected and has probably contributed to the public's definition of fear of crime as a social problem (Lawton, 1980; Conklin, 1976; Henig and Maxfield, 1979; Yin, 1980). Not only have television, movies, newspapers, and popular magazines created an inflated impression of crime rates, they have also selectively focused on how fear of crime adversely affects the lives of older people. For example, notice the title of a *New York Times* (1976) story, "Way of life of older people curbed by fear of crime," or one in *Time* magazine (1976) "Elderly Prisoners of Fear."

(b) Bureaucratic administrators have accepted the phenomenon of fear of crime as a social problem for the elderly. A national program called "Criminal Justice and the Elderly" was funded in 1978 "to learn how urban service programs can reduce the impact of crime and fear of crime that poisons the lives of many older Americans" (Criminal Justice and the Elderly, 1978). The program is a part of the National Council of Senior Citizens' Legal Research and Services for elderly people. Initially, the program was supported by grants from the government (Law Enforcement Assistance Administration, Department of Housing and Urban Development, Community Services Administration, and Administration on Aging) as well as from the private sector (The Ford Foundation, and the Edna McConnell Clark Foundation).

(c) Legislators have also accepted the problematic nature of fear of crime. The U.S. Congress (1977:44), for example, reported that, "the sub-committee is convinced that fear of crime is a pervasive and onerous problem for older Americans."

(d) Gerontologists, in general, also see the elderly as suffering from fear of crime (Leibowitz, 1975; Lawton et al., 1976; Butler, 1976; Clemente and Kleiman, 1977). They believe that the impact of fear of crime includes curtailing social activities, avoiding going out at night, loss of morale, limited or no hospitality to strangers or even neighbors on the street, and moving out of neighborhoods. In fact, these ill-effects of fear of crime are not restricted to the elderly but to the general population as well. Brooks (1974) summed up the sentiment very well when he wrote, "the fear of crime in the United States is a fundamental social problem which has not yet received attention in proportion to its severity and which may well prove to be more difficult to treat than criminality itself."

(e) Probably the most significant factor in the acceptance of fear of crime as a problem for the aged is that, according to a national study, more elderly people consider fear of crime as a "very serious" or "serious" personal problem than any of the other eleven issues included in that study (National Council on the Aging, 1977:130). In fact, fear of crime outranks prominent problems such as poor health or low income. Since that study became public, many researchers have asserted that fear of crime is *the most serious* problem facing the elderly (Braungart et al., 1979; Braungart et al., 1980; Patterson, 1979; Pollack and Patterson, 1980; Yin, 1980). Fear of crime has moved from being merely a problem facing the elderly to the number one problem for the old.

Yin (1980, 1982) pointed out that the problematic nature of fear of crime lies not in fear of crime, per se, but in its ill-effects. Fear of crime in and of itself should not be considered a problem, especially if we find that the fearful ones enjoy life as much as the non-fearful. Fear only becomes a problem when it inhibits people's well-being.

There are two different strategies to assess the problematic nature of fear of crime (Yin, 1982): first, simply to see if the aged themselves define fear of crime as a problem in their lives. In this instance, whether fear of crime actually leads to ill-effects for the aged is less relevant; what is more important is how the elderly define and see fear of crime. As Thomas and Thomas (1970) argued long ago, "Situations defined as real are real in their consequences." If fear of crime is defined and perceived as a problem by the aged, they will lead and adjust their life styles accordingly.

As mentioned earlier, one national study, conducted by Louis Harris and Associates for the National Council on Aging (1977), which surveyed a national sample of people aged sixty-five and over, reported that elderly people consider crime and its fear to be their most serious problem. Respondents were read a list of twelve problems of daily living. For each, the respondents were asked if the issue was "a serious problem," "a somewhat serious problem," "hardly a problem at all," or "not sure." The result of the NCOA study is presented in Figure 4.1.

Yin (1982) reported on data that assessed elderly people's definition of fear of crime with a different measurement. The study was a survey of a random sample of elderly people in Ramsey County, Minnesota. Two open-ended questions were asked. "What are your biggest problems in life?" and "What are your biggest worries in life?" Two responses to the former and one to the latter were coded. The combined list is also shown in Figure 4.1. The most astonishing element of this comparison is that while the relative ranking of many of the items are nearly equivalent in the two studies, fear of crime is not. Fear of crime was named by only one percent of elderly people in Yin's (1982) data ranking seventh among the twelve items, whereas in the NCOA study fear was named by 23% and was ranked first.

Yin accounted for this difference in findings by comparing the measurement procedures used in the two studies. With the closed-ended format, NCOA's question has the effect of sensitizing

Items*	NCOA (1977)	Yin (1982)
Fear of crime/crime	23%	1%
Poor health	21%	28%
Not enough money	15%	10%
Loneliness	12%	5%
Not enough medical care	10%	1%
Not enough education	8%	0%
Not feeling needed	7%	1%
Not enough to do to keep busy	6%	3%
Not enough job opportunities	5%	2%
Not enough friends	5%	1%
Poor housing	4%	0%
Not enough clothing	3%	0%

*Other items identified in Yin's data include the following:
health of family members or care of family members (9%), transportation
or winter weather problem (6%), home maintenance (5%), family relations
(4%), afraid of moving (1%).

Source: Based on data partially reported by Yin (1982).

Figure 4.1. Most serious personal problem. Source: Based on data partially reported by Yin (1982).

respondents to the issue of crime and its fear. Note that crime/ fear is an item that is categorically different from any of the other items. Crime victimization is an acute event. It involves an unknown situation over which a victim feels little control. Victimization reminds one of danger, trouble, and hazard, when one's life may be in jeopardy. The other items of poor health, not enough money, loneliness, medical problems, not enough education, and so on, are more enduring problems of life, problems which are not imminently life-threatening. If crime and fear of crime are used as sensitizers, they may arouse a sense of threat that is not actually there. As a result, more of the aged responded by defining crime and fear of crime as extremely serious problems in the NCOA study. On the other hand, when no suggestive questioning techniques were used in Yin's data, only one percent of the respondents considered crime or its fear as a serious problem or worry. This implies that the issue of fear and crime is not one that the elderly consider highly serious. At least it is not kept at a conscious level and readily identified.

In sum, Yin's study points to measurement issues in the NCOA data, and argues that fear of crime as the most pressing problem facing the elderly is an overstatement. Nevertheless, fear of crime may still be a secondary problem for the elderly and this fear may affect the lives of the elderly. To ascertain this, Yin (1982) identified a second approach to assessing the problematic nature of fear of crime: testing for the presence of any inverse relationship between well-being and fear. Does fear of crime detract from and lower older people's sense of well-being? If so, in what sense? As before, the concept of well-being is divided into a psychological component and a behavioral component.

Two aspects of the psychological dimension of well-being have been shown to be adversely affected by fear of crime. The first is morale. Lawton and Yaffe (1980) found that, among public housing elderly residents, those who are fearful have lower morale compared to those who are not. Similarly, Yin (1982) found the same relationship among community residents of an urban county. In both instances, the strength of the relationship is notable, though by no means strong. Based on the measurements used in the two studies, it can be concluded that the fearful elderly suffer from less happiness and satisfaction in life, feel sad more often, and believe things get worse with aging.

The second aspect of psychological well-being diminished by fear of crime is neighborhood satisfaction (including city satisfaction, and housing satisfaction). Both Lawton and Yaffe (1980) and Yin (1982) found this in their analyses of their elderly samples. Furthermore, Hartnagel (1979) reported that fear of crime has the same negative effect on neighborhood satisfaction among his all-age sample in Edmonton, Canada. In all cases, the inverse relationship between neighborhood satisfaction and fear of crime appears stronger than that between morale and fear.

These findings suggest that when any person feels unsafe on the neighborhood street, the satisfaction to be gained from living in that particular neighborhood, housing, and community is drastically reduced. This blends with Rainwater's (1966) notion of the home as a haven. When the neighborhood is perceived in dangerous terms, the ability for that setting to serve as shelter and refuge from the "outside world" is gone and one's satisfaction with it is diminished. What this may mean is suggested by the National Crime Survey (Law Enforcement Assistance Administration, 1977c): those who are fearful tend to think seriously about moving elsewhere more often, although the relationship is a weak one. The strength of this relationship should not be surprising since there are numerous other factors that have to be taken into consideration in actual moves. Research on moving behavior confirms that crime and its fear have little or no effect on people's actual move out of their neighborhoods (Skogan and Maxfield, 1981). In short, the impact of fear of crime on neighborhood preference remains a psychological one.

It has been suggested that other aspects of psychological well-being are also reduced by fear of crime, although none have been tested empirically. Liska, et al. (1982) suggested that feelings of anxiety, mistrust, and alienation may develop when one is fearful and there is more possibility that one may take drugs to reduce fear. Similarly, Braungart, et al. (1980) claimed that fear leads one to take tranquilizers. More research is needed in this area to substantiate these claims. Reductions in one or two dimensions of well-being does not automatically imply the decrease of others.

This apparently is the case with the presumed adverse effect of fear of crime on the behavioral aspect of well-being. Limiting social activity is probably inferred most often as the problem that the fearful aged have to face. The assumption is that if the elderly are fearful of crime or feel unsafe on the neighborhood street, they will stay at home more often. This curtails their social activities. This line of logic comes in various forms. For example, Butler (1976) used the term "house arrest," and *Time* (1976) portrayed the elderly as "prisoners of fear." An extremely dramatic account is presented in a news story recounted by Braungart et al. (1979:22):

> Perhaps one of the saddest stories came from the Bronx policeman who told reporters about "Mary." Mary was 75 years old and,

after being mugged, never left her apartment. She was so fright-
ened that she did not even carry out the garbage, which accumu-
lated day by day, month by month. Systematically, each room in
her apartment was filled with garbage and then sealed. Mary did
not go out for food; she tossed money out the window to children
who bought her candy bars. Even the children abused her by
overcharging for the candy. One day Mary let down her guard and
went out to mail a letter. She was mugged again. It was only then
that the police learned about her plight and the devastating effect
of fear on her life.

To what extent is this story of "Mary" typical of the elderly? Is
Mary's reaction to her perceived threat of victimization common
among those who are fearful? Does fear of crime turn elderly
people into "prisoners" in their own homes? In his Edmonton
general population sample, Hartnagel has two sets of measurements for social activities—neighborhood cohesion and social
activities. The former set includes measures of "number of neighbors known" and "talk to neighbors"; the latter includes numbers of social evenings with friends and entertainment. None of
these measures was related to either fear of neighborhood crime
or of city crime. Having higher levels of fear did not lower the
quantity of social activities with neighbors or friends. Likewise, Lawton and Yaffe (1980) studied the relationship between
amount of social activity and fear of crime. They used six types
of measures for social activities (off-site activities, on-site activities, contact with friends, social space, aggregate walking time,
and percentage of resources used that are the closest to the
housing site). Again, fear of crime did not adversely influence
any of these activities. Both of these studies failed to find any
support for the claim that because of the threat of crime victimization, people isolate themselves, avoid the street, or have fewer
social activities. No significant differences were found between
the fearful and the non-fearful aged. Similarly, in a survey of 150
elderly respondents in an East London borough, Clarke and
Lewis (1982) did not find fear of crime to be related to frequency,
duration, and quality of social contacts.

One of the problems with these three studies on the isolating
effects of fear is their conceptualization and, consequently, measurement of social activities. These studies quantified the degree
of social activities. Social isolation was signified by few nighttime activities, little involvement with neighbors, few interac-

tions with friends, limited on-site/off-site activities, reduced social space, and so on. Social involvement was indicated by the
reverse. The implication is that social activity can be measured
by a continuum from high social involvement, which is good, to
utter isolation, which is bad. Yet, the literature has cautioned
against conceptualizing social activities this way. Lowenthal
and Robinson (1973) argue, for example, that "composite indices
which assess only the extent of social interaction tended to give a
holistic emphasis to the concept of social activity (one of the
dangers when methodology precedes conceptualization)." The
drawback of seeing social involvement as "good" and isolation
as "bad" became apparent first in the debate between the disengagement theorists and the activity theorists. One of the several
conclusions derived from the debate is the significance of involving symbolic interactionism and phenomenology in the conceptualization of isolation (Hochschild, 1975). The meaning of
social involvement and isolation for specific aged, particularly
whether the isolation is voluntary or involuntary, should not be
neglected. Cumulative indices of isolation like the ones used by
Hartnagel and Lawton and Yaffe conspicuously neglected this,
confounding the difference between loneliness and aloneness
(Shanas, 1970).

Lowenthal and Boler (1965) illustrated the significance of the
lonely/alone distinction. They reported that those who were involuntarily withdrawn but socially deprived ranked similarly
and consistently lower in morale than those who were not deprived of social activity and those who were voluntarily withdrawn. Similar results were obtained by Tallmer and Kutner
(1970) who reported that voluntary disengagement yields high
morale while forced disengagement is associated with hopeless-
ness and despair.

In light of this discussion, Yin's (1982) finding on fear's effects
on social activities becomes more significant. Yin conceptualized
isolation as *involuntary* isolation. In this instance, Yin defines
those who are involuntarily isolated as only those persons who
have low levels of social activity and who desire to have more.
Persons who have low levels of social activity and who are content that way would be included in the same category as those
who are socially active. For measurements in Yin's data, respondents were asked first how often they went out of their homes
each week. Those who went out less than "several times" a week

were asked if they would "like to go out more often." Those who expressed a desire to go out more often were coded as one group indicating involuntary isolation. Those who did not desire to go out more often were the voluntary withdrawers and were coded the same as those who went out several times a week.

Yin found that almost all older people had the amount of social activities they desired. In fact, only 5% of older people were isolated involuntarily. When the relationship between this variable and fear of crime was assessed at the bivariate level, Yin found a weak association. Those who are fearful of crime do tend to be involuntarily isolated. This finding is in contradiction to other studies which found no relationship between the amount of social activity and fear. Yin attributed the discrepancy in finding to conceptualization and measurement differences.

To further support his conclusion that fear does reduce social activity, albeit only slightly, Yin presented additional data. In the survey Yin analyzed, respondents were asked at different points during the interview, whether they had trouble participating in six different types of social activities: going to the neighborhood senior citizen center, going to a particular senior citizen center in St. Paul, taking part in religious services, taking a hobby course, going to shows or concerts or other activities, and taking part in activities of respondent's voluntary association groups. Those who responded positively to any of the six were asked the source of trouble. A combined frequency distribution of the factors, as reported by Yin, is shown in Figure 4.2. Notice first that there are many factors that constrain social activities; crime and its fear are only one. There is no reason to assume that when an elderly person feels restricted from engaging in more social activities, fear of crime is the only constraining factor. As a matter of fact, Figure 4.2 shows that fear of crime or crime were considered by only 4% of Yin's sample to be a factor which gave them trouble in participating in at least one of the six activities mentioned. Notice that the three factors of lack of time, poor health, and transportation, identified by more respondents all had 12% or more of the sample naming the item, much more than fear of crime. In addition, fear's inhibiting effects on social activity are comparable to a host of other factors, such as lack of interest, winter weather, and no company. Based on this data, as well as the bivariate relationship discussed earlier, Yin concluded that fear of crime is a conscious but minor factor that deters a small fraction of people from participating in social events.

Law Enforcement Assistance Administration (1977c) provided a comparable set of data, which also allowed respondents to suggest factors that deter them from social activities. The survey item asked those respondents who replied that they were going

reasons for not participating in social events	Yin (1982): six social events	LEAA (1977c): "less now than a year ago"
lack of time	16%	----
poor health	13%	23%
transportation problem	12%	2%
fear of crime	4%	18%
lack of interest	3%	7%
winter weather	3%	----
no company	3%	3%a
age	2%	27%
care of family members	2%	4%b
lack of money	2%	5%
others	8%	2%

[a]no opportunity

[b]family reasons

Sources: Law Enforcement Assistance Administration (1977c)
Yin (1982)

Figure 4.2. Factors inhibiting social activities. Source: Law Enforcement Assistance Administration (1977c), Yin (1982).

out less now than a year or two ago to identify the most important reason for reducing their activities. The responses of those aged sixty-five or older are also shown in Figure 4.2. Because of the difference in nature between LEAA's and Yin's data, the two are not entirely comparable. For example, while Yin's data showed lack of time as the most often identified reason for not going out more often, no respondents mentioned limited time as a response in LEAA's survey, or at least not often enough to have it coded separately. This is not surprising given that one would hardly anticipate a sizable portion of elderly people to have less time available compared to "a year or two ago." On the other hand, it is reasonable to see time limitation as a factor that prohibits older people, as well as younger people, from engaging in more social activities.

Given the difference in the nature of the two data sets, it is interesting to notice that more respondents (18%) in the LEAA study identified crime or its fear as the reason for not going out more frequently. Despite the fact that the two factors of age (27%) and poor health (23%) came ahead of fear of crime, the 18% who saw crime as threatening enough to deter activity were significantly more than the 4% in Yin's data. The reason may lie in the orientation of the two surveys. Yin's data came from a needs assessment survey of the elderly. In this survey, only a very small portion of questions were devoted to crime. Whereas, LEAA's data is part of the National Crime Survey. Respondents for this survey were faced with a lengthy interview guide entirely devoted to crime. Hence, the 18% reported by LEAA may be inflated. After engaging in a long interview on victimization experience, elderly respondents may find it natural to say fear of crime reduced the level of their going out.

The conclusion, then, is that fear of crime does inhibit social activities, but only slightly. Earlier research which failed to uncover this relationship may have erred in neglecting to consider the meaning of isolation for the elderly person. But, research also shows that just because the aged are fearful of crime they are not imprisoned in their homes nor are they house-arrested. On the other hand, as will be seen shortly, while the threat of crime does not have much adverse effect on the desired frequencies of social activities, the fear does influence the patterns of going out for older people in other more subtle ways.

In summary, available research shows that fear of crime has a strong adverse effect on neighborhood satisfaction and a modest effect on morale. The ill-effects of fear of crime have more to do with the deterioration of older people's psychological well-being and less with behavioral well-being. Furthermore, given that only one percent of Yin's sample identified fear of crime/crime as a major problem or worry, it would be a mistake to consider fear as the most serious problem the elderly face. The problematic effects of fear may need to be more diverse and intense before more older people consider it as the most pressing problem they face.

COPING

The previous two sections look at how actual victimizations and the fear of crime affect elderly people. In this segment, the focus is on how elderly people respond to crime. In light of the possibility that one may be victimized, what type of behaviors do older people engage in to minimize the chance or the impact of victimization?

How people cope with crime has been a major research area since the pioneer work of the President's Commission on Crime in the mid-sixties. The national study of victimization (Ennis, 1967) as well as the Washington, D.C. one (Biderman, et al., 1967) both studied how people change their lives to prevent victimization. There are two major problems with this body of literature. First, as the detailed literature review by Dubow et al. (1979) showed, the vast majority of these studies were not published. Most of them were in-house reports for commissions, anti-crime programs, or local government agencies. Only published reports will be examined here. Second, almost all of this research studied the general population; age distinctions are often not made. Hence, despite the research efforts in this area, little knowledge exists on the exact coping behaviors in which elderly people engage. Yet, to some extent, the problem is not so much the lack of gerontological orientation in this research area. Rather, it is the diverse and elusive nature of coping behaviors. Coping includes a wide variety of behaviors with complex patterns.

How do people cope with crime? Coping behaviors will be defined as all activities that people deliberately engage in or avoid with the intention of reducing the likelihood of victimization or the severity of its impact if victimization does occur. With this definition a large variety of activities can be considered coping behavior. For example, in a study of the elderly population in Multnoma County in Oregon, Rifai (1976) included the following activities as coping behaviors: carry no wallet/money/ purse, avoid going out at night, own weapons, add locks, mark properties, go to crime prevention block meetings, turn on lights when going out, and own dogs. Rifai reported that 63% of the elderly surveyed reported using at least one of these measures. A quick glance at Rifai's list will reveal that the list is by no means inclusive of all coping behaviors. Further, the list includes items for different purposes: for example, not carrying money reduces the financial impact of victimization; leaving on lights gives the appearance that someone is at home; carrying weapons allows more effective defense against offenders. One way to capture the diverse ways people cope with crime and the numerous purposes for coping behaviors is to create a typology of coping behaviors which serves as a first step to systematic understanding of the issue at hand.

Typologies of coping behaviors in the literature are bountiful. Numerous researchers have proposed conceptual schemes for dividing and sub-dividing coping behaviors. The first group of typologies all share the characteristic of having only two categories. The first one proposed by Furstenburg (1972) makes a distinction between avoidance and mobilization behaviors. Avoidance refers to strategies for isolating oneself from exposure to victimization (e.g., staying off the street, locking doors, ignoring strangers); mobilization refers to the purchase and/or installation of anti-crime devices (e.g., burglary alarms, window bars, guns). Conklin (1975) presented a different typology which separated individual responses from collective responses. Individual responses refer to anti-crime activities undertaken by individuals; collective responses refer to anti-crime activities carried out by citizens as groups (e.g., neighborhood watch). Similarly, the Law Enforcement Assistance Administration (as discussed in Lavrakas and Lewis, 1980) proposed a distinction between public-minded vs. private-minded crime prevention. Public-minded efforts refer to programs designed to promote social responses to crime and its fear at the neighborhood level; private-minded efforts refer to individual activities that do not contribute to neighborhood organization.

The second group of typologies, with more than two categories, are more complex in that further sub-categories may exist. Skogan and Maxfield (1981) discussed three different categories: personal precaution, household protection, and community action. Personal precaution refers to measures that reduce one's chance of being victimized, such as driving instead of walking, taking an escort, and avoiding certain places; as well as measures that reduce one's chance of being attacked if victimized, such as taking something for protection—a weapon or a dog. Household protection refers to efforts to protect one's household against property crime. Again there are several sub-types. Target-hardening, a term frequently found in the literature, refers to efforts to make the household more difficult to break into, e.g., window bars, special locks, and solid core doors. Surveillance refers to measures that create the appearance that someone is at home, e.g., turning on the lights and radio, stopping delivery of paper and mail, and having neighbors watch one's house when away for prolonged periods. Finally, loss reduction measures are strategies that minimize financial losses if and when a burglary occurs, e.g., insurance, or engraving of identification on valuable items.

The third group of coping behaviors, according to Skogan and Maxfield (1981), is community actions. Included here are participation in groups whose sole purpose is to fight crime, such as neighborhood watches or neighborhood patrols, and participation in community groups which include anti-crime programs as one of their functions.

Lavrakas (1981) presented a typology for coping behaviors mainly designed for home protection. His is similar to Skogan and Maxfield's (1981) for household protection in that it also includes target-hardening, surveillance (which Lavarkas called occupancy proxy), and loss reduction. However, Lavarkas introduced a new type called psychological access control measures, which includes installing alarms or outdoor spotlights.

Finally, after an exhaustive review of the literature, Dubow, et al. (1979) proposed five different types of "reactions to crime": behavior, protective behavior (home and personal), insurance behavior, communicative behavior, and participatory (organizational) behavior. Aside from communicative behavior, which is a reaction to crime and not a coping behavior, all the others have already been noted.

This discussion of the various typologies of coping behaviors does not include all those which exist in the literature. Rather, the purpose is to highlight the diversity of coping behaviors and also the various ways in which these behaviors can be categorized. Notice that all of these typologies are constructed conceptually rather than empirically. They are designed to make sense out of the various ways in which people cope with the threat of crime victimization. They do not represent, however, the clusters of coping behaviors that people actually undertake (see Lavakas and Lewis, 1980, for an alternate position on this). For example, window bars, security doors, and dead-bolt locks are all considered target-hardening devices because these various mechanisms all serve the same purpose, but not all of them are installed as a group by people. Using one target-hardening device in no way implies other devices will also be used. Similarly, people who avoid going to certain parts of town at night, which is a type of avoidance behavior, may not necessarily avoid strangers on the street altogether.

Given the conceptual nature of these typologies, it becomes somewhat difficult to evaluate them or to choose a best one. The typologies of Furstenburg (1972), Conklin (1975), and LEAA appear to be too simple to fully capture the complexity of the behaviors people perform to prevent victimization. On the other hand, the typologies by Dubow, et al. (1979), Skogan and Maxfield (1981), and Lavarkas (1981) may be too detailed to present a succinct perspective on coping behaviors. In addition, these latter typologies contain categories that overlap one another. For example, home protection may also be considered as a personal precaution in the home setting. Yet another typology will be presented below which one hopes captures the most salient criteria for differentiating coping behaviors while remaining brief.

For this typology, two criteria of demarcation will be used, primarily because they can be conceptually linked to other discussions in this book. An important distinction that has emerged in these discussions is that some coping behaviors aim to lower one's chances of being victimized while others aim at reducing the impact of victimization if and when one is victimized. This difference is similar to the two aspects of victimization, prevalence and impact, discussed earlier in this chapter, or perceived likelihood and perceived seriousness, the two aspects of fear of crime discussed in Chapter 3. The second distinction to be examined is the coping behavior as designed for the household versus the street.

The typology created when cross-tabulating the two criteria of differentiation is shown in Figure 4.3. Four different types of coping behaviors emerge. The first type refers to street crime prevention behaviors. This refers to any measures that will lower one's chance of being victimized on the street. Avoiding certain places (e.g., downtown or subways), or particular streets, at certain times (e.g., night time), and certain people (e.g., teenagers) are all considered part of this strategy. Also included are protective measures that are conspicuous (e.g., going out with other people, or with a dog). All of these are designed to lower one's chance of being victimized on the street. The second type of coping behaviors refers to street victimization loss reduction behaviors, if and when victimized on the street. In this category are habits such as carrying less money when going out, not carrying jewelry, and carrying concealed weapons such as a gun, knife, or mace. Carrying less money and jewelry lowers potential losses by reducing the amount of available goods to be taken; the weapons have the same result of offering effective resistance. The third type of coping behaviors are household victimization prevention measures. Included here are the various target-hardening devices: locking doors and windows, surveillance, occupancy proxy, and the posting of signs that indicate household property is marked. These are all ways to deter criminals from entering one's household illegally, whether someone is home or not. Finally, the last type is household victimization loss reduction, which refers to methods of minimizing household losses if victimized. Included here are insurance of household goods, storing expensive items in bank safe deposit boxes or away from home, and marking property to allow easier retrieval.

This typology allows for easy comprehension of the numerous coping behaviors people engage in. It includes all of the types and sub-types proposed in the literature. The only exception not

	VICTIMIZATION PREVENTION	LOSS REDUCTION
STREET VICTIMIZATION	• AVOIDANCE • CONSPICUOUS PROTECTIONS	• CARRY LESS PROPERTIES • CARRY WEAPONS
HOUSEHOLD VICTIMIZATION	• TARGET HARDENING • LOCKING BEHAVIORS • SURVEILLANCE • OCCUPANCY PROXY	• INSURANCE • MARK PROPERTIES

Figure 4.3. A typology of coping.

included is what Conklin (1975) called collective responses, what Law Enforcement Assistance Administration (as discussed in Lavrakas and Lewis, 1980) termed public-minded crime preventions, what Skogan and Maxfield (1981) called community actions, or what Dubow et al. (1979) considered participatory behavior. Despite the differences in terminology, they all refer to collective coping behaviors rather than individual ones like those presented in the typology under discussion. Actually, collective coping behaviors can also be classified according to the four types in Figure 4.3, depending on the nature of the activities. For example, citizen patrol of neighborhoods or neighbor watch programs are meant to reduce both street and household victimizations. On the other hand, the engraving of property, a type of crime prevention that is often done in groups (Dubow, et al., 1979) belongs to loss-reduction of household victimization. Finally, self-defense courses that are organized by community groups can be considered as a measure of street victimization loss reduction. In short, the classification scheme for individual coping can also be applied to collective coping behaviors.

With this typology in mind, it is reasonable to inquire next into the type(s) of coping behaviors the elderly engage in. Among the four types of coping behaviors, which type do elderly people practice most often? And then, among the elderly population who will have a greater tendency to engage in coping behaviors? Finally, does the pattern of coping behaviors for elderly people established by the previous two questions differ from the pattern among the younger population? All of these questions appear to be basic to research done in this area. But no fast and easy answers exist. There are several reasons for this absence of knowledge. First, as noted earlier, little research in this area has been focused exclusively on the elderly population. The questions raised by victimization interest criminologists far more than gerontologists. In existing research, if age is entered as a predictor variable, there are usually no explicit comparisons between the old and the young. Thus, age, as a continuous variable, may be related to certain coping behaviors but it is still not certain whether old people are or are not coping that way. Second, rarely are there national studies on coping behaviors. What exist instead are a variety of regional, small-scale surveys. The results of these surveys vary considerably in terms of the prevalence of people practicing various coping strategies. For example, as Dubow, et al.'s (1979) review of these small-scale regional studies shows: the percentage of respondents who claim they stay off the street at night ranges from 7% through 80%, and the percentage of respondents who indicate owning guns for protection ranges from 4% through 43%.

Finally, it is fair to say that this is an extremely confusing area of research. The major problems lie in the numerous types of coping behaviors that people practice. There are simply too many dependent variables. In examining the relationship between the characteristics of people and whether they practice coping behaviors or not, the common strategy is to treat each specific coping strategy in turn as the dependent variable. When this is done, the results often become confusing. For example, Clotfelter (1977) statistically regressed ten different coping behaviors on six predictor variables in turn, and what emerged was no systematic or ultimately interpretable patterns among the ten coping behaviors. Different relationships of coping were found for the ten different coping behaviors. Lavrakas and Lewis (1980) used factor analysis as a data reduction technique to cluster coping variables; the common factors they discovered are often not conceptually meaningful. Furthermore, it is even questionable whether people should be expected to practice coping in meaningful clusters. Skogan and Maxfield (1981) probably presented the best way to measure coping: they reported the presence of a Guttman scale for household surveillance behaviors. According to these two researchers, the following four items are practiced by people in a hierarchial pattern: turn lights on at night if out, have neighbors watch home, stop mail and paper delivery, and join neighborhood-watch programs. The idea of Guttman scaling for coping behaviors is interesting. It awaits further work to see if other types of coping behaviors form such a hierarchial pattern. Unless analysis schemes for coping behaviors are improved, knowledge of who and why people practice which types of coping will remain muddled.

Despite these problems, some accumulation of knowledge about these questions does exist. The following discussion is based on the literature without singling out the elderly people. It is hoped that more research will be developed in the future that makes comparison between the old and the young, or at the very least, focuses on the elderly exclusively.

Street Victimization Prevention

Street victimization prevention is divided into two major groups: avoidance behavior and conspicuous protection. Avoidance is the more prevalent of the two and is researched far more. Readers may have noticed by now the conceptual resemblance between avoidance behavior as a coping behavior and involuntary isolation or deliberate isolation due to the threat of victimization. If, as argued earlier in this chapter, fear of crime has a weak effect on limitation of frequency of activities, why then is avoidance discussed as a frequent form of street victimization prevention?

Actually, avoidance and involuntary isolation are not identical concepts. The distinction between the two is this: involuntary isolation because of crime threat is one kind of avoidance, i.e., the avoidance of going out even when one wants to or needs to. As those noted earlier, there are other types of avoidance: avoiding strangers or teenagers, certain areas such as parks, downtown, or some neighborhoods, certain public transportation such as the subway, or nighttime in general. Those who avoid some people, places, and transportation modes do not necessarily reduce the total amount of their desired activities, which would be involuntary isolation. Thus, despite the fact that 42% of the NCS (8) city samples responded that they have limited or changed their personal activities because of crime, Hindelang et al. (1978) concluded that the limitation comes more in terms of how activities were carried out rather than the actual frequency of going out. He wrote,

> ...the most reasonable inference we can make from the eight-city data, as well as other sources, is that for most people, the behavioral effects of crime appear more as subtle adjustments in behaviors than as major shifts in what can be called "behavioral policies." That is rather than making substantial changes in what they do, people tend to change the ways in which they do things.

In other words, Hindelang and his associates believe that people do not necessarily reduce desired frequency of activities because of crime. Desired frequency of going-out depends more on one's occupation, friends, and leisure habits, and much less on crime or its threat. Rather, fear of crime affects the way people do things, such as taking taxis instead of using public transportation, taking walks with family members around safe neighborhoods instead of parks, selecting theaters in safe neighborhoods and avoiding those in high crime areas, and going out for groceries before dark. Without the threat of crime, these activities will certainly be more care-free. People can go out wherever, whenever, and however they feel. There is little doubt that crime changes people's behavior and that most people use avoidance as a way of coping. Nonetheless, one should not leap to the conclusion that people, whether young or old, isolate themselves or reduce the desired frequency of going out because of the threat of fear of crime. When researchers (e.g., Skogan and Maxfield, 1981) reported that fearful respondents go out less often in the evening, what is not known is whether those respondents make up those (desired) frequency during the day. Evidence on involuntary isolation presented earlier in this chapter suggested that they may do that. Hence, when avoidance is used as a coping strategy, it is not the same as reducing the desired frequency of going out.

What sort of people are more likely to practice avoidance? Skogan and Maxfield (1981) reported a positive relationship between fear of crime and avoidance. Those who are fearful are more likely to practice this coping strategy. Likewise, demographic groups such as females, the old, the poor, blacks, and those in high crime areas, or those who are more fearful of crime are also more likely to practice avoidance. Both conclusions are supported in Dubow, et al.'s (1979) review of unpublished reports.

Household Victimization Prevention

Among the four types of coping behaviors, the different ways of preventing household victimization is the most varied. Among the different means of coping in this category, Dubow, et al. (1979) pointed out that it is difficult to measure target-hardening devices, such as the installation of solid-core doors, security gates, alarms, special locks, and window-bars; they are all "one-time" events. For example, a person may install a dead-bolt lock once which fulfills the need (unless a second one is desired). Hence, studies that asked respondents if they had changed door locks in the "last few years" may not be an accurate assessment of target-hardening as a coping strategy since the existence of previously installed suitable door locks is not controlled for. Likewise, answers to questions that asked the quantity and quality of respondents' various target-hardening devices may also be erred in that a house may be full of such devices but all were installed by the previous owner. This measurement issue, however, does not influence other household victimization preventions, such as, locking behavior, surveillance, and occupancy proxy, given that they are "recurrent" rather than "one-time" events.

Although it appears reasonable to assume that fearful individuals and (demographic) groups partake in household victimization prevention more than their counterparts, research, in general, has failed to support this. Rather, the most frequently found participants in household victimization prevention are homeowners, those in high income brackets, white, and living in single-family residences (Skogan and Maxfield, 1981; Dubow, et al., 1979). Lavrakas (1980), on the other hand, added two non-demographic determinants to the list, that of perceived efficacy of the particular coping strategy and participation in anti-crime programs. Note that fear of burglary, a variable that is often tested in relation to household victimization prevention, is not part of the list. Furthermore, it is primarily the high income white home-owners who are more likely to take these anti-crime measures despite being considered, usually, a group with lower levels of fear.

A closer look at the above determinants may reveal the conceptual reasoning behind these relationships. For instance, target-hardening involves purchases which at times may cost a sizable amount of money. Furthermore, installing target-hardening devices, such as window bars and special locks, also involves permanent changes in the household. Hence, it is not surprising to find homeowners, especially those with higher incomes, engaging in target-hardening more often. Renters are typically financially less able, and, with good reason less willing, to install security devices permanently on a residence they do not own. And owners of rental properties do not live there themselves. Hence, this scenario emerges: lower SES, black, and renters have fewer target-hardening measures in their home.

Skogan and Maxfield (1981) suggested a good explanation of an unexpected relationship they discovered: white, homeowners and high income persons are more likely to have neighbors survey their property when they are gone. Skogan and Maxfield believe that in order to have neighbors do surveillance, one has to be integrated into one's neighborhood. Along with neighborhood integration comes frequent communication and, consequently, trust between neighbors. Request for surveillance can then be established based on such a neighborhood network. Whereas, a tight network can be found in neighborhoods with homeowners, this is missing in low-income rental neighborhoods. Therefore, despite stronger need for surveillance in the latter neighborhoods, such activity is less frequent.

Similar explanations may be designed for locking behavior and occupancy proxy to account for the lack of such coping behaviors among those who need them more. For example, one can argue that low SES households are less conscious of locking doors and windows and providing occupancy proxy because they have fewer valuables to lose in a burglary. Nonetheless, it is important to realize that these explanations, like others noted here, are ad hoc in nature and their validities are less obvious. More important, all these rationales simply point to the conclusion that the practice of coping behavior is determined by many factors, in addition to consideration of crime victimization. Hence, studies show that for household crime prevention, it is often those demographic groups who are typically less fearful who use these coping strategies. Yet, it is still crucial to notice that the variable fear of crime, or specifically, fear of burglary, has not been found to be related to the usage of home security measures even by multivariate analyses. That is, among those with similar demographic characteristics, those who are fearful are still no more or no less likely to be more protective of their homes. It is this enigma that awaits additional research and conceptual attention.

Street Victimization Loss Reduction

The two types of street victimization, loss reduction measures shown in Figure 4.3 mean carrying less property and carrying some sort of weapon to ward-off offenders. Dubow, et al. (1979) noted that elderly people are more likely than youth to practice the former. Research shows that older people try to carry less money on their persons to avoid major losses in the event of being victimized on the street. On the other hand, carrying weapons is usually practiced by youths, males, and blacks. The logic behind this is probably that for those who are fearful, such as, the aged and females, weapons such as knives and guns tend to intimidate them even when they are in their own possession. Indirect support for this contention may be drawn from an interesting analysis of the NORC General Social Survey data by DeFonzo (1979). He reported that high levels of fear of crime do not lead to handgun ownership. Rather, ownership of a handgun appears to have the effect of lowering one's fear for safety on the street. The absence of a relationship between gun ownership and fear of crime has also been reported in the research by Lizotte and Bordua (1980).

Household Victimization Loss Reduction

Household victimization, loss reduction refers to carrying home theft insurance policies and marking properties. The former facilitate financial recuperations of lost properties; the latter facilitate retrivials of lost properties. Not much is known about either one of these two coping strategies.

SUMMARY

A victimization event can have three different impacts on its victims: financial loss, physical injury, and diminution of well-being. One earlier study concluded that older victims do not suffer more than younger victims in terms of financial loss and physical injury. However, upon closer scrutiny, the earlier researchers failed to distinguish between the seriousness of the victimization and the sufferings of the victim. When this distinction is made, the available data showed that older victims do suffer more from victimization than younger victims even though the victimizations they are involved in are usually less serious in nature. Nonetheless, the differences are not great. On the other hand, research has failed to show a noticeable difference between recent crime victims and non-victims in terms of well-being.

The research interest on fear of crime among the aged grew out of the attention on victimization of the aged. Fear of crime is always assumed to be a problem for the aged. In fact, some gerontologists considered it the most serious problem facing the aged. Studies have, however, shown that this belief is largely exaggerated. First, fear of crime was not a problem readily identified by the aged as serious. Second, when the inverse relationships between well-being and fear of crime are considered, they are mostly modest in size. Nevertheless, fear of crime does have an adverse impact on the aged. Most notably, fear of crime lowers the neighborhood and housing satisfaction of the aged substantially. In addition, fear of crime was found to be related to lower morale.

While virtually all studies failed to show that fear of crime is related to reduced social activities, the position here is that social activities need to be conceptualized and measured differently. Instead of measuring the quantity of social activities, researchers should measure older people's desire for more social activity. Hence, the concept of involuntary isolation is created. With this new concept, fear of crime was found to be related to involuntary isolation of the aged. Yet, this is a weak relationship. Older people are generally not turned into prisoners in their home because of fear of crime. There are many factors that deter older people's participation in social activities and fear of crime is found to be only a minor one.

To clarify the different ways people cope with their fear for victimization, a typology was constructed. This typology was constructed along two dimensions: victimization preventions vs. loss reduction, and street victimization vs. household victimization. Street victimization preventions refer mainly to avoidance behavior. Avoidance behavior is not equivalent to involuntary isolation. There are different ways to avoid crime, not going out is but one type. Studies show that people practice avoidance by altering their patterns of going out without necessarily reducing their desired frequencies of going out. Those who are fearful of crime, e.g., the aged, tend to practice avoidance.

Household victimization prevention includes target-hardening, locking behaviors, surveillance, and occupancy proxy. The most interesting finding here is that those who are fearful do not practice these coping behaviors any more than those who are less-fearful. In fact, it is often those who are not fearful and who are living in better neighborhoods who practice them more. Various post-hoc explanations exist for these known patterns of coping. The question of why the fearful ones do not practice household victimization prevention remains.

Street victimization loss reduction refers mainly to carry less property or carry weapons while going out. Old people tend to practice the former but not the latter. Finally, not much is known about household victimization prevention which refers to insurance and the marking of property.

Chapter 5

FRAUD

There are different types of thefts (Nettler, 1982). Robbery refers to theft by force. Burglary and larceny refer to theft by stealth. Fraud refers to theft by deception. The former two types of thefts were discussed in Chapter 2. This chapter focuses on fraud, and its special implication for elderly people.

In many ways, fraud is a more interesting type of theft to study than is robbery, burglary, or larceny. Fraud involves drama between predator and the victim (Nettler, 1982). The predator presents a phony role to the victim and communicates a message that is largely false. To succeed in defrauding, a fraud predator has to understand the victim's motive and definition of the situation, as much as he understands his own. In other words, predators of fraud have to be intelligent.

From the victim's standpoint, fraud is also categorically different from other types of victimization. Rather than succumbing to brute force or its threat, as in other crimes involving face-to-face confrontation with offenders, a victim of fraud voluntarily transfers his own money or property to the fraud predator. The transfer, of course, was done by the victim because of the fraud predator's false pretenses. Another unique characteristic of fraud is that the financial loss from a fraud is often believed to be more severe than other types of thefts. Ducovny (1969), for example, estimated that as far back as the late sixties, elderly people lost one billion dollars annually.

TYPES OF FRAUDS

In the Uniform Crime Report, the FBI defines fraud as: "Fraudulent conversion and obtaining money or property by false pretenses. Includes bad checks except forgeries and counterfeiting. Also includes larceny by bailee." This definition does not come close to communicating the complexity of the nature of fraud. Fraud can be carried out in a great variety of ways. The saying that there are as many types of frauds as fraud predators is probably not an exaggeration.

For the purpose of discussion, three types of fraud will be differentiated here: fraud against organizations, bunco, and consumer fraud. Fraud against organizations refers to thefts where the victim of deception is not an individual but a formal organization. Examples of this type of fraud include insurance fraud, embezzlement, medicare/medicaid/social security fraud, and counterfeiting. Although the direct victims of these frauds are organizations, individuals would also be affected indirectly. Insurance fraud increases insurance payments for consumers; embezzlement cuts into organization profits which in turn results in higher prices for organization products; medicare/medicaid/social security fraud hurts all taxpayers; finally, counterfeiting means phony monies or sub-standard products for those who exchanged for them. Yet, given that the link between fraud against organizations and individual victims is less direct than other frauds, this type of fraud will not be discussed here.

Bunco refers to theft by trick and devices (Glick and Newsom, 1974). The legal principle of a bunco may be stated as "the victim did not intend to relinquish title to his property but only possession, giving it over to the con-men to be used for a specific purpose such as a loan, investment, purchases or other similar reason, but the con-men had no intention of putting it to such use, intending from the outset to steal it or divert it to their own use" (Glick and Newsom, 1974:35).

Bunco can also be called short con or street con. Glick and Newsom (1974:33) described bunco as a "fast-moving, short duration, high mobility operation with a commensurately smaller take but with a higher frequency rate." Bunco is referred to as a con because its key feature is the ability of the predator to gain the confidence of the victim. The bunco predator is, therefore, called a con-man or a con-artist. There are numerous schemes in the art of bunco, two common ones are described here.

The *pigeon drop* is probably the most talked-about bunco (Carey and Sherman, 1976; Elmore, 1981; Glick and Newsom, 1974; Hahn, 1977). In this con, as in many other street cons, there are two operators who pretend to be strangers. The first operator alerts the victim (the pigeon) to a second operator who is picking up a wallet apparently left on the street. The first operator together with the victim then confronts the second operator and claims that all three discovered the wallet simultaneously. The three agree to split the contents of the wallet. Upon opening the wallet, they discover several thousands of dollars inside. Realizing the size of the loot, the two operators express a concern with keeping the money. The victim at this point probably suggests turning it over to the police. The operators, however, suggest that the police are corrupt and that the money will never be returned to the owner. The first operator then points out that he has a lawyer friend who may know the best way to handle the money. The three then go to an office building supposedly to consult the lawyer, but the victim and the second operator are told to wait outside. The first operator then returns with the good news that the lawyer's advice is that it is all right to split the money so long as the victim and the second operator are able to put up good faith money equal to their one-third share. The victim is told that the good faith money is to ensure that all three have enough cash to mix with the discovered money so that their serial numbers are harder to trace. The second operator then immediately pulls out a roll of bills, counts the right amount, and hands it to the first operator. In return, the first operator gives the second operator one-third of the loot plus his own good faith money in an envelope. Seeing this, the victim becomes convinced that he can be benefited by doing the same. The victim then goes to the bank, withdraws a large sum of money, and hands it over to the first operator. Dutifully, the first operator puts the good faith money and an equal amount from the loot into an envelope. But before he hands it over to the victim, a quick exchange is made. After the victim leaves the two operators, he opens the envelope to discover a stack of newspaper cuts.

Another common con is *the bank embezzler* (Carey and Sherman, 1976; Elmore, 1981; Glick and Newsom, 1974; Hahn, 1976). In this con, an impersonator of a bank official would call up the victim and request his cooperation in apprehending a bank embezzler. The victim is told that the embezzler has taken money out of the victim's account. The suggestion to the victim is that he should withdraw his whole account so that the embezzler has to immediately steal from another account to cover the withdrawal. The bank would then apprehend the embezzler. The victim is also promised a small sum of money for his cooperation. The victim concurs with the plan and withdraws the money. The next day, the same impersonator phones the victim again, thanks the victim, and tells him that the plan worked perfectly. Rather than having the victim take the trouble of going to the bank again, the impersonator suggests that the bank would send an official to come to the home of the victim to pick up the cash and deposit it for the victim. In a short while, this "bank official" shows up with proper identifications and receipts from the bank, and the victim hands over the money. The money, however, is not deposited.

Both the pigeon drop and the bank embezzler can be carried out in variant forms. In addition, there is "the switch," sometimes in conjunction with the pigeon drop and sometimes not, where the victim's attention on his money, usually in an envelope, is diverted momentarily, and the con-artist does a quick switch of envelopes (Glick and Newsom, 1974). Then, there is "the shake" where the victim is induced to do something wrong by the con-artist, e.g., sex with inappropriate partners, who then extort money or property from the victim (Glick and Newsom, 1974). Alternatively, there is "the city inspector" where con-artists impersonate city inspectors, charge that homes and buildings are defective, and demand an exorbitant amount of money for fixing the defects (Haskell and Yablonsky, 1974). The forms of bunco are numerous, and their variations attest to the ingenuity of con-artists.

The third type of fraud is consumer fraud. The legal principle against consumer fraud is theft by false pretenses: victim's consent for releasing properties or monies is given but only as a result of misrepresentation or deceit (Glick and Newsom, 1974). Like bunco, consumer fraud comes in a great variety of forms. Some are carried out by big legitimate corporations, others by small operators not unlike the con-artists.

Frauds committed by corporations against consumers represent the most complicated types of fraud (Comer, 1977; Russell, 1977). Examples include price-fixing, defective merchandise, tax evasion, and anti-trust. Casual observations of daily news would suggest that corporate frauds are not uncommon. The unique characteristic of corporate fraud is that the loss to an individual victim is small, but large numbers of victims are involved. The result is that the total loss due to corporate fraud is astronomical (Conklin, 1981).

On the other hand, consumer frauds are also committed by smaller companies and individuals as well. Several types of such frauds are discussed quite frequently in the literature. Medical fraud is one such example (Glick and Newsom, 1974; Butler, 1975; Elmore, 1981; Ducovny, 1969). Consumers are frequently offered a variety of drugs or medical equipment whose manufacturers provide false claims in their healing power.. Chronic and terminal diseases, the types most often suffered by older people, are especially favorable targets for medical quacks because there are no known cures for them. Illustrations include arthritis, hearing loss, denture problems, cancer, and epilepsy. Despite policing by the Food and Drug Administration, fraudulent claims of cures for these afflictions can be successful in attracting consumers, because chronic and terminal patients are often willing to try anything to alleviate their suffering, in the hope of a slim chance that it may just work.

Along the same line, health and nutrition frauds also find readily available markets, especially among elderly people. The claims of these frauds is usually that the nutritional requirements of older people are different, therefore diet supplements of various types are essential. Some manufacturer quacks go as far as claiming that the drug can bring back vitality and quicker responses in old age (Ducovny, 1969).

Real estate fraud is another common type of consumer fraud. Many people have strong desires to own land, and this desire can be preyed on easily by fraudulent entrepreneurs. Newman and Strauss (1977) believe that many retiring people may be especially suspectible because of their plan to move to warmer climates. Fraudulent presentation of the assets of lands can easily be made when the buyer is living miles away from the property and is not able to see it first hand. Swamps and marshes have been sold as prized real estate this way (Ducovny, 1969; Glick and Newsom, 1974).

Mail-ordering is another common medium to defraud consumers (Elmore, 1981; Newman and Strauss, 1977). This can come in several forms: failure to deliver pre-paid merchandise, late delivery, sending unsolicited merchandise, and overcharging on credit cards. The postal inspector is charged with the responsibility of protecting consumers from mail order frauds (Elmore, 1981).

Finally, investment is also a popular way to defraud consumers. The pyramid game, for example, is a scheme that re-emerges from time to time. Investors are promised returns which are simply numerically impossible to keep. Promise of work at home is another scheme. In this instance, people are asked to purchase machinery, e.g., sewing machines, at exorbitant prices as an investment for future orders for work at home. Except that the orders never come. Yet, the heaviest loss in investment fraud is probably in the area of commodity futures. Stocks and bonds are at times sold to buyers with claims of security which in reality are financially unsound. Recent history has seen several cases where stock and bond holders were cheated out of millions of dollars (Elmore, 1981; Glick and Newsom, 1974; Haskell and Yablonsky, 1974).

Like the examples for bunco, this list of examples of consumer frauds is for illustrative purposes only. The numerous ways in which consumers can be cheated is simply beyond the scope of coverage here. Neither can anyone be sure that such a list is ever complete. At the same time, it is also important to distinguish between what may be considered unethical practices of businesses and, fraud, theft by deceit. The confusion between the two appears when aggressive sales tactics are, at times, considered fraud. Butler (1976), for example, includes the following activities as frauds: aggressive door-to-door salespersons who convince older people to purchase unnecessary merchandise, funeral directors who may exploit the sorrow of the elderly survivor by pushing for an expensive funeral, or cosmetic companies that produce and market cosmetics for older people. Clearly, these practices may be considered unethical, but whether they can be considered frauds from the legal standpoint is less certain. As Butler himself acknowledged, in protecting older people against fraud, it is important to preserve the rights of the aged to make their own decisions.

PREVALENCE AND DETERMINANTS
OF FRAUDS

Just how prevalent buncos and consumer frauds are is not at all certain at this point; neither is there any apparent research strategy to resolve the enigma. Like victimizations of ordinary crimes, the rate of non-report for these two frauds may be high, making official statistics an unreliable form of data. Blum's (1972) interviews with approximately seventy fraud victims, for example, suggest that the pride and shame of fraud victims as well as the perception that nothing could be done are the primary reasons for their not reporting their victimizations to the police.

Whereas victimization surveys appear to be an adequate strategy to uncover unreported crimes, the same may not be true of fraud victimizations. After all, the best type of fraud is supposed to be the type where even after the incident, the victim still does not realize that he has been defrauded. This is true of buncos but is especially the case for consumer fraud. Listerine, for example, has long been advertised as a cure for the common cold until it was stopped by the Food and Drug Administration. It is hard to determine how many other common products with fraudulent claims still exist on the market. At any rate, consumer fraud is probably more prevalent than ordinary crimes. On the other hand, it seems safe to presume that the victimization rate of bunco is considerably lower than those for both consumer frauds and ordinary crimes.

The issue of determinants of frauds can be divided into four different components and they are illustrated in Figure 5.1. First, in line with the distinction between bunco and consumer fraud made earlier, it makes sense to believe that the determinants of the two may be different since the nature of the two are not the same. Bunco particularly appeals to the trust some people have in strangers, and in most instances, it also attests to the greed of the victim. Consumer fraud, on the other hand, is successful largely due to the particular needs of the victim, as in medical fraud and real estate fraud; while at the same time, the element of trust, as in bunco, is also there. Secondly, when investigating determinants of frauds a distinction should also be made between why some people are approached, and then among those who are approached, why some people take the bait and become victimized. This distinction is necessary in that it is obvious that not all those who are approached would go on to be victimized. Knowing the characteristics of those who are approached assists in the understanding of how con-artists and fraudulent business people choose their targets. Knowledge of who and why some proceed to be defrauded explains the successes of bunco and consumer frauds.

Unfortunately, given the problems of assessing the prevalence of frauds identified earlier, a method to study fraud has yet to be found, and systematic empirical data on the pattern of frauds are simply missing. None of the four questions raised can be addressed adequately.

To find out the type of people who would be approached by con-artists, Box a in Figure 5.1, it may appear that a reasonable strategy is to simply survey the public on their experience of being approached by con-artists. However, this may not yield meaningful data since con-artists oftentimes would retreat from a potential victim when initial interactions suggest that the

RESEARCH ISSUES ON THE DETERMINANTS OF FRAUD

	BUNCO	CONSUMER FRAUD
APPROACHED BY PREDATOR	a	c
VICTIMIZED BY PREDATOR	b	d

Figure 5.1. Research issues on the determinants of fraud.

individual is not an appropriate target. Victims would, therefore, not realize that they had been approached. In addition, as pointed out earlier, some victims may not even realize that they have been conned. The alternate method would then involve interviewing con-artists themselves in their selection of subjects. This is exactly the strategy used by Blum (1972). Blum interviewed thirty-five con-artists, and they were asked how they select their "marks" (potential victims). Surprisingly, the general response was that just about everybody can be "marks." The average person is perceived as greedy and stupid. Some people desire attention, some seek romance and love, others hope for fame, while still others look for fortune. The point is that everybody has at least one weakness, every person is vulnerable to at least one type of bunco.

The con-artists interviewed by Blum were not helpful in distinguishing between those marks who do and those who do not fall for the cons either (Box b in Figure 5.1). Blum (1972:41) reported the sentiment of the con-artists:

> Merely because someone rejected an approach was no proof of honesty. Rather, the conmen suggested that those who didn't "go" were "crybabies," "afraid of the police," "ashamed to admit they don't have any money," "gullible but just not stupid that time," "skeptical" or "immune because they have jobs" or "haven't time." Either directly or indirectly, all citizens were seen as greedy and thieves at heart; the difference was that the marks who did not go had not been approached with the right game and at the right time.

Despite the fact that con-artists were reluctant, or simply unable, to identify desirable traits in their marks, it is hard to believe that none exist. It appears that a successful con-artist is one who is not only polished in his presentation to marks, but also discriminating in his selection of them. Even if all people can potentially fall victim to a bunco, it should still be possible to differentiate the vulnerable and gullible ones from those who are not. Blum (1972) believed that the idea that all people can be conned since they are greedy and stupid, may be popular among con-artists because it is used as an ideology to justify their crime of bunco. In essence, the implicit message is that ordinary people are no different from con-artists, and that marks deserved to be cheated.

If little is known about the pattern of bunco victimizations, the same is true of consumer frauds, Box c and d in Figures 5.1. This is true because the range of consumer frauds is just as variant as buncos. At one extreme are frauds committed by large corporations, at the other end the culprits are not unlike the con-artists. In short, the nature of both buncos and consumer frauds have restrained systematic investigations on their patterns of victimization.

Despite the lack of data on the characteristics of victims of fraud, many believe that older people are particularly vulnerable (Butler, 1976; Ducovny, 1969). Butler (1976) proposed several explanations to support this belief. First, older people are often in poor health, requiring medical, health, dental, and diet aids of various kinds. Second, some older people suffer organic brain damage making them less than rational and alert at times. Third, many older people, such as the widowed, are lonely and suffer from grief and depression, which makes them vulnerable to pretentious fraud predators. Fourth, older people have various fears, such as aging and death, which exposes them to frauds in seeking comforts to these fears. Fifth, the current cohort of older people have generally poorer educations, allowing fraud predators to prey on their ignorance. Finally, older people are financially poor compared to younger people, which pushes them to seek ventures to improve their conditions. All of these appear to be reasonable suggestions, yet their validity should be assessed if and when data are available. The errors in presuming older people are victimized more often than young people in ordinary crimes (see Chapter 2) point to this need.

SUMMARY

Fraud refers to theft by deception. Three types of frauds are are differentiated. The first type is fraud against organizations which refers to cases where the victim is an organization rather than an individual. The second type, bunco, refers to theft by trick and devices. The predators of buncos are called con-artists. The pigeon drop and the bank embezzler are but two of the more common buncos. Finally consumer fraud refers to theft by false pretenses. This can range from fraud by large corporations to those by individuals like the con-artists. Numerous types of consumer fraud exist including medical fraud, health and diet fraud, real estate fraud, mail-order fraud, and investment fraud. Though the types of buncos and consumer frauds are numerous, it is important to exclude those exchanges which are more un-ethical than illegal, such as high pressure sales.

The prevalence of buncos and consumer frauds cannot be assessed with official statistics given that many fraud victims may not report their victimizations. The method of victimization survey does not appear to be appropriate here given that the natures of bunco and consumer fraud are complex, and its actual occurrence is at times uncertain even to the victim. Thus, no reliable estimates of the prevalence of buncos and consumer frauds are available.

The issue of the determinants should be considered separately for consumer fraud and bunco, and then differently for being approached and actually falling prey to the scheme. However, given the lack of an appropriate method to study fraud, no empirical data are available to show the pattern of fraud victimization. The problem is shown clearly in one study where con-artists were asked to identify the characteristics of those whom they approach. The finding is that all people are considered likely fraud victims. Despite this lack of data, many believe that older people are particularly vulnerable. Whether this position is valid awaits empirical verification if and when an appropriate method to study fraud is devised.

Chapter 6

ELDER ABUSE

W hen people imagine crime victimization, the scene is
usually one in which the aggressor and the victim are
strangers, e.g., a teenage gang mugging passers-by. Criminologists, however, long ago pointed out that in many crimes, the
aggressor and the victim are actually people who know each
other, sometimes rather well. Examples: an argument between
neighbors erupts into an assault, a casual date ends up with a
rape, a visiting friend returns later as a burglar, or a domestic
quarrel between spouses becomes settled by a homicide. The
National Crime Survey in the 1970s confirmed the belief that a
significant proportion of crimes, whether against the young or
the old, are indeed committed between perpetrators and victims
who are known to each other (Bureau of Justice Statistics, 1980a).

In this chapter, this issue of non-stranger victimization is
lodged in the intimate social world of the aged. Here, the criminal
not only knows the elderly victim, but is actually a person in
whom the older victim trusts and believes. Examples of such an
intimate perpetrator include the older person's spouse, siblings,
children, other kin, or someone who is in the position of caring
for the aged. Yet, despite the intimacy of these relationships,
these persons sometimes do commit crimes against the aged.
These crimes can be either physical or financial in nature, though
physical attacks have drawn far more attention, probably because
they violate people's conscience to a much larger extent. The
literature on intimate perpetrator/elderly victim offenses is rather

105

new, and in fact, has been studied more by gerontologists and social workers than criminologists. Increasingly, this offense is being referred to as elder abuse.

The idea that an elderly person can be abused by his family members or persons he relies on for care has been captured by two different sets of literature. The first is that on nursing homes. Nursing homes as a form of long-term care for the aged have never been viewed favorably by the public. Negative stereotypes of nursing homes are strong and pervasive. Nursing homes are often perceived as inhumane, nightmarish, and at the very least, uncaring to and undesirable for the aged (Fontana, 1977). Lawton (1981) summed up the sentiment well by noting that if an alternate environment is available, an older person should never be institutionalized in a nursing home. This image of the nursing home is reinforced by periodic horror stories reported by the mass media that some older patients are abused by nurses and nurse aides. Stannard (1973), for example, did a participant observation study of a nursing home in order to uncover the social conditions where abuses occur in such a setting. When Stannard was doing his study in this nursing home, an elderly man died one night. According to Stannard's informant, the elderly man had cursed at an orderly. Infuriated, the orderly then punished the elderly patient by placing him in a tub of hot water. As a result, the skin and tissue of the elderly patient became severely burned and began to fall off. The man died shortly thereafter. Stannard's observations suggested that such abusive treatments can occur in nursing homes mainly because of a shortage of workers and the invisibility of nurse aide/patient interactions.

Despite the gruesome nature of Stannard's tale, more systematic studies of elder abuse in nursing homes are virtually non-existent and writings on this subject are infrequent (see also Hacker, 1977). Nonetheless, in the late 1970s and the early 1980s, the concept of elder abuse re-appeared in a totally different literature. In this second instance, the abuser is not a nurse or an orderly but a family member of the aged person, and the setting changes from the nursing home to the homes of the aged in the community. This time, the interest among professionals appears far stronger, and in fact, it is here that the term elder abuse is coined (Callahan, 1982).

The nature of elder abuse in the homes of the aged, in contrast to nursing homes, can be illustrated by a couple of case histories reported by Rathbone-McCuan (1980:299, 300).

> Sally was an eighty-year-old black woman who owned her own home but preferred spending a great deal of her time at the home of her sister. A nephew, who had been living with her, kicked her in the abdomen. A week later she was admitted to the hospital through the emergency room and became progressively weaker; she was anorexic. The local department of social services was aware of the problem. The nephew drank a great deal and on several occasions, when he was inebriated, had beaten the aunt. The social services department reported that it could do nothing as Sally refused to consider other living arrangements and refused to enter into legal action against her nephew for fear of a reprisal at home.

> Mrs. J was a seventy-one-year-old white woman who lived with her son and daughter. Both children were in their thirties and were retarded. There was documentation of several minor physical attacks on Mrs. J by her son. The third attack was major and required that she be hospitalized. She remained in the hospital for a month and was then transferred to a foster home placement center. Her absence from the household led to the eventual institutionalization of the two adult children.

If the attention to elder abuse in nursing homes arises out of people's ambivalence towards the nursing home, the switch in focus to elder abuse in the home setting can certainly not be attributed to people's feeling about the family. After all, the family is supposed to be filled with love, harmony, and good-will. While this image of the family is not incorrect, professionals in the 1960s and 1970s began to challenge it. In a well-received paper in the early 1960s, "The battered child syndrome," Kempe and his associates (1962) began a research tradition on parental abuse of children that still remains active today. In the 1970s, the study of child abuse was extended to the study of spouse abuse, husbands and wives physically attacking each other. And, as Pedrick-Cornell and Gelles (1982) and Steinmetz (1978) noted, professional interest in elder abuse appears to be a natural extension of research on these two types of domestic violence.

In sum, the picture that is emerging is this: elder abuse occurs in nursing homes as well as in the community. In the nursing home, it is the nurse and nurse's aide who are the abuser, and in the community, it is the family member of the aged or related kin. Although anecdoctal cases illustrate the nature of elder abuse in these two settings, numerous issues remain unanswered: What exactly is elderly abuse and how may this be defined? How prevalent are elderly abuses in nursing homes and in the community? What are the causal factors of elder abuse? These and other issues will be addressed in this chapter.

DEFINING ELDER ABUSE

Abuse is a term that carries extremely negative connotations. Hence, before any person is accused of abusing an aged, it is imperative to have a clear definition of elder abuse. A murky definition will create a large grey area where whether an incident should be classified as elder abuse becomes difficult to decide. When this is the case, it becomes impossible to conduct research on the prevalence of elder abuse as well as its causal factors.

Currently in the literature, little attention has been paid to explicitly defining elder abuse. On the other hand, there are numerous "listings" of types of behaviors that are considered to be elder abuse, and the consensus among these listings is remarkably high (Brock, 1980; Champlin, 1982; Chen et al., 1981; Hickey and Douglass, 1981; Lau and Kosberg, 1979). In general, there are five types of elder abuse. The first type is physical abuse and neglect. Included are physical battering, physical neglect, and sexual abuse. Physical and sexual abuses may be likened to the violent crimes of rape, assault, and robbery. On the other hand, physical neglect may also be a crime if there is a legal duty to act in the particular case (e.g., see Reid, 1982). The second type is financial abuse. Financial abuse is analogous to property crimes, i.e., personal larceny with or without contact, household larceny, burglary, auto-theft, and fraud. The third type of elder abuse is psychological abuse. Brock (1980) referred to this as psychological torment; Hickey and Douglass (1981) called this verbal/emotional abuse. No category of officially defined crimes can be linked to psychological abuse. Besides these three types of elder abuse which are invariably listed by all writers, there are two others that have been noted occasionally. Champlin (1982) and Lau and Kosberg (1979) listed violation of individual rights (e.g., institutionalization of an aged); Lau and Kosberg (1979) included the idea of self-abuse (e.g., refusal of food).

A quick glance of these various types of elder abuse would suggest that the term abuse, as used in relation to the aged, is much broader than when used in lieu of children and spouse. The terms child abuse and spouse abuse usually refer restrictively to physical abuse. One seldom hears of people financially or psychologically abusing their children and wives. Hence, the literature on elder abuse has seen several critics who believed that the term abuse has been used too liberally. Callahan (1982:15) noted that, "With some of these definitions [of elder abuse] there seems to be a drive to include all forms of troubled interpersonal relationships under the rubric of violence and abuse rather than family breakdown or social ills." Likewise, Pedrick-Cornell and Gelles (1982) believed that, "...the concept of elder abuse has become a political/journalistic concept, best suited for attracting public attention to the plight of the victims. But while elder abuse may be a fruitful political term, it is fast becoming a useless scientific concept." Similar sentiments have been expressed by Faulkner (1981) and Katz (1980).

To a large extent, these criticisms are not inaccurate. Take psychological abuse, for example: regardless of the term used (e.g., mental abuse, psychological torment), the fact remains that virtually all human conflicts of a non-physical nature involving an old person can be classified as psychological abuse of the aged. Hence, disagreements between elderly siblings, friction between kin, quarrels between spouses, an angry nurse raising her voice, or even an unloving son can all be interpreted as psychological abuse of the aged. Likewise, two other types of elder abuse, violation of individual rights and self-abuse, suffer the same shortcomings. Besides being extremely vague with regard to what is and is not individual rights, it is hard to think of any individual rights, besides freedom from physical injuries and financial exploitation, whose violation is severe enough to warrant the term abuse. Similarly, an elderly person inflicting harm onto oneself is so categorically different from harm inflicted by another person that to label both as abuse is simply preposterous. Most importantly, psychological abuse, violation of individual rights, and self-abuse are simply not crimes. Inclusion of these three activities as components of elder abuse would trivialize the term abuse.

On the other hand, the same cannot be said of financial abuse. Although financial abuse is usually not considered as a part of child or spouse abuse, there are good reasons to include this as a type of elder abuse. One seldom reads about financial abuse of children or spouse simply because children usually do not have much in the way of financial resources to be abused, and, normatively, married couples are supposed to share their finances. Yet older persons, in the role of parents for example, do have financial resources and are not under normative obligations to share them with their children. Any extraction of finances from older people against their will by an intimate person, with the exception of their spouse, can and should be considered a form of abuse. In addition, as pointed out earlier, financial abuse of the aged violates criminal laws.

After these considerations, two types of elder abuse are left, that of physical and financial. Although both are frequently discussed in the literature, neither has been defined explicitly. This is particularly problematic for financial abuse since this type of abuse is unique to the aged, and research on other forms of family violence provides no guidance. Hence, financial abuse of the aged will be defined from a legal perspective here: any types of property crimes committed against an elderly person by his family members or persons to whom he has entrusted his care is financial abuse. This includes all types of larcenies, fraud, burglary, and auto-theft.

On the other hand, physical abuse has been studied in relation to the child and spouse for many years, and this literature provides suggestions for a definition of physical abuse of the aged. Gil's (1970:6) definition for child abuse is revised here for the aged. Physical abuse of the aged is the intentional, non-accidental use of physical force, or intentional, non-accidental acts of omission, on the part of an intimate person or a care-taker interacting with the aged in his care, aimed at physically hurting, injuring or destroying that aged.

Four aspects of this definition should be noticed. The first is the specification of intent on the part of the perpetrator. The perpetrator must have knowledge that his behavior or the lack of it would injure the aged. Accidental causes of injuries are not considered abuse. Second, omission of acts with the intent of injuring the aged is included with actual acts. Hence, physical neglect, just as physical battering, is also part of elder abuse. Third, the perpetrator is an intimate person, including the elderly person's family members, or a care-taker the aged entrusted for his care. This highlights the fact that elder abuse can occur in the actual homes of the aged as well as in nursing homes. Finally, the act or its omission must have the consequence of hurting, injuring, or destroying the aged before it is considered elder abuse. Notice that relatively mild forms of violence, such as slapping an elderly person, which causes physical pain but not necessary injury, are also considered elder abuse.

It is interesting to note that this definition of physical abuse works much better for the aged than for either children or spouse. Numerous researchers have noticed that parental violence towards children and violence between married couples are at times considered normatively acceptable. Given that parents are delegated the responsibility of socializing their children, society also grants parents the right to use physical punishment (Gil, 1970). According to a national survey conducted by Strauss and his associates (1980), for example, over 70% of adult Americans find spanking a twelve year old child an acceptable form of punishment. With regard to marital violence, the same survey showed that one-fourth of wives and one-third of husbands approve of slapping one's spouse at times. Hence, what constitute abusive behaviors towards children or spouse depends very much upon whose definition of abuse one relies.

Physical violence towards an elderly person, however, is an entirely different matter. Although no data is available to confirm this, the suspicion here is that normally any sort of physical violence towards an aged is unacceptable. This includes even relatively moderate violent behaviors, such as pushing and shoving an older person. This is so especially when the elderly person is one's parent. People are supposed to take care of their parents, to love, and to honor them. If people find beating up an elderly man by a young teenager discomforting, a similar attack by the elderly man's son becomes outrageous.

THE PREVALENCE OF ELDER ABUSE

If elder abuse is being defined as physical abuse and financial abuse, how prevalent, then, are these two types of abuse? Some professionals, apparently, believe that this is a critical social problem. Brock (1980:191), for example, argued that, "...abuse of the elderly is serious and growing." Is this belief valid?

Several empirical studies on elder abuse have been reported at this point, however, they are all exploratory in nature and their data do not give any indication of how prevalent is elder abuse. Chen et al. (1981), for example, mailed survey questionnaires to ninety practitioners in various social, medical, homemaker, and legal services; likewise, Hickey and Douglass (1981) interviewed 228 respondents in similar professional roles. The two studies were partly designed to measure the practitioner's awareness of elder abuse. Several problems exist for using this type of research design in estimating the prevalence of elder abuse. First, the respondents were clinical practitioners, not older people. Most aged, including some who have been abused, never come to the attention of clinical workers. Second, these respondents were not randomly selected among practitioners who may have contacts with elderly clients. Hence, findings cannot be generalized beyond the sample itself. Finally, the practitioners interviewed were not asked to estimate the total number of elderly cases they have handled, regardless of abuse. The denominator for estimating an elder abuse rate is, therefore, missing. Any one of these three problems alone would have prevented making estimates on prevalence based on a data set. All three are present in both the Chen et al. and the Hickey and Douglass studies.

What these two studies do show, however, is that almost all clinical professionals in the role of helping the aged are, indeed, familiar with elder abuse. Of the thirty professionals in Chen et al.'s study, twenty-nine indicated that they had dealt with cases of elder abuse; Hickey and Douglass also reported that virtually all professionals in their study had some contacts with some forms of elder abuse. However, notice that in both studies, elder abuse is defined rather broadly. Both, for example, included psychological torment as a type of elder abuse. In fact, Chen et al. (1981:8) noted that several respondents in their sample favor expanding the definition to include, "...criminal activity, evictions, ageism and depreciation of elder persons." Given such an inclusive outlook on what constitutes abuse, it is not surprising to find that almost all service-oriented clinical practitioners are familiar with elder abuse.

Instead of studying elder abuse through the eyes of practitioners, two other studies examined elder abuse more directly. Harbin and Madden (1979) presented data on fifteen psychiatric cases of parent battering; Rathbone-McCuan (1980) provided case descriptions of nine elder abuse cases to which she had access. Both studies are, however, designed more for exploring and suggesting causal factors of elder abuse than for assessing the prevalence of elder abuse.

Finally, two other studies had somewhat different designs from those just noted. Lau and Kosberg (1979) conducted their study at the Chronic Illness Center of the County Hospital System in Cleveland, Ohio. Workers at this center were asked to review all cases involving a client over age sixty within a twelve-month period for instances of physical, psychological, and material abuse, and "violation of rights." Among the 404 elderly clients this center had served, 9.6% or thirty-nine aged, were identified as victims of abuse. Seventy-four percent of these cases involved physical abuse/neglect; 31% were victims of psychological abuse; 51% suffered psychological abuse; 18% had their rights violated. Even though this study provides some sort of elder abuse rates, the value of these rates is still highly questionable. The rates only represent those of one health service center in Cleveland, and, furthermore, unreported elder abuse cases remain undetected. On the other hand, Steinmetz (1983) interviewed seventy-seven adult children who have the experience of caring for an elderly parent. The respondents were asked the method they usually use to resolve conflict with their parent. The data showed that five per cent of the adult child respondents had threatened their parent with physical force, while one percent had actually slapped, hit with an object, or shook the elderly parent. However, the seventy-seven respondents in the Steinmetz sample were not randomly selected. They were volunteers who responded to advertisements requesting respondents with the experience of caring for an elderly parent. Hence, the rates reported may not be generalized. Nonetheless, the research method Steinmetz (1983) used forms the basis for part of the following discussion.

This quick review of the literature shows that no study at this point provides any reasonable estimates of the prevalence of elder abuse. The current state of knowledge on elder abuse is close to that of child and spouse abuse in the 1960s. Although numerous research studies were being conducted during that decade, all were based on studies of officially known cases not unlike those currently available for elder abuse (Gelles, 1980). Hence, no reliable estimates of child and spouse abuse were available. This situation has, however, changed today. This is largely the result of two studies, Gil (1970) and Strauss et al. (1980). Both used the survey method and both had national samples of American adults. A close examination of these two studies provides numerous insights into how the prevalence of elder abuse could be assessed.

Gil (1970) surveyed 1520 respondents on their opinions, attitudes, and knowledge of child abuse. He found that three percent of his sample reported knowledge of specific instances of child abuse. Based on this, Gil's estimate was that between two and one half million to four million adults knew of a child being abused. Despite the overlap arising from different adults reporting the same case, this estimate is still substantially higher than all previous estimates, and it is also a considerable distance from the 6000 confirmed cases of child abuse reported nationally the same year (Gil, 1970).

Strauss et al. (1980) took this survey strategy for the study of family violence one step further. Rather than making estimates based on respondents' awareness of child abuse, Strauss and his associates surveyed people in terms of their own actual experience of family violence. Their study showed that nationally 3.6% of all children have been physically punished to a rather severe extent each year. Severe violence, according to the researchers, refers to kicking, biting, hitting with fist, hitting or trying to hit with something, beating up, threatening with a knife/gun, or actually using a knife/gun. With the same measurement, Strauss et al.'s data showed that 3.8% of husbands use severe violence on their wives and 4.6% of wives use similar measures on their husbands annually. All of these rates put child and spouse abuse well into the millions.

The studies by Gil (1970) and Strauss et al. (1980) have several major implications for future research on elder abuse. First and most importantly, these researchers, especially Strauss and his associates, have shown that it is entirely possible to have the respondents volunteer information on their own experience of family violence in the roles of both victim and perpetrator. This is similar to what Steinmetz (1983) did in her study of elder abuse, where she asked volunteering respondents whether they have used physical force against their parents. It appears that surveys of the elderly population, even local ones, are needed to provide reliable estimates of the extent of elder abuse in the community. Continual reliance on the opinions of clinical professionals or detected cases of elder abuse as data would not improve current knowledge of the prevalence of elder abuse. At the same time, it should be pointed out that the survey method would probably be less applicable among the nursing home aged. In nursing homes, the average age of elderly residents is often in the neighborhood of eighty years and the proportion of mentally impaired, who would not be able to participate in a survey, may be high.

A second implication of the studies by Gil, and Strauss and his associates is that many victims of family violence never seek help nor report the violence to authorities. Whether this is also true of elder abuse, of course, requires empirical confirmation. The suspicion here is that whatever the proportion of non-reporting for physical abuse is for the aged, those proportions for neglect and financial abuse would be higher. These are exactly the type of questions that a survey could address.

A third implication from surveys of family violence is one of Strauss and his associates' discoveries noted above: the prevalence of husband battering is equivalent to that of wife battering. This is a rather surprising finding. The meaning of this has generated much discussion (see Gelles, 1979; Pleck et al., 1977; Steinmetz, 1977; Strauss et al., 1980). Suffice it to say that although wives are physically weaker than their husbands, they are perfectly capable of being violent toward their husbands (some of which is most likely in self-defense). The suggestion for elder abuse research is to measure violent behavior of older people toward their family members or caretakers. An older father may, for example, choose to show his discontent by slapping or biting the daughter with whom he is living. Needless to say, this is not to imply that elderly abuse occurs mainly because of the violence behaviors of the aged themself. Rather, the possibility for such occurring at times should be allowed for in the research design. In the Steinmetz (1983) study, for example, while only one percent of the adult children interviewed indicate experiences of physical violence towards the parent, 18% responded that their elderly parent had recently been physically violent with them.

Finally, it is interesting to inspect the way Strauss et al. (1980) measure violence, and judge its applicability to elder abuse. Strauss and his associates designed what they called the Conflict Tactics Scale (see Figure 6.1). The scale measures the way conflict and disagreements are resolved between family members. This can occur in three different ways: rational discussions/arguments, verbal or non-verbal expression of hostility, or use of physical force or violence. Violence is measured with a continuum of intensities, from throwing something to using a knife/gun. Notice that Strauss and his associates used the term violence instead of the customary term abuse. This is probably a strategy to overcome the normative problem of what constitutes abuse discussed earlier. Different people have different definitions of what abuse is. In fact, Strauss and his associates eliminated threw something, push, grab, shove, and slap from a reduced version of the Conflict Tactics Scale, the severe violence scale, in studying violence towards children and spouse since these types of violence are mild and may be considered acceptable by many. This, however, may not be necessary for studying elder abuse. As pointed out earlier, the norms concerning elderly parents as well as the aged in general appear to be one where violence of any kind is unacceptable. Hence, the Conflict Tactics Scale may actually be a better measure of abuse toward elderly parents than it is of abuse toward children and spouse. Even mild forms of violence toward elderly parents, such as throwing something, pushing, grabbing, shoving, or slapping, can be labeled as elder abuse. (A different version of the Conflict Tactics Scale was apparently used in Steinmetz's study, 1983:146.) On the other hand, notice that the Conflict Tactics Scale only measures physical abuse of the elderly, the other two types of elder abuse, neglect and financial abuse, require additional independent measures.

THE CONFLICTED TACTICS SCALE FOR ELDER ABUSE

No matter how well a parent and (his/her) child get along, there are times when they disagree, get annoyed with each other, or just have fights because of a bad mood. They also use many different ways of trying to settle their differences. I'm going to read a list of some things that your child might have done when (he/she) had a dispute with you. I would like you to tell me for each one how often (he/she) did it in the past year.

a.	Discussed the issue calmly	0	1	2	3	4	5	6	X
b.	Got information to back up (your/her) side of things	0	1	2	3	4	5	6	X
c.	Brought in or tried to bring in someone to help settle things	0	1	2	3	4	5	6	X
d.	Insulted or swore at you	0	1	2	3	4	5	6	X
e.	Sulked and/or refused to talk about it	0	1	2	3	4	5	6	X
f.	Stomped out of the room or house (or yard)	0	1	2	3	4	5	6	X
g.	Cried	0	1	2	3	4	5	6	X
h.	Did or said something to spite you	0	1	2	3	4	5	6	X
i.	Threatened to hit or throw something at you	0	1	2	3	4	5	6	X
j.	Threw or smashed or hit or kicked something	0	1	2	3	4	5	6	X
k.	Threw something at you	0	1	2	3	4	5	6	X
l.	Pushed, grabbed, or shoved you	0	1	2	3	4	5	6	X
m.	Slapped you	0	1	2	3	4	5	6	X
m.	Kicked, bit, or hit with a fist	0	1	2	3	4	5	6	X
o.	Hit or tried to hit with something	0	1	2	3	4	5	6	X
p.	Beat you up	0	1	2	3	4	5	6	X
q.	Threatened with a knife or gun	0	1	2	3	4	5	6	X
r.	Used a knife or gun	0	1	2	3	4	5	6	X
s.	Other (PROBE): _____	0	1	2	3	4	5	6	X

Source: Revised from Strauss et. al. (1980:256)

Figure 6.1. The conflicted tactics scale for elder abuse. Source: Revised from Strauss et al. (1980:256).

A FAMILY TRANSITIONAL THEORY
OF ELDER ABUSE

What are the causal factors of elder abuse? What makes some aged the victims of abuse and others free from this type of harm? Numerous suggestions of the determinants of elder abuse are available in the literature at this point. However, it must be pointed out that all of these causal factors are suggestive in nature, and have not been tested systematically. Furthermore, most of these efforts have been directed toward physical abuse of older parents by children. Attention has not been on abuse by other family members, abuse that occurs in nursing homes, or financial abuse.

As reviewed in the previous section, existing research on elder abuse can be divided into two types: those which studied clinical professionals who may have experience with elder abuse (Hickey and Douglass, 1981; Chen et al., 1981), and those which studied clinical cases of elder abuse (Lau and Kosberg, 1979; Harbin and Madden, 1979; Rathbone-McCuan, 1980). One of the problems of the former set of studies is that data on elder abuse are obtained indirectly, through the eyes of the clinical professionals. Hence, when these researchers investigated the causal factors of elder abuse, the data they obtained appeared to reflect as much the biases of the professionals as elder abuse itself. Hickey and Douglass (1981), for example, noticed that the different causes of elder abuse respondents ascribed to reflect the professional lives of the respondents. Thus, mental health workers favor explanations of abuse based on irrational reactions to life-crises; adult protective and aging services workers prefer the vulnerability or dependency of the victim as explanations.

On the other hand, those research studies that examined clinical cases of elder abuse, all suffered from the lack of appropriate sampling procedures. For example, when Rathbone-McCuan (1980) reported that victims of abuse are overwhelmingly female, one still cannot conclude that the variable sex is related to elder abuse. Given that there are more older women than older men in the general population, it makes sense to expect more victims of elder abuse to be women than men. Women are more likely to be victims of abuse only if the proportion of elderly women who are abused is higher than that for elderly men. With only a clinical sample, this cannot be assessed.

Although existing research has not been able to systematically identify determinants of elder abuse, a large number of determinants have been hypothesized through these exploratory studies as well as other conceptual works. As noted above, many have held that females are more likely to be abused (*Medical News*, 1980; Pedrick-Cornell and Gelles, 1982; Rathbone-McCuan, 1980). In combination with sex, another demographic characteristic, age, is also thought to be related to abuse. Females at advanced ages have been observed or suggested to be the most likely victims (Pedrick-Cornell and Gelles, 1982; Rathbone-McCuan, 1980).

An often suggested social determinant is the stress created by an increasingly dependent parent (Chen et al., 1981; Hickey and Douglass, 1981; Hooyman et al., 1982; *Medical News*, 1980; Pedrick-Cornell and Gelles, 1982; Rathbone-McCuan, 1980; Steinmetz, 1983). In relation to this factor of dependency, others have hypothesized that those aged who are more impaired, either physically or mentally, are more difficult to care for and are therefore more likely to be abused (Chen et al., 1981; Katz, 1980; Pedrick-Cornell and Gelles, 1982; Steinmetz, 1983). Still others have suggested that the competency of the child to take on the caretaker role is a major factor (Hooyman et al., 1982; *Medical News*, 1980).

Borrowing from the child and spouse abuse literature, the cycle of violence is another favorite explanation of elder abuse (Hickey and Douglass, 1981; Kosberg, 1983; Pedrick-Cornell and Gelles, 1982; Rathbone-McCuan, 1980). The violence the abuser child received from an abusive parent during youth is now reciprocated. Previous violence is, therefore, perpetuated; however, the roles are reversed. Faulkner (1981:89) noticed a traditional rhyme: "When I was a laddie/ I lived with my granny/ And many a hiding me granny di'ed me/ Now I am a man/ And I live with my granny/ And I do to my granny/ What she did to me."

This focus on the abusive characteristic of the previous relationship between the parent and the child has also been conceptualized in less violent terms. Rather than necessarily having an abusive relationship in the past, some hypothesized that a poor or strained parent-child relationship in earlier years may be sufficient to create a higher likelihood of elder abuse (Chen, et al., 1981; Katz, 1980; Rathbone-McCuan, 1980).

Although the psychological traits of the abuser appear to be a reasonable causal factor of elder abuse, it has been virtually ignored in the literature. This is in sharp contrast to the earlier history of the child abuse literature where the abuser was often portrayed as suffering from psychopathology of various types: immaturity, depression, sadomasochism, poor emotional control, hypersensitivity, and so on (see Gelles, 1973). However, due to the lack of any systematic research on any of these psychological traits, this emphasis was reduced by the late 1970s. Social and social psychological variables were hypothesized, instead, to be related to child abuse. Maybe because of this, psychopathology of the perpetrator has seldom been hypothesized as an explanation of elder abuse (except for Chen et al., 1981, and Rathbone-McCuan, 1980).

Finally, there is a set of other variables which has also been hypothesized as being related to elder abuse, though only rarely. Chen et al. (1981) believed that the sub-culture of violence of some segments of society may contribute to a higher incident of elder abuse. Chen and his associates also argued that an elderly parent may, at times, be held as a scapegoat for other problems with which the abuser-child is confronted. Katz (1980) held that ageism on the part of society and the individual abuser also contribute to elder abuse. Finally, Hickey and Douglass (1981) hypothesized that elder abuse is more prevalent among the lower class, and that a situational crisis is needed to erupt into an elder abuse incident.

This quick review of the various hypothesized explanations of elder abuse points to one conclusion: at this point, all of these explanations remain to be a group of unrelated and disperse hypotheses. Although each of them appeal to common sense, there is no interrelationship among them. No structure has been imposed on these hypotheses. Ultimately, the implication is that little intuitive understanding of elder abuse is achieved by these relationships even if they are all verified empirically. To achieve an understanding of elder abuse, a theory is needed.

The theory that will be presented here is called a family transitional theory of elder abuse. The family transitional theory aims at explaining physical abuse of the elderly parent by the adult-child, although it may also be applied to an abuser who is the elderly victim's spouse or sibling. What the theory will not explain is financial abuse of the aged. The dynamics of violence towards one's parent is categorically different from that of theft, and it appears that a theory on physical abuse would not do for financial abuse. At this point, research and discussions on financial abuse are simply not sufficient to build a theory. Likewise, elder abuse in nursing homes would also not be covered by the family transitional theory. For abuses within this latter long-term care setting, organizational variables unrelated to the family have to be involved.

The family transitional theory of elder abuse is grounded in two different bodies of literature. The first is the family development literature. Christensen (1964) in his *Handbook of Marriage and the Family* identified family development as one of five theoretical perspectives on the family. The uniqueness of the family development perspective is that the family is seen as an organization that goes through a life career (Hill and Rodgers, 1964). Beginning with the initial establishment stage, where a man and a woman are married, this family career evolves through various stages (such as family with an infant, with teenage children, family in the middle years, and so on), and terminates with the stage of the aging father, after which the family is dissolved through the death of one member of the couple (Rollins and Cannon, 1974). Note that these stages are demarcated by the addition of new family members (through birth) or their subtraction (through departures), and also by the maturing and aging of all family members. Because of the dissimilarity between stages, the role relationships and interaction patterns of family members change from one stage to another. Hence, the family development perspective is one which attends to changes in the family over time, specifically changes that are "normal" and "not unexpected."

For the present purpose, the concept of developmental task is particularly pertinent. According to Aldous (1978), each developmental stage of the family is associated with a set of tasks. A newlywed couple, for example, is supposed to build the foundation for a mutually satisfying partner relationship; a family with a young child is charged with the nurturing and caring of the child whose mere survival depends entirely on the parents. Not only is the successful accomplishment of these tasks required by the norms of society, failure to accomplish assigned tasks at a certain stage would also adversely affect task performance at later stages of the family. Thus, the newlywed couple that fails to achieve a partnership life style may end up with a divorce, and the young couple that falls short of being attentive and nurturing parents may have to contend later on with a problem teenager. The relevance of the family development perspective and especially the developmental task concept to elder abuse will be discussed shortly.

The second body of literature on which the family transition theory of elder abuse is based is on stress. Early research on stress has mainly focused on the effects a stressor has on individuals. A stressor may be defined as: "a demand made by the internal or external environment of an organism that upsets its homeostasis, restoration of which depends on a non-automatic and no readily available energy-expending action" (Antonovsky, 1979:72). Classical examples of stressors that have been studied include air battles for World War II pilots (Grieken and Spiegel, 1945) and examinations for post-graduate students (Mechanic, 1962). Many studies have documented that stressors such as these can lead to physical illnesses of all intensities (Antonovsky, 1979). Later research, however, has switched attention to the resources people have to cope with stressors, and the success of these coping resources in alleviating the ill-effects of stressors (Antonovsky, 1979). Resource may be defined as "any characteristic of the person, the group, or the environment that can facilitate effective tension management" (Antonovsky, 1979:99). Socio-economic status, health, and social support have generally been considered valuable resources that assist in coping with many types of stressors (George, 1980).

Overall, the stress literature may be summed up by a conditional relationship: The predictor is a stressor, the dependent variable is the set of ill-effects, and resources serve as a conditional variable. Under the condition of few resources, the stressor will lead to many ill-effects; under the condition of abundant resources, the same stressor produces few ill-effects. Although the interest here is not on stress per se, but rather elder abuse as an outcome, the relevancy of the stress literature will be apparent later.

Besides this basic formulation of studying stress, a topic of major concern for stress researchers is whether the severity of a

stressor can be measured objectively or should individual perceptions of the stressor be taken into consideration as well. The
Holmes and Rahe (1967) study best illustrates the former approach. Holmes and Rahe compiled a list of forty-two stressful
life events, and they asked a panel of judges to score them in
terms of the required amount of readjustment in life. Marriage,
for example, received a score of fifty, marital separation a score
of sixty-five, and retirement a score of forty-five. This list of
stressful events together with their scores is called the Schedule
of Recent Events (SRE). According to Holmes and Rahe, individuals experiencing several of such stressful events with a high
total score will suffer health problems.

The assumption of the SRE is, of course, that the same stressful
event will have the same impact on everyone experiencing it.
This, however, has been challenged by other researchers (George,
1980). Their main criticism is that the meaning a stressful event
has for individuals should be taken into consideration. Two
persons experiencing the same stressful event may suffer different
ill-effects if the perception of the experience is different. Some
married individuals, for example, may find the death of their
spouse almost alleviating if their marital relationship has been
extremely unsatisfactory, while most others may find the experience close ot SRE's scoring of 100, extremely stressful. This issue
of conceptualizing a stressor both objectively or subjectively,
together with the basic conditional relationship for studying
stress will be used in conjunction with the family development
theory in constructing the family transition theory of elder abuse.

The family transition theory of elder abuse is shown in Figure
6.2. This theory aims at explaining physical abuse of elderly
parents by adult children. The theory has four predictors: degree
of dependence of the elderly parent, resources of the adult child,
normative inputs, and the quality of previous parent-child relationship.

Drawing on the family development perspective, the theory
begins by noting that as a parent ages into the elderly years and
the child becomes a middle-age adult, the family moves into a
new stage where previous interaction patterns may not hold.
Whereas previous stages of parent-child relationships are characterized by the parent helping the child, the elderly parent may
now be in need of aid. This emerging need of the parent is most

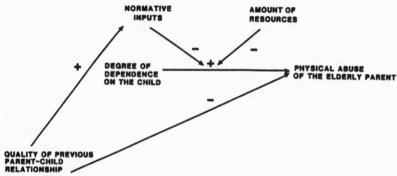

Figure 6.2. The family transition theory of elder abuse.

likely created by the declining health that comes with increases in age. In turn, the parent may become dependent on the child for maternal care, illness care, financial assistance, shared residence, among others. In many ways, this increase in dependence of the parent may be viewed as a stressor. Hence, when professionals with case experience on elder abuse suggest characteristics of old age, fraility, difficulty to care, impairment, hostility of the aged, and dependence as correlates of abuse, the hypothesis is that the higher the degree of dependence, the higher the chances of elder abuse.

Of course, dependence alone does not necessarily lead to elder abuse. Goode's (1971) Resource Theory of Intrafamily Violence may be used to explain why. According to Goode, a family member with many resources, such as control of finance and respect, would use these resources to resolve conflicts and problems he encounters within the family. Violence is, hence, unnecessary. However, for those family members who do not possess many resources, or in cases when even large amounts of resources are inadequate, violence becomes a method of conflict resolution. In other words, violence serves as a last resort when other resources are either unavailable or ineffective. The implication of Goode's theory on elder abuse is that dependence of the elderly parent would not lead to abuse so long as the child has plenty of resources to cope with the dependence. For example, if the elderly parent is increasingly demanding of the adult child in terms of financial assistance, time, and physical help, and the child possesses these resources, abuse as a coping mechanism would not be necessary. On the other hand, if the child is already lacking in these resources, the child may resort to abuse in dealing with the dependency.

An analogy may be drawn with the conditional relationship on stress derived from that literature. Among families where the adult child possesses many resources, the relationship between elder abuse and dependency of the parent is hypothesized to be weak. On the other hand, under the condition of little resources, a high level of parental dependency is hypothesized to be strongly correlated with elder abuse. Relevant resources for the adult child may very well include factors that have been hypothesized to be inversely correlated with elder abuse: being employed, high socio-economic status, emotional stability or lack of psycho-pathology, physical health, as well as a relative absence of other stressors that may deplete available resources.

In previous discussions on stress, the issue was raised that a stressful event, such as dependence of the parent, should be conceptualized and measured both objectively and subjectively. In other words, similar dependence of the parent may be perceived differently by the child in different families. Some children may see it as their obligation to care for their elderly parent; other children may consider this a burden; while still others may feel no responsibility towards their aged parent at all. Hence, a second conditional variable, normative input, is hypothesized here for the relationship between elder abuse and dependence of the aged parent. Normative input refers to the extent to which the adult child believes in the norm that a person should be responsible for the well-being of one's elderly parent. If norma-tive input is strong, meaning the adult child holds to this norm of filial responsibility, dependence of the parent is not expected to lead to elder abuse. On the other hand, among those who do not see filial responsibility as a meaningful norm, dependence is hypothesized to be correlated with elder abuse.

Finally, the last factor in the family transition theory of elder abuse is the previous parent-child relationship. In this instance, the family development concept of developmental task is utilized. At this late stage of the family, the developmental task that is most apparent is to care for the well-being of the elderly parent. However, as Aldous (1978) noted, the extent to which tasks are performed adequately at any particular stage depends on how developmental tasks were performed in earlier stages. If previous tasks have not been accomplished successfully, current tasks may be met with difficulty. This conforms with the cycle of violence suggestion in the elder abuse literature. Those elderly parents who have failed to perform the task of caring for their children properly when they were young, as in child abuse, may now have to contend with children who are ready to respond in kind. Note that this relationship, based on the developmental task concept and the cycle of violence, is hypothesized to hold regardless of whether the elderly parent is dependent on the adult child. The adult child may use violence in interacting with the elderly parent even when the parent makes little request for assistance.

On the other hand, an abusive or simply strained parent-child relationship in earlier years may also lead to elder abuse through normative input and dependence of parent. Because of earlier problems with the parent, the adult child feels little filial responsibility towards the same parent at old age. In turn, normative input is weakened. If the elderly parent with such a family background becomes dependent on the adult child, the result is likely to be elder abuse. Conversely, if the parent has performed the developmental task of nurturing the child adequately in earlier stages, and the two have a close relationship, the child is hypothesized to have a stronger acceptance of the filial responsibility norm. For such elderly parents, dependence on the adult child is not expected to lead to elder abuse.

In sum, the family transition theory sees abuses as an outcome that is inherent during the later stages of family development. The stresses that are part of the late family life includes the dependence of the elderly parent on the adult child. In coping with this dependence, the adult child may resort to violence, if the child does not possess enough resources to cope or if the child does not believe in his normative obligation to support his parent. Finally, it is also suggested in the theory that previous parent-child problems, especially in the parent abusing the child, may continue at this family stage as elder abuse.

SUMMARY

Elder abuse is a peculiar form of crime in that the perpetrator and the elderly victim are intimates. Earlier research on elder abuse was primarily conducted in nursing homes, and the abuser was a nurse or nurse's aide. Recent attention, however, has turned to abuses of the aged by family members.

Five types of behaviors have been previously considered as elder abuse: physical abuse and neglect, financial abuse, psychological abuse, violation of individual rights, and self-abuse. Several researchers believe this conceptualization of elder abuse is too inclusive and, in doing so, may have trivialized the severity the term abuse suggests. The last three types of abuses are, therefore, eliminated from a definition of elder abuse, primarily because these activities do not violate any criminal laws. On the other hand, physical and financial abuses can be likened to personal and property crimes respectively. The nature of physical abuse of the aged is further clarified by modifying Gil's (1970) definition of child abuse.

Several empirical studies of elder abuse exist at this point. Some studied clinical professionals who have contacts with elder abuse cases; other studies utilized known cases of elder abuse as data; still others interviewed volunteer respondents from especially at-risk groups. All of this research suffered methodological problems of various kinds, e.g., small and non-random samples and reliance on officially known cases. As a result, no reliable statistics exist on the prevalence of elder abuse, and the severity of the problem is simply not known. To overcome these methodological problems, surveys of the elderly population are recommended. Such surveys would allow for a more accurate assessment of the rate of elder abuse. Furthermore, the Conflict Tactics Scale by Strauss et al. (1980) can easily be modified and be used in surveys to measure physical abuse of the aged.

Existing research has also failed to uncover the causal factors of elder abuse. Although many such factors have been hypothesized, none have been tested systematically. This set of suggested causes include dependence of the aged, severity of impairment, competency of the child to care for the aged parent, being female and very old for the parent, cycle of violence, psychopathology, and so on. These suggested causes of elder abuse, when considered as a whole, reveals that they lack any systematic relationships among them. As a result, intuitive understanding of elder abuse is not enhanced. Hence, a family transition theory is proposed to explain and predict physical abuse of the aged by adult children. The theory is based on two different bodies of literature. The first is the family development perspective with special attention on the concept of developmental task; the other is the literature on stress, in particular the need to conceptualize the meaning of stressful events for people. The family transition theory predicts that elderly parents with the following two conditions will have a high likelihood of being abused: heavy dependence on a child who feels little filial obligations and who has few resources to cope with the dependence, and a previous history of the parent abusing the child.

Chapter 7

THE JUSTICE SYSTEM

W hen an elderly person is victimized, as in ordinary crimes or abuse, the aged is confronted with the decision of whether or not to report the crime to the police. If the victim chooses to report the incident, what will happen next may be a series of interactions with the police, the public prosecutor, the judge and so on. The interactions between the elderly victim and personnel within the criminal justice system constitute the focus of this chapter. Three aspects of this focus will be examined: (a) the victim's decision to report the crime which, in essence, alerts the justice system to the victimization, (b) the role the victim plays within the justice system, and (c) the efforts of the justice system to restore the victim.

The relationship between the victim and the criminal justice system is a new area of inquiry for social scientists. This interest is part of a new literature called victimology. In the late 1960s, when victimology first became formalized, the primary interest was on victim-offender interaction, or, the behaviors of the victim which may contribute to the victimization (Schafer, 1977; Viano, 1976, 1983). Hence, although both criminology and victimology focus on crimes, the approaches of the two perspectives are different. Criminology concentrates on the criminal, whereas victimology focuses on the victim. The interest in victimology grew considerably in the 1970s. The decade saw the development of several international conferences on victimology, specialized victimology journals, public policies on crime victims, and an increase in research attention on victims (Galaway and Hudson, 1981). In turn, the scope of victimology became broadened to include victim-justice system interaction, among other topics.

With this background of the literature, it is not surprising to find that the elderly victim is rarely singled out in works on the victim-justice system relationship. Instead, the victim is usually discussed without age differentiations. This may not create any problems for our purpose here in that the unique characteristics of older victims may not affect their relationship with the criminal justice system. Certainly, this issue of victim's age is an empirical one, and more research is required. At any rate, given the current status of knowledge, the following discussion is largely applicable to the experience of both younger and elderly victims, unless otherwise stated.

VICTIM AS GATE-KEEPER TO THE CRIMINAL JUSTICE SYSTEM

Although the criminal justice system is the institution within society that is responsible for monitoring crimes and punishing offenders, the system is not primarily designed to detect the occurrence of crimes. Rather, the justice system is more akin to a consumer oriented agency. Crimes usually have to be reported by victims or witnesses to the police before the justice system is aware of their occurrences and can do anything about them. Even though many officers spend the majority of their time on patrol, the chances of them actually detecting a crime is small. Instead, they typically interact with offenders and victims when they respond to citizen calls. As Reid (1982:328) puts it, "... police work is *reactive* rather than *proactive*." This is well illustrated by the finding of Reiss (1971)—95% of all crimes that the Chicago police have records of are citizen-reported incidents.

In this sense, the victim plays a vital role in the criminal justice system. The victim may be conceived as its gate-keeper (Hindeland and Gottfredson, 1976). If the victim decides not to report the crime to the police (and no witness reports it), the crime did not occur so far as the justice system is concerned. Most importantly, no victim-justice system interaction would occur.

In Chapter 2, it was pointed out that the proportion of unreported crime is substantial, as evidenced by Ennis' (1965) pilot victimization survey which showed that only approximately half of all crimes are reported to the police. Subsequent data from the National Crime Survey, however, show that as low as Ennis' estimation may seem, the actual report-rate may be even lower. Results of the 1980 National Crime Survey (Bureau of Justice Statistics, 1982) show that for the entire population, the report-rate was 47% for crimes of violence, 27% for crimes of theft, and 39% for household offenses. On the other hand, older people have slightly higher report rates. For those victims sixty-five years of age or older, report-rates were 55% for crimes of violence and 38% for crimes of theft. (The report-rate for household crime against the aged was not published.) In short, over half of all victimizations were never reported to the police, though older victims tend to report crimes slightly more often.

The meaning of such a low report-rate among victims has been investigated on several occasions. The main concern is its implication towards the victim's perception of the criminal justice system. For example, Schneider et al. (1976) wondered if non-reporting signifies the victim's lack of trust of the justice system. In general, there are two different methods of investigating the meaning and implications of non-reporting. The first is to ask the victims directly for their own perceived reasons for reporting or non-reporting. A second method is, instead, to assess correlates of reporting/non-reporting. Hence, factors which respondents may have failed to identify as contributing to their decision would be also detected here.

Data from the National Crime Survey have been analyzed with the second method to identify determinants of victimization reporting. Skogan (1976) found that personal characteristics of the victim are not related to crime reporting. There was little difference in report rates between Blacks and Whites, males and females, or young and old for that matter. In addition, whether the offender was a stranger or a non-stranger also made virtually no difference. Instead, it was found that reporting is strongly correlated with the seriousness of the crime—the more serious the crime, the higher the report rate. Seriousness of the crime has been measured in a variety of ways—whether the victimization was successful, whether the victim was assaulted, whether weapons were used, whether injuries were sustained, whether the crime occurred at home or on the street, and also, property loss in actual dollars (Skogan, 1976; Hindeland and Gottfredson, 1976). Regardless of the measure used, the relationship holds consistently. At the aggregate level, this is reflected in the report rate of the different crimes. Aggravated assault has a higher report rate than simple assault; personal larceny with contact has a higher report rate than personal larceny without contact; burglary has a higher report rate than household larceny (Bureau of Justice Statistics, 1982).

Using the same approach to uncover determinants of crime reporting, Schneider et al. (1976) reported on results with a data set, collected in Portland, Oregon, that is not part of the NCS. Because Schneider et al.'s study was independent from the NCS, they were able to include other predictors of crime reporting that were not contained in the NCS. Yet, at the multivariate level, seriousness of crime still emerged as the most powerful predictor of crime reporting. Other predictors include the victim's integration into the community, the victim's beliefs about the chances of the police catching the offender, and the general attitude of the offender towards the police.

When victims were asked directly why they did not report their victimization to the police, three reasons emerged repeatedly (Bureau of Justice Statistics, 1982). The most common reason is that the victim considered the crime "not important enough": 26% of personal crime victims and 28% of household crime victims used this response. This coincides with the finding that seriousness of crime is the most powerful predictor of crime reporting. The other two often cited reasons are "nothing could be done/ lack of proof" and "police would not want to be bothered." These two reasons may be interpreted as lending support to Schneider et al.'s (1976) finding that the victim's negative perception of the police also contributes to crime non-reporting.

In a unique study, Smith and Maness (1976) asked victims why they reported the crime to the police, instead of why they did not report the crime. Among those victims who did report, the most common response was that they saw it as their responsibility to do so, a sense of civic duty. Another common response was that they desire to have the offender apprehended.

In sum, crime victims often failed to report their victimization to the police. This is particularly true for victims of less serious crimes. By not reporting, the implication is that they would not be interacting with the criminal justice system in the role of a victim.

THE INTERACTION BETWEEN THE VICTIM AND THE JUSTICE SYSTEM

The Police

When a person is victimized in a crime, and if he chooses to report the crime, the first persons he would be interacting with are police officers. With information supplied by the victim, the police may record the crime, investigate the incident, and make an arrest of suspects. Oftentimes, police officers are the only justice system personnel with whom the public ever has contact.

When police officers respond to a citizen's call, the victim is often in a highly emotional state (Goldstein and Wolf, 1979a). Victimization is a rare occurrence event, and frequently victims experience at the crime scene a feeling of helplessness or even a state of shock. When police officers arrive, the victims usually expect sympathy and understanding from the officers. However, Arcuri (1981) has observed that the police are entering the situation from a totally different perspective. Seeing victimization is part of the everyday experience of a police officer. Rather than being caught off-guard by the victimization, the officers are likely to react to the victim and the crime scene calmly and matter-of-factly. At the same time the officers are routinely taking down the information and recording the crime, the victim is expecting comfort and empathy from the officers. Hence, Arcuri (1981) believed that some victims find the "bedside manner" of the police less than desirable.

Arcuri (1981) further asserted that older victims may fare worse in their interaction with the police because older people have low status in society and police do not understand the aged. Hence, Goldstein and Wolf (1979a) proposed ways that the police can calm an elderly victim, such as presenting a non-hostile authority, showing empathy, and modeling calmness, among others. In a related article, Goldstein and Wolf (1979b) also discussed specific techniques to train police to work with elderly victims, e.g., role play, modeling, and so on.

The extent to which victims are dissatisfied with police performance in responding to calls to victimizations is, however, not certain. Anecdoctal cases certainly exist, but generalizability of these cases is questionable. In at least one study, crime victims have rated the performance of the police highly. Knudten and Knudten (1981) interviewed 1,553 victims who are at various stages of the trial process in Milwaukee County in Wisconsin, and found that 76% to 86% of the victims rated the police excellent or good in terms of their effort, effectiveness, and courteousness.

In another study, the position that older victims received worse treatment from the police was also challenged. Sykes (1976) systematically observed and coded police-citizen interactions by riding with police patrols. Variables coded included the content and the emotional tone of each statement by officer or civilian and acts of special salience (such as violence). Comparisons of young-citizen/police and old-citizen/police interactions yield little difference. One exception that warrants special attention here is that older people are more likely to get away with disrespectfulness than are younger people. When older citizens are disrespectful to the police officer, the officer is less likely to respond with verbal control behaviors. It may be that older people are less of a threat to the police, and therefore, disrespectful behaviors are more likely to be tolerated. Although Knudten and Knudten's (1981) and Sykes' (1976) studies are by no means conclusive, they do dampen the position that victims are generally not satisfied with officers' "bedside manner" in responding to calls or that the problem is especially severe with older victims.

An interesting idea that has emerged out of the attention on the elderly victim-police interaction is the potential role police officers can play as a social service referral for older people (Brostoff, 1976; Sykes, 1976). One of the problems that social workers for the aged face is that the extremely isolated older individuals are oftentimes hard to reach and difficult to be detected, even though they may be the ones who need services the most. The police have the unique capacity to reach this segment of the population in that they are often called upon to provide emergency services of medical or other natures. Wilson (1968), for example, found that among a sample of citizen calls to the Syracuse police department, 38% are requests for services, such as accidents, illnesses, and assistance to individuals. In other words, when people are in need of emergency help, rather than calling social workers or hospitals, they would, instead, call the police. Data from Sykes' (1976) systematic observation study provide support to the belief that this may be especially true with older people. Sykes found that although only 14% of police-citizen contacts were of service in nature, 25% of police contacts with older people were for services. Hence, the police are in an unique situation that allows them to identify older people in need of help and services.

Sykes further noted that the additional chore of referring older people in need of social services to the appropriate agencies would not retard the officer's primary duty of fighting crime. There are several reasons for this. First, as noted above, requests for police assistance are seldom for criminal violations. Second, since police usually arrive at the crime scene after the offenders are gone, their role is reduced to record-keeping. Third, crimes often occur in private spaces, e.g., homes, that are not accessible to the police unless by request. Finally, in patrolling, the likelihood of police actually stumbling onto a crime scene is slim. All of these considerations mean that the referral role would not reduce the effectiveness of the police to fight crime and that they are in an excellent position to provide referral services to the aged.

Brostoff (1976) described one such police department that had experimented with adding referrals for older people to the roles of its patrol officers. The police station was in Washington, DC, and between 1970 and 1971, a referral office was opened adjacent to the police station. Some older people who needed social services were referred to this office by the police who were handling the case while other elderly were identified as in need of services by reviewing police reports of crimes. Based on interviews by the project staff, these older people were in turn referred to social agencies. Brostoff described several cases in which the intervention of the police officers was essential in placing these older people in appropriate social services agencies. Given that Brostoff's account was more of an exaltation of the program than an evaluation, it is not certain to what extent and in what sense the program was a success. Nonetheless, the idea that the police have the capacity to act as referrals for the aged appears to be a concept that is well worth further attention.

Arrest and the Trial Proceedings

Not all crimes reported to the police are investigated. Crimes with little clues, for example, burglaries, are seldom investigated. Not all investigations lead to arrests of suspects. And unless arrests are made, the victim would not have to interact with any justice system personnel other than the police.

The Federal Bureau of Investigation's (1982) Uniform Crime Report provided the arrest rates for seven types of ordinary crimes that formed their crime index. These statistics are shown in Figure 7.1. Murder has the highest rate of arrest, 74%, followed by aggravated assault, 60%, forcible rape, 51%, and robbery, 25%. On the other hand, the three types of property crime have far lower arrest rates: 15% for burglary, 19% for larceny-theft, and 14% for motor vehicle theft. The four types of violent crimes all have higher arrest rates because the police spend more time investigating them, the victims are more cooperative with the police, and because of the greater availability of witnesses (Reid, 1982). It is important to note that the prevalence of property

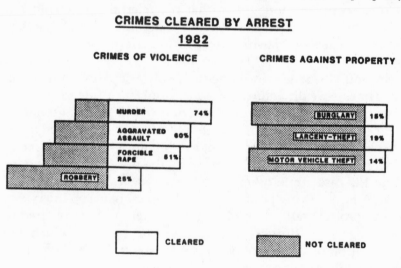

Figure 7.1. Crimes cleared by arrest.

crimes is much higher than that of violent crimes (see Chapter 2). The implication is that by far the majority of crime victims who report their victimization to the police do not participate in any trial proceedings.

For the small proportion of victims whose suspected offenders are apprehended, they will proceed on to interact with the rest of the criminal justice system in the role of victim-witness. Depending on the complexity of the case, the role of victim-witness can be demanding. The following represents the *most* complex sequence of events for the victim-witness if the case proceeds on to the trial stage.

Upon the arrest of the suspect, the victim will be asked by the police to identify the offender. If the correct identification is made, the victim will then be interviewed by the public prosecutor to collect information for establishing the case. The first time the witness may appear before a judge is during the *preliminary hearing* (Reid, 1982). During this hearing, the judge will examine the evidence presented by the public prosecutor, possibly including testimonies from the victim. The judge will decide two things: whether there is probable cause to believe that a crime has been committed and whether the evidence points to the suspect. The judge will then either dismiss the charges or send the case to the grand jury.

The *grand jury* is a group of randomly chosen private citizens, charged with the responsibility of deciding whether or not the suspect should go to trial (Reid, 1982). The evidence presented by the public prosecutor, including possibly in-person testimonies from the victim, are examined at this stage again. After studying the evidence, the grand jury may vote to return an "indictment," which means the suspect should go to trial, or they may "fail to indict," which means the case proceeds no further in the judicial system. All federal felonies must go through a grand jury, but individual states vary in their use of the grand jury system.

The final appearance for the victim as a witness is during the *trial*. Television and movies have familiarized the lay public with the proceedings of a trial. Both the public prosecutor and the defense attorney, with the help of witnesses, present their positions to a judge or a jury, who will then decide on the verdict.

Although the above sequence of events for the victim-witness is allowed in justice system procedures, in reality, the role of victim-witness is less demanding. In most cases, the victim does not have to appear in-person during either the preliminary hearing or the grand jury, a sworn statement is usually sufficient. Furthermore, *plea bargaining* diverts most cases away from an actual trial. Plea bargaining refers to the suspected offender pleading guilty to the crime in return for consideration of favor from the prosecutor, such as a less serious charge, a recommendation for lenient sentencing, and so forth (Reid, 1982). Studies have shown that as many as 90% of cases terminate with plea bargainings.

Victim's Characteristics and Case Outcomes

Given that the victim plays a pivotal role in the victimization and that the victim may be required to testify on numerous instances during the justice proceedings, some have wondered if the victim's characteristics may not affect the outcome of the case. For example, if the rape victim is a disabled elderly woman, would this not arouse the sympathy of the judge and jury which may in turn affect their judgement of the case? The hypothesis that victim's characteristics somehow affect the case outcome falls in line with other research in jurisprudence. This literature suggests that the demographic characteristics, clothings, and mannerisms of the judge, public prosecutor, defense attorney, witnesses and juries, as well as that of the victim, may all be used to predict the outcome of a case. This essentially implies that the final verdict of a case depends on factors other than the merits of the evidence presented in court.

At least two studies have examined the relationship between the case outcome and the characteristics of the victim. Demo and Cramer (1976) observed the trial proceedings of 161 cases in Toronto. To prevent observation intrusions, prior consent from the justice system personnel and the victims was not solicited. The in-court observation focused on two variables, the judge's reaction to the victim in court (favorable or unfavorable) and the defendant's sentence. Demo and Cramer found that neither variable is related to the age, ethnicity, appearance, or physical attractiveness of the victim. In a similar study, Williams (1976) analyzed 5,042 criminal cases in Washington, D.C. Williams inspected three variables: whether the prosecutor filed charges after the arrest, whether the prosecutor dismissed the case before trial, and whether cases that went to trial resulted in a guilty verdict. Hence, Williams studied not only the possible influence of the victim's characteristics on the judge, but on the prosecutor and jury as well. In general, Williams found little support for the hypothesis that the victim's characteristics affect the outcome of the case. In short, although disposition of cases in the court system is oftentimes highly irregular, this irregularity has not been found to be a function of the victim's characteristics. Victims that may appear to be more helpless, such as an aged, do not receive preferential treatment from the courts in the disposition of cases.

Victim's Input and Case Outcomes

Normatively, the lack of any correlation between the victim's characteristics and case outcome is desirable in that such a relationship is, at best, idiosyncratic. Prosecutors and judges are not supposed to punish suspects just because the victim appears to be old, helpless, and vulnerable. On the other hand, a related issue that needs to be addressed is the amount of input a victim has in the disposition of his own case. For example, how much influence does an elderly woman have in influencing how her burglar is being handled by the criminal justice system? Does the elderly woman have a say if the prosecutor decides not to file charges, to drop charges, or to plea bargain? Can the elderly victim advise the judge in sentencing if the offender is convicted? Whereas the concern earlier was on the indirect effects victims may have on case disposition, because of their characteristics, the current focus is on the amount of direct power a victim has on the justice system. In other words, the interest is on how large a role a victim-witness has in convicting and punishing his offender.

The consensus among victimologists is that the victim has little input in the prosecution of his offender and that his role is restricted to that of a witness. Wolfgang (1972) pointed out that the criminal justice system ignores the victim except when the victim's contribution in evidence is required. Likewise, Dubow and Becker (1976) believe that the victim is used at the discretion of the prosecutor. The prosecutor may dispense the case or plea bargain with the defense without even informing the victim. The only power left to the victim is the decision to provide information and testify. Similar sentiments have been expressed by Schneider and Schneider (1981) and Ziegenhagen (1976): the preference of the victim on case disposition is not officially represented in the justice system, and no justice personnel formally solicit their opinion.

Whereas the needs of the victim are virtually ignored, the justice system appears to overextend itself in protecting the offender (McDonald, 1976; Schafer, 1976). The rights of the offender to be informed of his right to counsel at the time of his arrest, to make a phone call shortly after the arrest, to receive counsel at public expense, and to appear before a judge within two or three days upon arrest, are just a sample of rules that the justice system is required to conform. Violations of any of these rights could lead to the freeing of the offender. Yet, the victim receives no such attention from the justice system.

Given that the system of justice works so independently of the victims, many believe that victims are frustrated by their role, especially when the judicial procedures become long and tedious (Dubow and Becker, 1976). Geis (1975:64) provided several telling illustrations of this frustration among victims. Take the following account of a larceny victim, for example.

> On October 19, I encountered a thief who had broken into my parked car and who was in the process of removing the FM radio tuner. I followed him for eight blocks and was fortunate enough to spot a police prowl car. The man was duly arrested and charged. In his possession was the FM tuner.
>
> That evening, playing the role of "good citizen," I spent three hours in night court waiting my chance to see justice administered. Taken before Judge Hyman Skolniker, the defendant pleaded "not guilty."... Because of a legal complication, the prisoner; to my great shock, was released without bail despite the fact that he admitted to being a heroin addict with a previous arrest record....
> The entire court appearance lasted between sixty to ninety seconds.
>
> On October 28, the defendant failed to appear in court. As one who took the trouble to follow, to apprehend, and to appear in

court, I am totally disillusioned with the results. I am informed
by the Appearance Control Project people at the District Attorney's
office that no one will attempt to locate the defendant. I was told
that his failure to appear in court will merely be recorded and that
should he ever be re-arrested, he will then face the music.

Basically what has happened is that this man has been given
license to commit more crimes. This has been effected by sixty-
second justice administered with help of Legal Aid Society lawyers.

From my point of view, I deeply regret being involved and
having wasted my time in the interest of justice. Should this
situation recur (and I have no doubt that it will), I will not
participate. Should I witness a crime, I will turn my back. It is
obvious that under our present court system the victim gets no
redress, and the petty criminal, when caught, goes free.

The powerlessness of the victim in the judicial process and his
alleged frustration with the justice system can be assessed empirically as well as normatively. From the empirical angle, the
issue is whether victims who have served as witnesses *are*, in fact,
as frustrated as some believed. From the normative standpoint,
the question is whether victims *should* have more say in the
exercising of justice on his behalf.

The dissatisfaction of victims towards prosecutors and judges,
or the lack of it, is documented in the study of approximately
1,600 victims in Milwaukee County, Wisconsin noted earlier
(Knudten et al., 1976; Knudten and Knudten, 1981). Between 69%
to 86% of the victims consider the performance of the district
attorney and judge excellent or good in terms of their effort,
effectiveness, and courteousness. Although the same group of
victims had rated police performance higher, the difference is
small, and the researchers believed that the higher evaluation of
the police is due to their more extensive interaction with the
victims. Knudten and her associates concluded that victims do
not have unrealistic expectations of the expedition of justice and
that they are generally satisfied with the justice system. The
result of this study clearly calls into question the belief that
victims are generally disillusioned with the justice system. Dissatisfaction is apparently not as widespread as some believed.
Nonetheless, more studies in various other locales are needed to
resolve this enigma satisfactorily.

From a normative viewpoint, there are substantial reasonings
behind the position that victims should not have more official
authority in the disposition of their cases. First, notice that the

entire justice system is established essentially to ensure that punishment is taken out of the hands of the victim. Private vengeance disrupts social order. If victims are allowed to participate in punishing offenders, they may very well demand punishments that far exceed the crime.

Furthermore, the justice system makes a distinction between tort and crime (Geis, 1976a; Reid, 1982). Torts are acts which civil laws prohibit and for which redress is allowed, e.g., personal injuries, defamation of character, and so forth. In torts, it is the victim who files the suit against the particular individual and the case is settled in a civil court. Crimes, on the other hand, are acts that violate criminal laws. Crimes are considered so serious that the well-being of the entire society is being threatened. Committing a crime is analogous to doing a public, not a private, wrong. Hence, the public prosecutor represents *the people*, not the victim, in seeking punishment of the offender for his crime. In spirit, the public prosecutor prosecutes the offender to preserve social order, not to seek vengeance for the victim. It is because of this distinction between torts and crimes, that the victim is only allocated the role of a witness in the judicial process. More active involvement of the witness in decision-making in a criminal trial proceeding, hence, violates the fundamental philosophy of the criminal justice system.

Yet, the distinction between torts and crimes is murky at best. The same offense, for example, assault, may be prosecuted in criminal courts by the public prosecutor and be sued in civil courts by the victim. If the victim is allowed to act as a prosecutor in the latter, there is little reason to treat the victim as an outsider in the former system. Hence, the literature contains the views of some advocates who strongly argue that the role of the victim should be extended in the trial proceedings (e.g., see Dubow and Becker, 1976). It is the victim, after all, who suffered the most from the crime, not society.

At least three different systems have been proposed to increase the input of the victim, all three have been put into practice to various extents: arbitrations, victim advocacies, and private prosecutors.

Ziegenhagen and Benyi (1981) believed that the goal of the criminal justice system is to minimize destructive behaviors and sometimes this goal can be reached without evoking the criminal justice system. One such alternate procedure is an arbitration system. In arbitration, the offender and the victim are brought together, and a resolution acceptable to all parties is sought. Most of the offenses brought to arbitration are of minor infractions of law, such as intrafamily crimes, or check offenses (Galaway and Hudson, 1981).

The "night prosecutor" system in Columbus, Ohio, illustrates how an arbitration program may work (Palmer, 1975). The program at Columbus is housed in the office of public prosecutors. Criminal cases are chosen out of police files for arbitration. These cases usually involve perpetrators who are known to the victim. A prosecutor playing the role of a mediator/conciliator meets with the victim and the perpetrator in half hour evening sessions to seek a private settlement to the case. Neither party is represented by lawyers. If a settlement agreeable to both parties can be reached, the case is terminated without criminal court involvement. Palmer (1975) reported the program works best when the victim does not want to prosecute.

A second approach that has been suggested to increase the input of the victim in the justice system is victim advocacies. Unlike arbitration, victim advocacies do not involve diverting cases out of the formal justice system. Instead, the purpose here is to involve the victim in the decision-making process in the case proceedings (Culp and Calvin, 1977), or specifically making the prosecutor and the judge more accountable to the victim (Dubow and Becker, 1976). The input of the victim is deemed crucial at two particular points of the proceedings, plea bargaining and sentencing (Schneider and Schneider, 1981). In both instances, the desired goal is to deter the justice system from overly lenient punishment of the offender. While this goal may be deemed worthwhile, its actual practice is problematic. Although victim advocacies may involve having attorneys represent victims, Ziegenhagen and Benyi (1981) believed that these attorneys are usually not well-accepted by judges and prosecutors. Unless a formal role is actually established for the victim in the trial proceedings, victim advocacies may actually be perceived as hindering the justice system.

In some sense, the third way to increase victim's input in case disposition, the private prosecutor, is also a form of victim advocacy. The major difference between the two is that the private prosecutor is a full-fledged member of the justice system. A private prosecutor is an attorney hired by the victim to prosecute the offender in criminal courts (McDonald, 1976). The private prosecutor may cooperate with the public prosecutor, or he may even prosecute the offender alone if the public prosecutor decides to drop from the case. Hence, the private prosecutor probably personifies the ultimate in victim advocacies in that the victim has the control and the responsibility of his own case. However, the drawback of the private prosecutor system is that it only exists in a small number of states. Private prosecutors also cost money, and many victims, such as the aged, would not be able to afford the attorney's fees. In North Carolina, where the system is the most active, it has been observed that cases which use private prosecutors virtually never result in plea bargainings (McDonald, 1976).

At the same time that different approaches are being suggested and experimented to expand the role of the victim in the justice system, Carrington (1977) pointed out that the victim has always had the right to litigate in the civil court system. As pointed out earlier, numerous offenses, such as assault and battery, violate both criminal and civil laws. Regardless of the outcome of the criminal court trial, the victim can sue the offender in civil court. In cases where the offender was found guilty in criminal court, the outcome of the civil suit is virtually guaranteed to be in the victim's favor. Yet, few victims file civil suits against their offenders. Carrington believed that the main deterrent is that the offender is often indigent, or in prison, which essentially make any judgement uncollectable. Another deterrent is the cost of using an attorney for the victim, both of which make a civil suit an impractical option for many victims. An alternate way is to sue not the offender, but a third party for negligence. In recent years, civil suits have been filed, for example, against psychiatric institutes and parole boards for releasing offenders who subsequently commit crimes against the victim.

The Cost of Being a Victim-Witness

While it is a consensus that the victim has very little impact on the outcome of his case, it is equally known that trial proceedings create numerous inconveniences for victims (Galaway and Hudson, 1981; Lynch, 1976). To be a witness, the victim may have to take time off from work without compensation, arrange for child care services, provide his own transportation, pay for the parking, and wait for court appearances in hallways together with defendants and their families. This process may occur more than once in that both the defense and the prosecutor have the right to request for postponements of trials, and victims may not be notified of the change in dates. To add to the aggravation, victims are seldom notified of the outcome of the case, and if it is a property offense, recovered stolen goods, e.g., a television, have to be held by the court as material evidence until the case is over. In short, the entire trial proceeding is operated to allow for the convenience of the justice system personnel at the expense of victims as well as other witnesses (Knudten et al., 1976).

The extent of the cost of being a victim-witness has been empirically documented in the Milwaukee study reported by Knudten, et al. (1976) and Knudten and Knudten (1981). Knudten, Knudten and their associates found that two problems were experienced by a majority of the 1,800 victim-witnesses interviewed: 79% indicated transportation and parking expenses and 57% time loss as problems. Interestingly, expenses incurred by transportation/parking were not considered serious by the victims. Among those problems that were rated as serious or very serious by at least 70% of the respondents were: income loss, exposure to threatening persons, unnecessary trips, time loss, difficulty arranging transportation, and long waiting time. Time loss, therefore, appears to be a problem that is both common and considered serious among victim-witnesses. It is also important to note that no particular group tends to monopolize these problems in confronting the justice system as witnesses. Elderly victim-witnesses, therefore, have to deal with these problems no more and no less than younger persons.

To make the role of witness less arduous for victims, a number of in-house services have been suggested (Culp and Calvin, 1977; Galaway and Hudson, 1981; Geis, 1975; Hamel, 1979; Lynch, 1976; Schneider and Schneider, 1981). In general, these suggested services can be divided into convenience services (Schneider and Schneider, 1981) and court-related services. Convenience services include provisions of escorts at courthouse entrance, comfortable reception areas, victims waiting rooms, child care, cafeteria services, transportation, parking facilities, early property release, and contacts with employer for paid leaves. Court-related services include a telephone system to alert victims for witness appearances (but only after confirmation that testimony is required that day), explanations and information on justice system, and information on case status and disposition.

In the 1970s, the then Law Enforcement Assistance Administration (LEAA) was active in funding demonstration projects that provide convenience and court-related services to victims (Schneider and Schneider, 1981). Most of these victim-witness assistance programs are located in urban areas (Hamel, 1979). The programs are usually housed in police departments, prosecutor offices, probation departments, or social services agencies. One such program in Tucson, Arizona has been described in detail by Lowenburg (1981).

While the rationale for victim assistance programs may rest entirely on normative grounds, victims deserve better treatment when they are willing to make the effort to become witnesses. It has also been speculated that these programs would increase the victims' cooperation with the justice system (Schneider and Schneider, 1981). If these programs do actually increase victim cooperation, then the money for them would appear well-spent. Given the various problems victims face, the no-show rate of the victim-witnesses is rather high. One study in Washington, D.C. found that of approximately 3,000 cases dismissed by the court or rejected by the prosecutor, 42% were due to a lack of witness cooperation (Lowenburg, 1981). Yet, empirical evidence, showing that victim assistance programs do increase victim cooperation, is still missing due to the lack of evaluation research (Schneider and Schneider, 1981). This may be especially detrimental to the future of assistance programs given that the LEAA funds were temporary in nature. Continued fundings are supposed to come from local governments. Without research to substantiate the effectiveness of these programs, this may prove to be difficult (Schneider and Schneider, 1981).

RESTORING THE VICTIM

Considering the numerous efforts the criminal justice system has made to rehabilitate criminals, the same system pays precious little attention to restoring victims. During incarceration, the convict may go through various rehabilitation programs: counseling, education, vocational training, and so forth (Reid, 1982). Upon release, the ex-convict may also be eligible for various programs, such as special manpower programs (Culp and Calvin, 1977). Yet, victims of crimes receive no such treatment. Until recently, few attempts had been made to restore victims to their former selves, to assist them in recovering from their physical injuries and property losses.

In the 1970s, three different types of attempts were made to restore victims: restitution, compensation, and social services.

Restitution

Restitution refers to the offender repaying the victim for the injuries or losses that the victim sustains as a result of the victimization. According to Schafer (1977), restitution as a form of punishment was customary during the Middle Ages. In those days, the state would seize the properties of the offender upon conviction, and give them to the victim as a form of justice. However, as time went by, the state retained the properties of the offender after confiscation, and no reparation was given to the victim. The victim's right to restitution was entirely overlooked when the separation between crimes and torts was formalized. The offender in committing a crime owes a debt to society, not the victim, and he repays his debt to society, not the victim, by incarceration.

In recent decades, the increasing realization is that crime not only violates the rules of society but also the rights of the victim. Interest in restitution, hence, has returned. Yet, it is important to note that justice for the victim is not the only rationale behind restitution. The offender is also supposed to benefit. Galaway (1977) believed that restitution is one of the more humane punishments and that it rehabilitates offenders. In addition, Barnett (1977) pointed out that restitution is a form of "self-determinant" sentencing, the hard-working offender may reduce his "time" by repaying the victim faster. Alternately, both Galaway and Barnett also noted that restitution as a form of punishment is advantageous to society in that it saves money for taxpayers. However, from the victim's standpoint, the most important rationale for restitution is simply that it offsets the losses incurred from victimization. Yet, restitution helps only a small proportion of victims (Galaway, 1977). As pointed out earlier, most crimes do not lead to arrests, and arrests do not necessarily result in convictions.

Restitution can be instituted in the justice system in any one of three ways (Galaway, 1977). First, restitution may serve as a pretrial diversion. Instead of prosecution, the police or prosecutor may arrange an agreement with the victim that involves restitution. A youth, for example, may pay for damaged properties of his vandalism, or a shoplifter may return his stolen goods. This is the idea of arbitration discussed earlier. A second mechanism is to use restitution as a condition for probation. Probation is a form of sentencing by the judge; the offender is allowed to remain in the community but with restrictions and supervision. Finally, restitution may also be used as a condition for parole. Parole refers to the early release of a convict but again with restrictions and supervision. The parole board can easily pronounce restitution as a condition for parole. These three methods of restitution have been used sporadically in various states.

Given that most offenders of ordinary crimes are from the lower class, some have wondered if expectations of restitution are realistic. In an interesting study, the Bureau of Justice Statistics (1980b) examined the losses incurred in property-related crimes. Using the 1974 National Crime Survey data, the amount of actual dollars in theft losses and property damages for six types of crimes were computed: unarmed robbery, larceny with contact, burglary, household larceny, larceny without contact, and motor vehicle theft. Surprisingly, the loss was less than $25 in 48% of the offenses, and less than $100 in 73% of the cases. In other words, restitution is well within reach of the poor offenders in most of the cases. (Note that this study focused only on property crimes and not violent crimes. If the medical cost incurred from personal injuries in violent crimes was considered, the amount of restitution would have been larger.)

Compensation

Whereas restitution refers to reparations by the offender, compensation refers to reparations by the state. If restitution appeals to the common sense because the offender is only repaying the victim for the harm incurred, what then are the rationales for having the state repay the victim? There are three such rationales.

First, it was pointed out that individuals in choosing to live in society forego certain freedoms. In exchange for the loss, the state undertakes to protect individuals from harm. Hence, when the state fails in its responsibility, the state is obligated to provide remedies for the victims (Harland, 1981; Schafer, 1976; Sutherland and Cressey, 1970; Ziegenhagen and Benyi, 1981). Second, in establishing the criminal justice system, the state is interfering into private disputes. The state has monopolized the right to punish offenders. In turn, offenders repay debts to the state, instead of to the victim. Compensation only means the state turns the debts it has collected from the offender to the victim (Harland, 1981; Ziegenhagen and Benyi, 1981). Finally, the welfare system of society assists all types of underprivileged people: the elderly, the poor, and the minorities. Given that victims are also unfortunate people, the welfare state should also be extended to help them (Harland, 1981; Stookey, 1981).

The idea of compensation is not new in history, but it was revitalized in the 1950s in Britain mainly because of the work of one woman, the late Margery Fry (Schafer, 1977). Her writings on the need to compensate crime victims have captured the attention of the public, and, in turn, influenced policy-makers. Switzerland, New Zealand, and Britain took the lead in establishing compensation programs. Currently, in the United States, the Congress, despite several attempts since the 1970s, has yet to pass a bill to create a federal victim compensation program. Given the current budget crisis and the political mood of the country, passage of such a bill appears to be unlikely in the near future. About half of the states, on the other hand, have created victim compensation programs (Hamel, 1979). The list includes Alaska, California, Delaware, Georgia, Hawaii, Illinois, Kentucky, Louisiana, Maryland, Massachusetts, Michigan, Minnesota, Nevada, New Jersey, New York, North Dakota, Ohio, Pennsylvania, Rhode Island, Tennessee, Texas, Virginia, Washington, and Wisconsin. These compensation programs are usually housed in a state social service agency, an existing state agency that processes monetary benefits, or in a justice system unit (Ashton, 1981). Doerner (1979) reported that several characteristics of the state are related to having state compensation programs: high welfare expenditures, high median family incomes, high violence rates, progressive in innovating new programs, and a low police/population ratio.

The ways in which these compensation programs are administered vary by state, but certain features are common (Ashton, 1981; Geis, 1976a; Hamel, 1979; Lamborn, 1981; Ziegenhagen, 1976). Harland (1981) provides the most systematic approach to understand these similarities and diversities in eligibility requirements.

A *compensable claimant* may be a victim of crime, the victim's dependent if the victim died, a bystander who intervened, or any third party who assumed medical/burial cost. To prevent fraud, the victim must not be closely related to the offender. The victim should also not be responsible for the crime. In many states, documentation of financial needs of the victim is required. In other words, a means-test is administered. In these states, older people should be in a better position to collect compensation given their generally lower economic status.

Compensable offenses are primarily restricted to crimes of violence, or simply where injury or death is sustained from the victimization. Arrest or conviction is not required. Automobile accidents are never included unless the automobile is used as a weapon. Property crimes are excluded because it may lead to careless behaviors on the part of victims, it may adversely affect the insurance industry, and the chances of fraudulent claims are high.

Compensable losses are usually restricted to unreimbursed (e.g., from insurance) medical expenses, opportunity for wages, and burial expenses. Except in a few states, awards are usually not made to compensate pain and suffering endured, such as in rape. Maximum benefit is usually no more than $10,000, although it goes as high as $50,000 in Louisiana. To eliminate the reimbursement of small losses, the majority of states set a minimum benefit of $100.

Aside from these eligibility requirements, there are some miscellaneous restrictions. In many states, the victim is required to report the crime within two or three days, to cooperate with the prosecution, and to file for compensation within one half to two years of the offense.

The current status of compensation programs in the United States faces numerous criticisms. The major one is simply that about half of the states do not provide compensation to victims. A federal program appears to be the best way to provide uniform

coverage. In an interesting analysis, the Law Enforcement Assistance Administration (1977e) showed that the cost of a federal
program may not be as high as some may think. Based on the
1974 National Crime Survey data, the analysis showed that of six
million victims, only one and half million were injured, out of
which only half a million victims required medical attention.
The cost of the medical bill is also rather low, only 15,000
victims had bills over $100. Finally, in 1974, if all compensable
victims were to claim their medical expenses, the total cost was
only $144 million if $100 was used as a minimum reimbursement,
or $261 million is no minimum was used.

Social Services

Whereas compensation aims at providing cash reparations to
the victim, social services restore the victim through in-kind
assistance. As in compensation, there are currently no federal
social services programs specifically designed for crime victims.
Such social services programs exist sporadically among the states.

Social services to crime victims have a short history, most
began in the 1970s, and the first ones were developed with
specific target groups (Dussick, 1981). Victims of child abuse
were, apparently, the first type of crime victims to receive services.
Crisis centers for victims of rape and spouse battering were
established soon afterwards. The umbrella approach, which service victims of all crimes, in fact, did not appear until later.

Different types of services have been provided by different
programs. In general, these services can be divided into two
types, crisis intervention and follow-up assistance. Crisis intervention refers to assistance at the scene of the crime, such as
transportation from the scene (Schneider and Schneider, 1981)
and counseling for fear or emotional trauma (Geis, 1975; Schneider and Schneider, 1981; Ziegenhagen and Benyi, 1981). A case
reported by Chesney and Schneider (1981:402) illustrates the
need for crisis counseling:

> The call on this case came in at 11 P.M. I met the police officer
> at the victim's house. She lived alone and was badly shaken. Her
> apartment had been ransacked and burglarized while she was out
> to dinner with friends. Appropriately, the police officer felt he
> could not leave her alone, as she was close to hysteria and had no

close friends she could call at that hour. I stayed with her until
2:30 A.M., at which time she and I both felt she was in control of
herself. During my stay with her, she was able to discharge all her
emotions. We went through her ransacked bedroom, listed items
that were missing, and made a list of things to be done the
following day....

Follow-up assistance may include more counseling, referral to
other social services agencies (Friedman, 1976; Lowenberg, 1981;
Lynch, 1976), and vocational rehabilitation (Geis, 1976a). A case
reported by Friedman (1976:114) illustrates the need for referral
services for elderly victims:

> An 83-year-old woman's husband was murdered by four youths
> in the hallway of their apartment house in the Bronx. We were
> called by police and were asked to see her. Severe signs of emo-
> tional trauma were evident while interviewing her. Following the
> violent death of her husband, she stopped eating and began to
> vomit and complain of abdominal pains. She was unable to sleep
> at night and was extremely agitated. Quickly her mental health
> deteriorated to the point where she developed a speech impedi-
> ment, was unable to sleep, and had a generalized tremor of the
> hands and feet. We referred her to an affiliated hospital psychiatric
> program for therapy that would deal with her problems. She was
> put on Thorazine and improved, but the drug treatment was dis-
> continued because of an allergic reaction. Her mental anxieties
> appear to be diminishing following a series of therapy sessions.

Social services programs for victims are usually established in
relation to police departments, rather than other social services
agencies, since cooperation with the police is crucial to their
success. This is the idea of police in the role of referral discussed
earlier. Detailed descriptions of specific programs exist: Lowenberg (1981) on the Tucson program, and Chesney and Schneider
(1981) on the Minneapolis/St. Paul program.

Early empirical data from these victim assistance programs
showed that victims' needs for these programs are, apparently,
not strong. Chesney and Schneider (1981) noted that when their
crisis intervention program was established, workers spent many
hours manning phone lines without receiving any calls from
patrols requesting assistance. At first, the belief was that the
police patrols were not calling the program for lack of trust.
Further investigations, however, showed that few victims indeed

require crisis counseling. Given this low demand, the cost of the Minnesota victim service program became rather high. Despite the fact that the program depends heavily on volunteers, the cost per victim served was $70, excluding community education and program evaluation costs. This conclusion has also been reached by Schneider and Schneider (1981), who reported that data from eight LEAA programs showed that only 4% of victims required services.

SUMMARY

The relationship/interaction between the victim and the justice system is usually studied without differentiating the age of the victim. Hence, the discussion in this chapter may be applicable to elderly as well as younger victims.

Victims play a vital role in the justice system in that if they do not report the crime, the incident would not be known to the system. The report-rate of all victimizations is less than 50%, but older victims have slightly higher report-rates than younger victims. Studies also showed that serious victimizations are reported much more often.

For those who report their victimization, the first justice system personnel they interact with are the police. It has been often asserted that the victim finds police officers unsympathetic when they respond to the victim's call, and that the elderly may especially fare worse in their interaction with police. Empirical research, however, has shown that neither assertion is true. One interesting suggestion on police-elderly interaction is that the police, upon detecting elderly in need of social services, may act as referrals for the aged. This added role is not considered to detract the police from crime fighting activities, and some police departments have reported success with such a police referral program.

When an arrest is made, the victim may also have to interact with the prosecutor and the judge. Despite the elaborate procedures of the justice system, many victims do not need to make an appearance in the role of a witness.

Although it has oftentimes been speculated that the characteristics of victims may indirectly affect the outcome of a case, available evidence tends not to support this. The structure of the justice system also does not allow for much victim input in the disposition of a case. This leads some to assert that the experience of being a witness leaves many victims frustrated with the justice system. The little available evidence on this, however, showed that this frustration is not widespread. Nonetheless, some advocates of victims believe that the role of the victim should be expanded simply because the victim is the one who suffers the most from the victimization. Three systems have been established to increase victim input. Arbitration is a method to settle a criminal case out of court by finding a resolution acceptable to both the victim and the offender. Victim advocacy promotes victims having legal representatives in trial proceedings, though oftentimes without much impact. Private prosecution, available only in a few states, allows the victim to hire attorneys to prosecute offenders in criminal courts.

Although the victim has generally little influence on the disposition of his case, the role of victim-witness is often considered to be arduous. Several attempts have been made to make the role easier and these can be classified as either convenience services or court-related services.

To assist the victim in recuperating from the victimization experience, three different types of programs have been implemented: restitution, compensation, and social services for crime victims. Restitution, or reparation to the victim by the offenders, may be operated in three different ways: as pre-trial diversion, as a condition for probation, and also for parole. Compensation programs, which provide monetary reparation to the victim by the state exist in about half of the states. Despite some differences, these programs do share some common features in terms of compensable claimants, compensable offenses, compensable losses, and other miscellaneous requirements. The last type of reparation are social services to victims. These services can be divided into two types: crisis intervention and follow-up assistance.

Chapter 8

IMPLICATIONS AND SUGGESTIONS

T he previous chapters in this book have examined a variety
of criminal victimizations: ordinary crime victimization,
fear of crime, elder abuse, and fraud. In this chapter, implications
and suggestions based on these discussions will be made. These
implications and suggestions are not for theory development or
future research, those have already been noted in the appropriate
sections in this book. Rather, the suggestions are of practical
concerns. In other words, the question is: "now what?" What
types of policies, programs, and activities can be recommended
to alleviate the problems created by crime victimization in the
lives of older people? These recommendations will be organized
into three levels: individual, neighborhood, and societal.

The strategy for making these recommendations is to focus on
the "malleable" variables. Malleable variables are factors whose
conditions can be changed or manipulated. For example, some
researchers have suggested, though not tested systematically, that
a person's sense of personal control is related to fear of crime.
Those who have a feeling of control hold less fear. If this hypothesis is valid, then recommendations may be made to increase
older people's perception of control since control is a malleable
variable. On the other hand, research on fear of crime indicated
that fear is higher among females, the aged, and those who have
been previously victimized. Given that a person's sex, age, and
victimization experiences cannot be changed, no personal recommendations can be made based on knowledge of these relationships.

Whether a variable is malleable or not is, of course, a matter of degree. For example, is one's residence in a neighborhood a malleable variable? Given that residence in a depleted neighborhood has been found to lead to fear of crime, can one then suggest that those older people who live in such neighborhoods should move to nicer neighborhoods? The judgment here is that this is not a malleable variable. The financial cost that would be incurred by such a move is prohibitive for many aged. In fact, the focus in this chapter will be only on those malleable variables which can "easily" be manipulated. Recommending suggestions and policies that cannot be readily implemented is but an exercise in futility.

Among the individual, neighborhood, and societal levels of recommendations, the first level may be the most controversial and requires some attentions here. First, remedies suggested to older individuals to combat crimes may, in turn, lead to undesirable side-effects. For example, installing various anti-burglary devices around the home can no doubt help in preventing burglary, but this may lead to a "fortress mentality" and induces a more intense level of fear. The financial cost of these anti-burglary devices is also prohibitively high for many older people. Alternately, staying home as much as possible will certainly reduce the chances of street crime victimization, and also burglary, but will also deteriorate the overall quality of life. Hence, recommendations at the individual level need to take these possible side-effects into consideration. Ultimately, the adoption of these recommendations by individual older persons will reflect their own personal values and priorities in life.

A second issue that distinguishes recommendations at the individual level from those at higher levels is that the former may be criticized as a way of "blaming the victim," borrowing the phrase made famous by the title of Ryan's (1972) book. Critics may point out that older people are not the culprits here, they are the victim. To reduce the magnitude of the victimization problem for older people, one should focus on how to change society, especially its patterns of crime, rather than how to change the lives of older people to adapt to the patterns of crime. Are recommendations to individual older persons, then, not a strategy to shift the blame from the victimizer to the victim, suggesting that older people are somehow responsible for their victimizations? While this viewpoint has considerable intellectual merits, it must be noted that making broad changes at the societal level is considerably more difficult than at the individual level. As pointed out already, recommendations at the neighborhood and societal levels will be made, but so long as changes in the patterns of victimizations have yet to occur, e.g., a dramatic reduction in victimization rates or a virtual disappearance of frauds against older people, individual older persons may be wise in taking note of some of the remedies that are available to them.

RECOMMENDATIONS AT THE INDIVIDUAL LEVEL

Ordinary Crime Victimization

The prevalence of ordinary crime victimization against older people is considerably lower than other age groups. Yet, one should not brush off this as a non-problem for the aged for several reasons. First, while it is true that older people have the lowest age-specific victimization rates, it does not imply that their rates cannot be lower nor does it mean that this level is acceptable. Comparisons between age groups yield a relative interpretation of rates, yet the rates of victimization against the aged per se may still be considered high. Second, Hindelang et al.'s (1978) theory of life-style and victimization points out that older people may have lower victimization rates because of their more sedentary life-style. While it is true that the magnitude of the differences in victimization rates between the old and young appears to be too great to be explained by the theory alone, it does point out that the "true" risk of victimization for older people may be considerably higher than that suggested by victimization statistics. Finally, victimization rates among sub-groups of older people vary much by demographic characteristics. In general, Blacks, males, those who are unmarried, and urbanites have significantly higher victimization rates. Liang and Sengstock's (1981) analysis of personal victimizations, for example, concluded that the victimization risk for an older divorced Black man, living in a community of one million population, is fourteen times higher than an older married white woman living in a suburban community. In light of these factors, several recommendations may be suggested to older people. These are divided into those against burglary and those against street crimes.

As discussed in Chapter 5, there are two different types of anti-burglary measures, household victimization loss reduction and household victimization prevention. Examples of the former include insurance and properties markings. Insurance, of course, definitely reduces the cost to replace properties lost, but the cost of insurance may be out of the reach of those aged whose income is low. To what extent property marking assists in the recuperation of stolen properties, however, has not been evaluated systematically.

On the other hand, there are numerous ways to prevent household victimization: target hardening, locking behaviors, survellence, and occupancy proxy. The ability of these measures in deterring burglars is best assessed in a study by Repetto (1974). Repetto interviewed ninety-two burglars, and they were asked the types of anti-burglary measures that would deter them from breaking into a home, as well as the types of anti-burglary measures they would recommend. Their responses are shown in Figure 8.1. Curiously enough, the responses to the two questions differ substantially. Yet, there is consensus with regard to the effectiveness of three measures between the two questions. The first measure is full-time occupancy. Since, full-time occupancy can only be guessed by a burglary, one can assume that a home can be manipulated to have the appearance of full-time occupany. Hence, timing devices may be attached to radios, televisions, and lights to create the appearance of someone inside the home. The other two measures that were especially noted by the burglars interviewed are evidence of an alarm, and a dog. Alternately, good lighting around the house, police security patrols, and steel doors and frames appear to be measures that would deter only a small proportion of burglars.

Anti-street victimization measures, like those for burglary, can also be divided into loss-reduction measures and victimization prevention. Examples of the former include carrying less property and carrying weapons. The success of carrying less property in reducing losses is self-evident. Carrying weapons, however, is less recommended. Unless the victim is skillful in using guns, mace, knives, or other similar devices, they may all be turned against the victim. Given that older people are physically less agile, it may be better for them not to carry weapons for protection. This is especially true given that data from victimization studies support

	Effective Deterrents[a]	suggested precautions[b]
Full-time occupant	88%	20%
neighbors checking	62%	---
police security patrols	51%	---
evidence of alarm	73%	20%
good lighting	33%	---
strong locks	38%	45%
steel door and frame	50%	7%
dog	61%	20%
window locks or bars	---	18%
lights on	---	14%

[a]Based on interviews with 92 burglars. Percentages shown combine "would prevent offense" and "might prevent offense" response categories (Repetto, 1974:151).

[b]Based on interviews with 92 burglars (Repetto, 1974:84).

Source: Repetto (1974)

Figure 8.1. Anti-burglary measures. Source: Repetto (1974).

the idea that those victims who resist have a higher chance of sustaining injuries.

In terms of street victimization preventions, the clearest method is to lead a sedentary life style, avoiding the street at all cost. As pointed out earlier, this has undesirable "side-effects," such as, lowering one's quality of life. A different strategy is, of course, to alter one's life-style—avoiding going out at night, avoiding going to certain neighborhoods, avoiding certain public transits, and so on. Studies have shown that the majority of the population are already engaged in these latter kinds of avoidance, and given that older people already have a more stay-home life-style, the possible undesirable "side-effects" of this latter strategy should be minimal.

Needless to say, the necessity of different older persons to practice these various measures depends on numerous factors: whether they live in high crime neighborhoods, whether they have a recent history of victimizations, whether they have an active life-style, and so forth. Individual prescriptions require considerations of far more factors than space allows here.

Fear of Crime

Among all age groups, the aged have the highest level of fear of crime in urban areas (and farming areas). Fear of crime has been shown to deteriorate psychological well-being among the aged, i.e., lower morale, and neighborhood dissatisfaction.

In the person-environment theory of fear of crime there are three sets of determinants of fear: victimization experience, neighborhood peril, and physical vulnerabilty. Victimization experience, either personal or vicarious, is not a malleable variable. As discussed earlier, neighborhood peril is also not considered malleable since it is unrealistic to expect older people to change residence simply because of crime and its fear. The only variable left is personal vulnerability.

While the objective status of an individual's physical vulnerability is also not malleable, some have suggested that the perception of vulnerability may be manipulated. An internal locus of control or a sense of mastery of the environmental may psychologically overcome the sense of vulnerability created by physical status. In turn, fear of crime may be reduced. Different methods have been suggested to increase one's sense of control, such as manipulating one's home external environment (see Patterson, 1979). Nonetheless, whether such methods do induce a sense of control or not, and whether a sense of control does lower fear or not, are questions that await empirical studies at this point.

Another suggestion is simply to educate older people that their physical vulnerability does not transform into higher likelihood of victimization. For example, one can communicate statistics on age and sex victimization rates to the public in the mass media. Yet, whether such efforts necessarily lower people's fear is unknown, and there are good reasons to suspect that they may have little impact. Casual observations suggest that people are more influenced by presentation of individual experiences than the use of statistics.

Elder Abuse

The family transition theory of elder abuse suggests that two of the determinants of abuse are a previous history of the parent maltreating the child and dependence of the elderly parent. Besides not having any research data to either support or disconfirm these hypotheses, another problem of providing recommendations is that neither determinants can be considered malleable. Previous parent-child problems are already history and dependence on the child, as well as the absence of resources of the child to cope with the dependence, may not be easily mitigated. Hence, attentions on elder abuse have focused instead on what to do after an aged has been abused, remedial assistances.

One of the problems with remedial works of elder abuse is that the elderly person, at times, is a consenting adult to the abuse, even when the abuses are not one-time occurrences but chronic in nature (Champlin, 1982). That is by not reporting the victimization to authorities, the elderly parent has explicitly determined not to prosecute the child nor to notify authorities. Several reasons have been proposed to account for the willingness of some older individuals to stay in an abusive situation. A common one is that the elderly parent prefers to stay with an abusive child more than the alternate choice of institutionalization. Another common explanation is that the parent is worried about the image of the adult child upon exposing such a scandal. Yet a third one is the older parent's fear for retaliation from the child.

How society may deal with such a consenting adult to elder abuse will be discussed later, suffice it to suggest here that some of these worries of the abused aged may be moderated. While institutionalization is, in fact, a likely way to allow the aged to leave an abusive home, its fear may be somewhat irrational. The quality of care in nursing homes and the quality of life in them are likely to be better than what stereotypes of nursing homes may suggest. Staying in an abusive situation is not only physically threatening, it most probably also deteriorates morale. In addition, given the health conditions of the aged, especially one who has to be dependent on the child, abuse could even become life threatening. The best way to terminate the abuse is to report it to the authorities and allow them to handle the situation.

Fraud

The best personal advice against bunco and consumer fraud is to be cautious. As the saying goes: "if it looks too good to be true, it probably is."

RECOMMENDATIONS AT THE NEIGHBORHOOD LEVEL

Ordinary Crime Victimization

Given that victimization rates against older people are lower than those against the younger population, it is reasonable not to single out older people in recommending policies to reduce victimization rates of a neighborhood. Rather, measures should aim at reducing victimization rates in general, benefiting everybody.

One of the most frequent attempts to control and reduce crimes in a neighborhood is to create neighborhood watch programs. In the 1970's, the Law Enforcement Assistance Administration was supporting police departments throughout the country in launching neighborhood watch programs. The rationale of these programs is that if neighbors watch out for each other, bystander intervention will increase, and this may deter potential offenders. Hence, signs indicating the presence of a neighborhood watch program may be seen posted on street corners. Though, systematic studies on the effectiveness of these programs have not been conducted, the study by Repetto (1974) (see Figure 8.1) showed that "neighbors checking" is considered by burglars to be the second most important deterrent of home break-ins. Gray (1983) believed that such programs may be more successful in small towns than in urban areas. In large cities, where cultural and ethnic backgrounds are diverse, and where mobility is higher, social cohesiveness is more difficult to attain by neighborhood watch programs. Furthermore, what constitutes suspicious behaviors in large cities is also less apparent.

Another program local police departments began initiating in the 1970s was crime education. Crime education involves having police officers give informal presentations to citizens on crime-related issues such as the correct way to carry a purse and how to improve home security measures. A study discussed in Schneider and Schneider (1981) provided some support to the contention that attending crime education programs is related to lower victimization risks. According to Schneider and Schneider, victimization surveys in Portland, Oregon showed that burglary victims who participated in crime education have a lower burglary victimization rate afterwards than those burglary victims who did not participate.

Among more affluent neighborhoods, private security patrols are another strategy to reduce crime. The prevalence of private security firms is not known. According to the mass media, the number has apparently swelled in recent years. Less certain is the success of these programs in curbing crimes. In experiments where the amount of police patrol of neighborhoods (or subways) was manipulated, the results were not conclusive with regard to the police patrol/victimization rate relationship (Wilson, 1977). In a well-known study in Kansas City, for example, researchers were surprised to find that when police patrols were completely withdrawn from one neighborhood, there was no appreciable increase in victimization rates.

Vigilante groups with para-military equipment, and sometimes police-looking uniforms, have also been formed by residents in some neighborhoods. The most notorious of such groups is probably the Guardian Angels who patrol the subways in New York City. As diverse as these groups may be, Gray (1983:369) pointed out five points they usually have in common: "(1) they fear crime; (2) they are essentially an urban phenomenon; (3) they cooperate with, but are not controlled by the police; (4) they are highly organized; and (5) the leadership tends to be socially and politically conservative." Like private security programs, whether vigilante groups deter crimes or not has not been systematically studied.

Fear of Crime

All programs designed to reduce victimization rates at the neighborhood level may have impact on fear of crime whether intended or unintended. In general, it is hypothesized that the presence of security personnel increases one's sense of security. Hence, increased police, vigilante, and private security patrols all are expected to contribute to the perception that the neighborhood is well-protected, and in turn, the level of fear of crime should be lowered. On the other hand, crime education, in teaching people anti-crime behaviors and measures, remind people of the threat and danger of crime victimization. Rather than contributing to a sense of security, crime education contributes to a sense of vulnerability. Hence, crime education is hypothesized to increase the level of fear of crime. Finally, the impact of the neighborhood watch on fear of crime depends on the success of the neighborhood watch program. If the program is successful in organizing neighbors, it is hypothesized that the effects on fear will be like increased security patrols, lowering fear of crime. Neighbors turn from strangers to acquaintances, and the perilous signs of the neighborhood become less threatening. Conversely, if the program is unsuccessful (i.e., the participation rate of the neighbors is low), it is hypothesized that the effects on fear will be like crime educations, heightened fear of crime. Going to neighborhood watch programs only results in another reminder of one's vulnerability to crime and the problems of the neighborhood.

Support to some of these hypotheses came from a study of 152 elderly people by Norton and Courlander (1982). These elderly people were studied because they reside in neighborhoods where police patrols increased and all the aged had also attended crime education programs. These two researchers found that communication with police officers on patrols is associated with lower levels of fear, and those highly affected by the crime education programs also exhibited higher levels of fear of crime.

Elder Abuse

According to the family transition theory of elder abuse, one of the hypothesized determinants of elder abuse is dependency of the elderly parents. One preventive measure at the neighborhood level is to establish respite care, day care, and/or home care of the aged (Katz, 1980; Steinmetz, 1978). These programs require support beyond the neighborhood, and all are already in existence to various degrees throughout the country. With the assistance of these programs, whether alleviating the dependency of the aged parent on the child has any impact on the prevalence of elder abuse remains to be studied.

Fraud

Given the current lack of knowledge on fraud, little can be recommended at the neighborhood level. Educating older people of the various common schemes of bunco and consumer fraud should help. Another measure, apparently already practiced at some banks, is to encourage older people withdrawing large amounts of money to take them in the form of bank drafts instead of cash.

RECOMMENDATIONS AT THE SOCIETAL LEVEL

Ordinary Crime Victimization. Similar to the previous discussions at the neighborhood level, recommendations on measures to reduce ordinary crime victimization at the societal level will also include all age groups in general, and not just the aged. Before recommending any such policies, however, it is necessary to first review the recent trends in victimization rates. Whether victimization rates have increased in the last decade or not, and if they have, the extent of the increase, are important issues in considering policy recommendations at the societal level. To the extent that victimization rates have remained stable in recent years, or have increased only slightly, the urgency of these recommendations has lessened.

There are two readily available sources of data to study overtime changes in victimizations—the Uniform Crime Report (UCR) and the National Crime Surveys (NCS). Whether victimizations have increased over the last decades depend largely on which of these two data sets one turns. In the UCR, the rates for seven types of serious crimes are summed to form the Crime Index: murder, rape, robbery, burglary, aggravated assault, larceny, and auto-theft. Between 1973 and 1980, the crime index increased by approximately 45%. Specifically, crime increased in the first half of the 1970's and the late 1970's, with little changes between 1975 and

1978. Closer examinations of the UCR's reveal that, although the magnitude of the increase is not uniform among the seven types of crimes, all of them did have an increase.

Data from the NCS between 1973 and 1980, on the other hand, provide a different pattern of change (see Appendices 1.1, 1.2, and 1.3). According to the NCS, the victimization rate for household larceny has increased, but the rates for rape, robbery, assault, personal larceny, burglary, and motor vehicle theft either remained unchanged or actually declined.

Despite various problems associated with the NCS, that data set is usually considered by criminologists to be superior to the UCR in measuring the prevalence of crime and victimizations. Yet, this by no means suggests that one can brush off the UCR and conclude that victimization rates have not increased in recent years. At least two considerations need to be noted. First, the rate for homicide, which is reported in the UCR but not the NCS, increased 10% between 1973 and 1980, or 20% between 1970 and 1980. UCR homicide rates are generally considered to be reliable. While this increase may or may not be indicative of victimization trends for other offenses, it does caution against an uncritical embracing of the NCS results. Second, the UCR in the 1960's and the early 1970's registered a sharp increase in the serious offenses of the Crime Index. Except for a few preliminary surveys, the NCS did not begin until 1973. Hence, the validity of the UCR data prior to 1973 remains unchecked. This leaves room for the possibility that crime rates might have increased between the 1960s and 1973 as described in the UCR.

In spite of the uncertainties with the trends in victimization rates in general, changes in the rates for homicide in the UCR have generated some systematic studies on explaining trends in crime victimizations. Interestingly enough, some of these explanations have strong policy implications. The study by Yunker (1982) is an illustration. According to Yunker, there are several traditional explanations of the fluctuation in homicide rates. All of them are based on findings from cross-sectional research. The first one is socioeconomic trends, based on the inverse correlation between violent offense rates and socioeconomic class. The second explanation is non White ratio, based on the higher offense rates among non Whites. The third is youth ratio in the population, based on the higher offense rates among youths. The

fourth is urban ratio of the population, based on the higher victimization rates in urban areas. Finally, the fifth is war, based on suggestions by some investigators that the psychological conditions of wartime affects homicide rates.

When Yunker regressed the homicide rates between 1907 to 1979 to these five predictors, he discovered that the predictions closely fit the actual homicide rates up till 1962. After 1962, the predicted course in homicide rates and the actual trend went in different directions: the predicted rates declined after 1962, and the actual rates increased. In other words, the five explanations of homicide rates operated well until 1962, after which the same explanations failed to account for changes in homicide rates.

Yunker pointed out that it was around 1962 that a virtual moratorium on the death penalty commenced. Between 1968 and 1978, there were no executions in this country. Hence, the deterrent effect of the death penalty was inoperative, and homicide rates increased correspondingly. According to Yunker, the moratorium on the death penalty lead to the increase of not only homicide rates, but rise in other crime rates as well. Yunker (1982:644) wrote, "Capital punishment is a highly visible symbol of society's determination to keep order in its ranks. To those involved in crime, or contemplating becoming involved, the retirement of the death penalty may have been taken as an indication that the overall strength of enforcement has declined and that leniency is becoming the order of the day."

Yunker's analysis is controversial since it is only an indirect test of the deterrent effect of capital punishment on crime, given that the annual frequency of execution was never directly involved in his analyses. This, however, was done in an earlier study by Ehrlich (1975) who did, in fact, find a relationship between execution risk and homicide rates. Based on Ehrlich's and other studies, Yunker concluded that the deterrent effect of the death penalty on crime, apparently, began only around the early 1960s when the death penalty virtually disappeared. The policy implication of Yunker's conclusion on crime control is self-evident.

Capital punishment is, of course, an issue of great moral concern. It is interesting to note that despite the demise of the various social movements of the 1960s, opponents of the death penalty are still highly organized and have remained potently vocal. Needless to say, additional research will never resolve the

moral issues on the death penalty, but they will shed additional light on the scientific basis of believing in its deterrent effects on crime and its policy implications. Despite the recent research by Ehrlich, Yunker, and others which support the deterrent effect of capital punishment, it is important to point out that most studies on this issue of deterrence have not supported the position that punishment deters crime (e.g., see Sellin, 1980).

Fear of Crime

Like ordinary crime victimization, it is instructive to first assess the trend in fear of crime. Knowing the trends will signify the severity of fear of crime as a social problem and its importance in a policy agenda.

In recent years, fear of crime has been a growing topic of interest in the mass media. Radio, television, newspapers, and magazines frequently report on the public's fear of being victimized. The general message is that the rising crime rate in recent years (according to the UCR) is reducing people's perception of safety and increasing their fear of crime (e.g., see the cover stories in *Newsweek* and *Time* during the week of, 1981). A variety of evidence has been cited by the mass media to support this contention. The public is believed to be purchasing firearms for personal and home protection more frequently. Special schools that teach the proper use of handguns are reported to be flourishing, other fearful individuals turn to karate and various self-defense classes, while still others resort to less dramatic measures of self-protection such as carrying mace or whistles while on the street. For home and business protection, people are presumably spending more money on locks, window bars, electronic surveillance devices, guard dogs, and so on.

The National Opinion Research Center, the Gallup Poll, and the Harris Survey have been inquiring into the public's level of fear of crime since the 1960's, and their findings are displayed in Figure 8.2. Two survey items best measure fear of crime, fear of walking alone at night, and feeling unsafe at home at night (see Chapter 3). Remarkably, the data for both items suggest that the level of fear of crime has not increased since 1974. If fear of crime has increased, the increase occurred primarily between 1966 and 1974.

	'67	'68	'69	'70	'71	'72	'73	'74	'75	'76	'77	'78	'79	'80	'81	'82
Fear of walking alone[a] at night	31%	---	---	---	---	42%	41%	45%	45%	44%	45%	---	42%	43%	45%	47%
Feel unsafe at home[b] at night	---	---	---	---	---	17%	---	---	20%	---	15%	---	---	---	16%	14%

[a] The exact survey question is: "Is there any area right around here—that is, within a mile—where you would be afraid to walk alone at night?" Percentages shown represent respondents who responded "Yes." Statistics for different years combine data from the National Opinion Research Center and the Gallup Poll.

[b] The exact survey question is: "How about at home at night—do you feel safe and secure, or not? Percentages shown are respondents who responded "Yes." Statistics for different years combine data from the National Opinion Research Center and the Gallup Poll.

Sources: Bureau of Justice Statistics (1982b)
Davis and Smith (1983)

Figure 8.2. The fear of crime trend. Sources: Bureau of Justice Statistics (1982b), Davis and Smith (1983).

In spite of the conclusion that fear of crime has not mushroomed into an issue of major concern in the last decade, the current level may still be considered high, and measures may be taken to reduce the fear. Given the conceptual link between ordinary crime victimization and fear of crime, an obvious question is whether attempts should be made to lower fear of crime without simultaneously lowering victimization rates? This question points to the position that it may be unethical to lead the public to reduce their level of fear of crime while the risk for victimization is as high as before. This position though is less valid if the public is holding an unnecessarily high level of fear, given the current victimization rates. However, after some discussions in Chapter 2, it was concluded that the public's fear of crime is not unnecessarily high, and neither is it irrational as some investigators believed. Warr, for example, is one of the researchers who believed the public has a fairly accurate perception of crimes in general (Warr, 1980, 1982; Warr and Stafford, 1983), suggesting that if and when victimization rates decline, the level of fear of crime will decrease likewise. Hence, the best way to reduce fear may be through lowering victimization.

Elder Abuse

Given the current lack of knowledge on the causes of elder abuse, attention at the societal level, like at the neighborhood level, has been on the treatment of elder abuse, instead of its prevention. In other words, the efforts thus far aim at the identification of cases of elder abuse and correcting situations in which the aged are abused. Few societal initiatives have been made to avert the occurrence of elder abuse in the first place.

Mandatory reporting appears to be the favorite remedy for elder abuse (Bragg et al., 1981; Brock, 1980). The consensus is that elder abuse has long been ignored as a problem confronting the aged. For various reasons, the aged tend not to report their abuses, and professionals, such as physicians and social workers, tend to disregard signs of abuse because of their ignorance. Hence, mandating professional and/or lay persons to report suspected cases of elder abuse to the authorities appears to be the ideal way to identify and help victims.

Currently, twenty states have legislation for mandatory reporting of elder abuse. These states are Alabama, Arizona, Connecticut, Florida, Hawaii, Kentucky, Massachusetts, Minnesota, Missouri, Nebraska, New Hampshire, North Carolina, Oklahoma, Oregon, South Carolina, Tennessee, Texas, Utah, Vermont, and Virginia. A description of these legislations can be found in a study by Salend et al. (1984). All of these legislations were passed in or after 1973.

The enthusiasm for mandatory reporting of elder abuse can be traced to similar legislations for child abuse. In the 1960s when child abuse emerged as an issue of major social concern, state legislatures all over the country were passing laws requiring mandatory reporting of child abuse. By 1967, all fifty states required physicians to report suspected cases of child abuse (Katz, 1980). Although, older people are not children, the parallel is apparent (Katz, 1980; Steinmetz, 1978). Both children and older people (to different degrees) are dependent on the adult generation. Both are politically weak and lack legal protection. Both are supposed to be protected from the middle generation by a norm of love and caring. The caring of both are sources of stress to the careprovider.

Although the merits of mandatory reporting may appear to be clear, critics of such policies have emerged in recent years. At least six such concerns have been raised. First, the meaning of elder abuse is rarely defined clearly (Faulkner, 1982; Katz, 1980; Salend, et al., 1984). The most problematic issue is the inclusion of emotional or psychological abuse. The Connecticut's Protection of the Elderly Act, for example, appears to be legally prohibiting unkindness to the aged (Katz, 1980). Another problem with the definition is the inclusion of self-abuse. While instances of self-abuse definitely exist, in fact, the prevalence of self-abuse is the highest among known cases (Salend et al., 1984), its nature is simply different from other types of abuses where the abuser and the abused are two different persons. Without a clear definition, it is difficult for those who are mandated to report to know when to report. Unwarranted intervention may also result.

Second, the majority of mandatory reporting legislation provided no fund for services. In fact, only Connecticut and Minnesota provided specific funding for implementing the new statue (Salend et al., 1984). If special services cannot be adequately provided, or simply are missing, what then is the rationale for mandatory reporting? Hence, mandatory reporting policies may be criticized in that they create an unmet expectation that services and treatments will follow (Faulkner, 1982).

Third, a mandatory reporting policy implies that elder abuse cases are currently not known to the authority. Yet, there is little evidence to support this contention. Hence, it has been suggested that mandatory reporting has little effect on discovering new cases. Rather, responsibility for registering and treating elder abuse cases will shift from one agency to another (Faulkner, 1982).

Fourth, by mandating physicians to report elder abuse cases, the traditional patient-physician privilege is breached (Faulkner, 1982). While the same seems to apply to the mandatory reporting of child abuse, the situation with elder abuse is categorically different. In child abuse, it is the abusive parent who seeks help, and the patient is the child not the parent. Hence, it is unfair for the parent to invoke the patient-physician privilege. In elder abuse, it is the elderly patient himself who is seeking help, and the desire of the patient to keep the incident from authorities is violated by the physician. Furthermore, it is even conceivable that mandatory reporting laws may discourage some abused aged from seeking medical help.

Fifth, mandatory reporting of elder abuse violates the civil liberty of the abused aged (Katz, 1980). Unlike an abused child who is helpless and ignorant, an abused aged is a competent adult with a right to self-determination. Even if the belief that many abused aged are not reporting their situation to the proper authorities is correct, should society not respect their decision? Mandatory reporting, in essence, strips the abused aged of individual civil liberty, and coercisively investigates and intervenes into the life of an unconsenting adult.

Finally, mandatory reporting promotes ageism (Faulkner, 1981). Seeing a parallel between child abuse and elder abuse, and therefore, legislating mandatory reporting for both, are but advocating the position that the aged are no different from children and should be treated similarly. It is interesting to note that public concern for wife battering, another type of family violence, never resulted in thoughts of mandatory reporting. Instead, efforts have been concentrated on providing the abused wife with temporary shelter, convincing her to prosecute the abusive husband, and assisting her to be independent. Possibly, policies on elder abuse should follow the wife-battering model, instead of the child-abuse model.

Ultimately, the problems with mandatory reporting of elder abuse legislation can be traced to the lack of systematic data on elder abuse. Without these data, policy-makers have no knowledge of the severity or prevalence of the problem, little information on the extent of underreporting, and no way to design policies to combat the causes of elder abuse directly.

Fraud

Geis (1976b) proposed that frauds against the aged should carry heavier penalty than those against the year population. The implication is that this will deter frauds against the aged. Whether or not this is true remains to be investigated, except to note here that there is little normative justification for choosing the aged for special treatment. Older people are not the only underprivileged in society. Little reason exists not to extend Geis' proposal to the handicapped, the mentally retarded, Blacks, the poor, and maybe even all women.

SUMMARY

Malleable variables are variables whose conditions can be manipulated. Based on known relationships of the malleable variables with crime victimization, policies may be recommended to reduce the prevalence of victimizations against older people. These recommendations are arranged into three different levels: individual, neighborhood, and societal.

For ordinary crime victimization, four measures are recommended for burglary and two for street crimes at the individual level. Against burglary, the measures are insurance, full-time occupancy at home or its appearance, evidence of an alarm system, and a dog. Against street crimes, the recommendations are to avoid going out to certain neighborhoods at night and carry less cash. To lower fear of crime, one suggestion for individuals is to learn to achieve a sense of control. Though the validity of this suggestion remains to be tested. Studies on elder abuse are not yet systematic enough to provide personal recommendations, except to note that older victims of repeated abuses should report their situations to the authorities. The current belief is that many abused victims are not reporting. Finally, older people are recommended to be cautious of financial transactions that appear too good to be true.

At the neighborhood level, several programs have been initiated to lower overall crime rates, not just those against the aged. These programs include neighborhood watch, crime education, private security, and vigilante groups. However, the success of these programs in lowering neighborhood crimes has not been tested rigorously. Programs designed to contain neighborhood crime rates also influence people's fear of crime. Increased police, vigilante, and private security patrols in a neighborhood are hypothesized to lower resident's fear, while crime education, and less successful neighborhood watch programs are hypothesized to have the reverse impact. For elder abuse, the suggestion is to provide relief for persons taking care of frail elderly parents, through programs such as respite care, day care, and home care programs. Given that the prevalence and determinants of elder abuse are currently not known, the effects of these programs remains uncertain. Likewise with fraud, the lack of research prohibts any extensive policies recommendation.

At the societal level, the urgency to implement policies to control victimization rates is uncertain given that the Uniform Crime Reports and the National Crime Surveys provided different assessments of the crime trend. The former indicates that crime rates have been increasing; the latter suggests that victimization rates have been stable. One interesting study concludes that the rise in the homicide rate during the past two decades is a result of the virtual moratorium on the death penalty in the late 1960s and the 1970s. The implication is that the death penalty may be used to deter crime. The merit of this position goes beyond science, however, in that ethical issues have to be considered as well. On the other hand, national polls have documented that the level of fear of crime has not increased since 1974, though an increase had occurred in the decade before 1974. To control this fear at the societal level, the best way may be to simply lower crime rates. In recent years, efforts to remedy elder abuse at the societal level have mushroomed. The most common strategy by state government is to require mandatory reporting of suspected cases. Despite the initial appeal of mandatory reporting, this strategy is not recommended because of possible adverse implications for the aged as well as the fact that such a policy rests on several untested assumptions on elder abuse. Finally, no policy was recommended for fraud against the aged due to the lack of research on this victimization.

REFERENCES

Aldous, Joan (1978) *Family Careers: Developmental Changes in Families.* New York: Wiley.

Antonovsky, Aaron (1979) *Health, Stress, and Coping.* San Francisco: Jossey-Bass.

Antunes, George E., Fay L. Cook, Thomas D. Cook, and Wesley G. Skogan (1977) Patterns of personal crime against the elderly: Findings from a national survey. *The Gerontologist* 17(4): 321-327.

Arcuri, Alan F. (1981) The police and the elderly. In David Lester's (Ed.) *The Elderly Victim of Crime.* Springfield, IL: Charles C Thomas.

Ashton, Nancy (1981) Senior citizens' views of crime and the criminal justice system. In David Lester's (Ed.) *The Elderly Victim of Crime.* Springfield, IL: Charles C Thomas.

Balkin, Steven (1979) Victimization rates, safety and fear of crime. *Social Problems* 26(3):343-358.

Barnett, Randy E. (1977) Restitution: A new paradigm of criminal justice. *Ethics: An International Journal of Social, Political, and Legal Philosophy* 84(4):279-301.

Baumer, Terry L. (1979) Research on fear of crime in the United States. *Victimology* 3(3-4):254-264.

Biderman, Albert D. (1967) Surveys of population samples for estimating crime incidence. *The Annals of the American Academy of Political and Social Science* 374:16-33.

Biderman, Albert D., Louise A. Johnson, Jennie McIntyre, and Adrianne W. Weir (1967) *Report on a Pilot Study in the District of Columbia on Victimization and Attitudes Toward Law Enforcement.* Field Surveys 1, conducted for the President's Commission on Law Enforcement and Administration of Justice. Washington, DC: U.S. Government Printing Office.

Biderman, Albert D. and Albert J. Reiss, Jr. (1967) On exploring the "dark figure" of crime. *The Annals of the American Academy of Political and Social Sciences* 374:1-15.

Block, Richard L. (1971) The fear of crime and fear of the police. *Social Problems* 19(1):91-101.

Blum, Richard H. (1972) *Deceivers and Deceived.* Springfield, IL: Charles C Thomas.

Bragg, David F., Larry R. Kimsey, and Arthur R. Tarbox (1981) Abuse of the elderly—The hidden agenda. *Journal of the American Geriatrics Society* 29(11):503-507.

Braungart, Margaret M., William J. Hoyer, and Richard G. Braungart (1979) Fear of crime and the elderly. In Arnold P. Goldstein, William J. Hoyer, and Phillip J. Monti's (Eds.) *Police and the Elderly*. New York: Pergamon.

Braungart, Margaret M., Richard G. Braungart, and William J. Hoyer (1980) Age, sex, and social factors in fear of crime. *Sociological Focus* 13(1):55-66.

Brock, Anna (1980) Editorial: Stop abuse of the elderly. *Journal of Gerontological Nursing* 6(4):191.

Brooks, James (1974) The fear of crime in the United States. *Crime and Delinquency* 20:241-245.

Brostoff, Phyllis M., Roberta B. Brown, and Robert N. Butler (1972) The public interest: Report no. 6; "Beating up" on the elderly: Police, social work, crime. *Aging and Human Development* 3(4):319-322.

Brostoff, Phyllis M. (1976) The police connection: A new way to get information and referral services to the elderly. In Jack Goldsmith and Sharon S. Goldsmith's (Eds.) *Crime and the Elderly*. Lexington, MA: D. C. Heath and Company.

Bureau of Justice Statistics (1980a) *Intimate Victims: A Study of Violence Among Friends and Relatives*. Washington, DC: U.S. Government Printing Office.

Bureau of Justice Statistics (1980b) *Restitution to Victims of Personal and Household Crimes*. Washington, DC: U.S. Government Printing Office.

Bureau of Justice Statistics (1980c) *Criminal Victimization in the United States, 1978*. Washington, DC: U.S. Government Printing Office.

Bureau of Justice Statistics (1981a) *Criminal Victimization in the United States, 1979*. Washington, DC: U.S. Government Printing Office.

Bureau of Justice Statistics (1981b) *Criminal Victimization in the United States, 1980*. Washington, DC: U.S. Government Printing Office.

Bureau of Justice Statistics (1982a) *Criminal Victimization in the United States, 1980*. Washington, DC: U.S. Government Printing Office.

Bureau of Justice Statistics (1982b) *Sourcebook of Criminal Justice Statistics, 1981*. Washington, DC: U.S. Government Printing Office.

Bureau of Justice Statistics (1983) *Criminal Victimization in the United States, 1981*. Washington, DC: U.S. Government Printing Office.

Butler, Robert N. (1976) *Why Survive? Being Old in America*. New York: Harper & Row.

Callahan, James J. Jr. (1982) Elder abuse programming: Will it help the elderly? *Urban and Social Change Review* 15(2):15-16.

Carey, Mary and George Sherman (1976) *A Compendium of Bunk or How to Spot a Con Artist*. Springfield, IL: Charles C Thomas.

Carrington, Frank (1977) Victims' rights litigation: A wave of the future? *University of Richmond Law Review* 11(3):447-470.

Champlin, Leslie (1982) The battered elderly. *Geriatrics* 37(7):115, 116, & 121.

Chen, Pei N., Sharon L. Bell, Debra L. Dolinsky, John Doyle, and Moira Dunn (1981) Elderly abuse in domestic settings: A pilot study. *Journal of Gerontological Social Work* 4(1):3-17.

Chesney, Steve and Carole E. Schneider (1981) Crime victim crisis centers: The Minnesota experience. In Burt Galaway and Joe Hudson's (Eds.) *Perspectives on Crime Victims*. St. Louis: C. V. Mosby.

Christensen, Harold T. (1964) *Handbook of Marriage and the Family*. Skokie, IL: Rand McNally.

Clarke, Alan H. and Margaret J. Lewis (1982) Fear of crime among the elderly: An exploratory study. *British Journal of Criminology* 22(1):49-62.

Clemente, Frank and Michael B. Kleiman (1976) Fear of crime among the aged. *The Gerontologist* 16(3):207-210.

Clemente, Frank and Michael B. Kleiman (1977) Fear of crime in the United States: A multivariate analysis. *Social Forces* 56(2):519-531.

Clotfelter, Charles T. (1977) Urban crime and household protective measures. *Review of Economics and Statistics* 59(4):499-503.

Cohen, Lawrence E., James R. Kluegel, and Kenneth C. Land (1981) Social inequality and predatory criminal victimization: An exposition and test of a formal theory. *American Sociological Review* 46(5):505-524.

Cohn, Ellen S., Louise H. Kidder, and Joan Harvey (1979) Crime prevention vs. victimization prevention: The psychology of two different reactions. *Victimology* 3(3-4):285-296.

Comer, Michael J. (1977) *Corporate Fraud*. London: McGraw-Hill (UK).

Conklin, John E. (1971) Dimensions of community response to the crime problem. *Social Problems* 18(3):373-385.

Conklin, John E. (1975) *The Impact of Crime*. New York: Macmillan.

Conklin, John E. (1976) Robbery, the elderly, and fear: An urban problem in search of solution. In Jack Goldsmith and Sharon S. Goldsmith's (Eds.) *Crime and the Elderly*. Lexington, MA: Lexington Books.

Conklin, John E. (1981) *Criminology*. New York: Macmillan.

Cook, Fay L. (1981) Crime and the elderly: The emergence of a policy issue. In Dan A. Lewis' *Reactions to Crime*. Beverly Hills: Sage.

Cook, Fay L., Wesley G. Skogan, Thomas D. Cook, and George E. Antunes (1978) Criminal victimization of the elderly: The physical and economic consequences. *The Gerontologist* 18(4):338-349.

Cook, Fay L. and Thomas D. Cook (1976) Evaluating the rhetoric of crisis: A case study of criminal victimization of the elderly. *Social Service Review* 50(4):632-646.

Culp, Marilyn W. and Mary L. Calvin (1977) Victim services programs. In Marlene A. Y. Rifai's *Justice and Older Americans*. Lexington, MA: D. C. Heath and Company.

Cunningham, Carl L. (1977) Pattern and effect of crime against the aging: The Kansas City study. In Jack Goldsmith and Sharon S. Goldsmith's (Eds.) *Crime and the Elderly*. Lexington, MA: Lexington Books.

Cutler, Stephen J. (1980) Safety on the streets: Cohort changes in fear. *International Journal of Aging and Human Development* 10(4):373-384.

Criminal Justice and the Elderly (1978) Cover story. *Criminal Justice and the Elderly Newsletter*, Washington, DC.

Davis, James A. and Tom W. Smith (1983) *General Social Survey Cumulative File, 1972-1982*. Ann Arbor, MI: Inter-University Consortium for Political and Social Research.

DeFronzo, James (1979) Fear of crime and handgun ownership. *Criminology* 17(3):331-339.

Demo, Deborah and James A. Cramer (1976) The effects of victim characteristics on judicial decision making. In William F. McDonald's (Ed.) *Criminal Justice and the Victim*. Beverly Hills: Sage.

Doerner, W. G. (1979) The diffusion of victim compensation laws in the United States. *Victimology* 1:503-516.

Doob, Anthony N. and Glenn E. Macdonald (1979) Television viewing and fear of victimization: Is the relationship causal? *Journal of Personality and Social Psychology* 37(2):170-179.

Dubow, Frederic L. and Theodore M. Becker (1976) Patterns of victim advocacy. and William F. McDonald's (Ed.) *Criminal Justice and the Victim*. Beverly Hills: Sage.

Dubow, Fred, Edward McCabe, and Gail Kaplan (1979) *Reactions to Crime: A Critical Review of the Literature*. Law Enforcement Assistance Administration. Washington, DC: U.S. Government Printing Office.

Ducovny, Amram (1969) *The Billion $ Swindle: Frauds Against the Elderly*. New York: Fleet Press.

Dussick, John P. J. (1981) Evolving services for crime victims. In Burt Galaway and Joe Hudson's (Eds.) *Perspectives on Crime Victims*. St. Louis: C. V. Mosby.

Ehrlich, I. (1975) The deterrent effect of capital punishment: A question of life and death. *American Economics Review* 65:397-417.

Elmore, Elizabeth (1981) Consumer fraud and the elderly. In David Lester's (Ed.) *The Elderly Victim of Crime*. Springfield, IL: Charles C Thomas.

Ennis, Philip H. (1967) *Criminal Victimization in the United States: A Report of a National Survey*. Washington, DC: U.S. Government Printing Office.

Erskine, Hazel (1974) The polls: Fear of violence and crime. *Public Opinion Quarterly* 38:131-145.

Eustis, Nancy N., Sharon Patten and Jay Greenberg (1984) *Long-term Care for Older Persons: A Policy Perspective*. Monterey, CA: Brooks/Cole.

Faulkner, Lawrence R. (1982) Mandating the reporting of suspected cases of elder abuse: An inappropriate, ineffective and ageist response to the abuse of older adults. *Family Law Quarterly* 16(1):69-91.

Federal Bureau of Investigation (1982) *Uniform Crime Report*. Washington, DC: U.S. Government Printing Office.

Fontana, Andrea (1977) *The Last Frontier: The Social Meaning of Growing Old*. Beverly Hills: Sage.

Friedman, David M. (1976) A service model for elderly crime victims. In Jack Goldsmith and Sharon S. Goldsmith's (Eds.) *Crime and the Elderly*. Lexington, MA: D. C. Heath and Company.

Furstenberg, Frank F. Jr. (1971) Public reaction to crime in the streets. *American Scholar* 40(4):601-610.

Furstenberg, Frank F. Jr. (1972) Fear of crime and its effects on citizen behavior. In Albert Biderman's (Ed.) *Crime and Justice: A Symposium*. New York: Nailburg.

Galaway, Burt (1977) The use of restitution. *Crime and Delinquency* 57-67.

Galaway, Burt and Joe Hudson (1981) Introduction. In Burt Galaway and Joe Hudson's (Eds.) *Perspectives on Crime Victims*. St. Louis: C. V. Mosby.

Gaquin, Deirdre A. (1979) Measuring fear of crime: The National Crime Survey's attitude data. *Victimology* 3(3-4):314-319.

Garafalo, James (1979) Victimization and fear of crime. *Journal of Research in Crime and Delinquency* 16(1):80-97.

Garafalo, James (1981) The fear of crime: Causes and consequences. *Journal of Criminal Law and Criminology* 72(2):839-857.

Garafalo, James and John Laub (1979) The fear of crime: Broadening our perspective. *Victimology* 3(3-4):242-253.

Geis, Gilbert (1975) Victims of crimes of violence and the Criminal Justice System. In Duncan Chappell and John Monahan (Eds.) *Violence and Criminal Justice*. Lexington, MA: Lexington.

Geis, Gilbert (1976a) Crime victims and victim compensation programs. In William F. McDonald's (Ed.) *Criminal Justice and the Victim*. Beverly Hills: Sage.

Geis, Gilbert (1976b) Defrauding the elderly. In Jack Goldsmith and Sharon S. Goldsmith's (Eds.) *Crime and the Elderly*. Lexington, MA: Lexington.

Geis, Gilbert (1977) The terrible indignity: Crimes against the elderly. In Marlene A. Young Rifai's *Justice and Older Americans*. Lexington, MA: Lexington.

Gelles, Richard (1973) Child abuse as psychology: A sociological critique and reformulation. *American Journal of Orthopsychiatry* 43(July):611-621.

Gelles, Richard (1979) The truth about husband abuse. In Richard Gelles' (Ed.) *Family Violence*. Beverly Hills: Sage.

Gelles, Richard (1980) Violence in the family: A review of research in the seventies. *Journal of Marriage and the Family* 42(2):873-885.

George, Linda (1980) *Role Transitions in Later Life*. Monterey, CA: Brooks/Cole.

Gerbner, George and Larry Gross (1976) Living with television: The violence profile. *Journal of Communication* 26(2):172-199.

Gerbner, George, Larry Gross, Michael Elley, Marilyn Jackson-Beeck, Suzanne Jeffries-Fox, and Nancy Signorielli (1977) TV violence profile no. 8: The highlights. *Journal of Communications* 27(2):171-180.

Gerbner, George, Larry Gross, Marilyn Jackson-Beeck, Suzanne Jeffries-Fox, and Nancy Signorielli (1978) Cultural indicators: Violence profile no. 9. *Journal of Communications* 28(3):176-207.

Gil, David G. (1970) *Violence Against Children: Physical Abuse in the United States*. Cambridge, MA: Harvard University Press.

Glick, Rush G. and Robert S. Newsom (1974) *Fraud Investigation: Fundamentals for Police*. Springfield, IL: Charles C Thomas.

Goldsmith, Jack (1976) Why are the aged so vulnerable to crime—and what is being done for their protection? *Geriatrics* April:40-42.

Goldsmith, Jack and Sharon S. Goldsmith (1976) Crime and the elderly: An overview. In Jack Goldsmith and Sharon S. Goldsmith's (Eds.) *Crime and the Elderly*. Lexington, MA: Lexington Books.

Goldsmith, Jack and Noel Thomas (1974) Crimes against the elderly: A continuing national crisis. *Aging* 236:10-13.

Goldstein, Arnold and Elizabeth L. Wolf (1979a) Police investigation with elderly citizens. In Arnold Goldstein, William J. Hoyer, Phillip J. Monti's (Eds.) *Police and the Elderly*. New York: Pergamon.

Goldstein, Arnold and Elizabeth L. Wolf (1979b) Training police for work with the elderly. In Arnold Goldstein, William J. Hoyer, Phillip J. Monti's (Eds.) *Police and the Elderly.* New York: Pergamon.

Goode, William (1971) Force and violence in the family. *Journal of Marriage and the Family* 33(November):624-636.

Gordon, Margaret T., Stephanie Riger, Robert K. Le Bailly, and Linda Heath (1980) Crime, women, and the quality of urban life. *SIGNS: Journal of Women in Culture and Society* 5(3):S144-S160.

Grieken, R. R. and J. P. Spiegel (1945) *Men Under Stress.* New York: McGraw-Hill.

Gubrium, Jaber F. (1973) Apprehensions of coping incompetence and responses to fear in old age. *International Journal of Aging and Human Development* 4(2):111-125.

Gubrium, Jaber F. (1974) Victimization in old age: Available evidence and three hypotheses. *Crime and Delinquency* 20(3):245-250.

Hacker, George A. (1977) Nursing homes: Social victimization of the elderly. In Marlene A. Y. Rifai's (Ed.) *Justice and Older Americans.* Lexington, MA: D. C. Heath and Company.

Hahn, Paul H. (1976) *Crimes Against the Elderly: A Study in Victimology.* Santa Cruz, CA: Davis.

Hamel, Robert (1979) Assisting the elderly victim. In Arnold P. Goldstein, William J. Hoyer, and Phillip J. Monti's (Eds.) *Police and the Elderly.* New York: Pergamon.

Harbin, Henry T. and Denis J. Madden (1979) Battered parents: A new syndrome. *American Journal of Psychiatry* 136(10):1288-1291.

Harland, Alan T. (1981) Victim compensation: Programs and issues. In Burt Galaway and Joe Hudson's (Eds.) *Perspectives on Crime Victims.* St. Louis: C. V. Mosby.

Hartnagel, Timothy F. (1979) The perception and fear of crime: Implications for neighborhood cohesion, social activity, and community affect. *Social Forces* 58(1):176-193.

Haskell, Martin R. and Lewis Yablonsky (1974) *Crime and Delinquency.* Second edition. Chicago: Rand McNally.

Henig, Jefrey and Michael G. Maxfield (1979) Reducing fear of crime: Strategies for intervention. *Victimology* 3(3-4):297-313.

Hickey, Tom and Richard L. Douglass (1981) Neglect and abuse of older family members: Professionals' perspectives and case experiences. *The Gerontologist* 21(2):171-176.

Hill, Reuben and Roy H. Rodgers (1964) The developmental approach. In Harold T. Christensen's (Ed.) *Handbook of Marriage and the Family.* Skokie, IL: Rand McNally.

Hindelang, Michael J. and Michael Gottfredson (1976) The victim's decision not to invoke the criminal justice process. In William F. McDonald's (Ed.) *Criminal Justice and the Victim.* Beverly Hills: Sage.

Hindelang, Michael J., Michael R. Gottfredson, and James Garafalo (1978) *Victims of Personal Crime.* Cambridge: Ballinger.

Hirsch, Paul (1980) The "scary world" of the nonviewer and other anomalies: A reanalysis of Gerbner et al.'s findings on cultivation analysis, Part 1. *Communication Research* 7(4):403-456.

Hochschild, Arlie R. (1975) Disengagement theory: A critique and proposal. *American Sociological Review* 40(5):553-569.

Holmes, T. H. and R. H. Rahe (1967) The social readjustment rating scale. *Journal of Psychosomatic Research* 11:213-218.

Hooyman, Nancy R., Eloise Rathbone-McCuan, and Karil Klingbeil (1982) Serving the vulnerable elderly: The detection, intervention, and prevention of familial abuse. *Urban and Social Change Review* 15(2):9-13.

House, J. S. Occupational stress and coronary heart disease: A review and theoretical integration. *Journal of Health and Social Behavior* 1974(15):12-27.

Janson, Philip and Louise L. Ryder (1983) Crime and the elderly: The relationship between risk and fear. *The Gerontologist* 23(2):207-212.

Jaycox, Victoria (1979) The elderly's fear of crime: Rational or irrational? *Victimology* 3(3-4):329-334.

Johnson, Kirk A. and Patricia L. Wasielewski (1982) A commentary on victimization research and the importance of meaning structures. *Criminology* 20(2):205-222.

Kahana, Eva, Jersey Liang, Barbara Felton, Thomas Fairchild, and Zev Harel (1977) Perspectives of aged on victimization, "ageism," and their problems in urban society. *The Gerontologist* 17(2):121-129.

Katz, Katheryn D. (1980) Elder abuse. *Journal of Family Law.* 18(4):695-722.

Kempe, C. Henry, F. N. Silverman, B. F. Steele, W. Droegemueller, and H. K. Silver (1962) The battered-child syndrome. *Journal of the American Medical Association* 181(1):105-112.

Kleinman, Paula H. and Deborah S. David (1973) Victimization and perception of crime in a ghetto community. *Criminology* 11(3):307-343.

Knudten, Richard, D., Anthony Meade, Mary Knudten, and William Doerner (1976) The victim in the administration of criminal justice: Problems and perceptions. In William F. McDonald's (Ed.) *Criminal Justice and the Victim.* Beverly Hills: Sage.

Knudten, Mary S. and Richard D. Knudten (1981) What happens to crime victims and witnesses in the justice system? In Burt Galaway and Joe Hudson's (Eds.) *Perspectives on Crime Victims.* St. Louis: C. V. Mosby.

Kennedy, Leslie W. and Robert A. Silverman (1983) Significant others and fear of crime among the elderly. *International Journal of Aging and Human Development* forthcoming.

Kosberg, Jordan I. (1983) The special vulnerability of elderly parents. In Jordan I. Kosberg's *Abuse and Maltreatment of the Elderly: Causes and Interventions.* Boston: John Wright.

Lamborn, LeRoy L. (1981) Victim compensation programs: An overview. In Burt Galaway and Joe Hudson's (Eds.) *Perspective on Crime Victims.* St. Louis: C. V. Mosby.

Lau, Elizabeth E. and Jordan I. Kosberg (1979) Abuse of the elderly by informal care providers. *Aging* 299:10-15.

Lavrakas, Paul J. (1981) On households in Dan Lewis' (Ed.) *Reactions to Crime.* Beverly Hills: Sage.

Lavrakas, Paul J. and Dan Lewis (1980) The conceptualization and measurement of citizens' crime prevention behaviors. *Journal of Research in Crime and Delinquency* 17(2):254-272.

Law Enforcement Assistance Administration (1975) *Criminal Victimization Surveys in 13 American Cities.* Washington, DC: U.S. Government Printing Office.

Law Enforcement Assistance Administration (1976a) *Criminal Victimization Surveys in Eight American Cities.* Washington, DC: U.S. Government Printing Office.

Law Enforcement Assistance Administration (1976b) *Criminal Victimization Surveys in Chicago, Detroit, Los Angeles, New York, and Philadelphia.* Washington, DC: U.S. Government Printing Office.

Law Enforcement Assistance Administration (1976c) *Criminal Victimization in the United States, 1973.* Washington, DC: U.S. Government Printing Office.

Law Enforcement Assistance Administration (1977a) *An Introduction to the National Crime Survey.* Washington, DC: U.S. Government Printing Office.

Law Enforcement Assistance Administration (1977b) *Local Victim Surveys: A Review of the Issues.* Washington, DC: U.S. Government Printing Office.

Law Enforcement Assistance Administration (1977c) *Public Opinion About Crime: The Attitude of Victims and Nonvictims in Selected Cities.* Washington, DC: U.S. Government Printing Office.

Law Enforcement Assistance Administration (1977d) *Criminal Victimization in the United States, 1975.* Washington, DC: U.S. Government Printing Office.

Law Enforcement Assistance Administration (1977e) *Potential Costs and Coverage of a National Program to Compensate Victims of Violent Crimes.* Washington, DC: U.S. Government Printing Office.

Law Enforcement Assistance Administration (1977f) *Criminal Victimization in the United States, 1974.* Washington, DC: U.S. Government Printing Office.

Law Enforcement Assistance Administration (1979a) *Criminal Victimization in the United States, 1976.* Washington, DC: U.S. Government Printing Office.

Law Enforcement Assistance Administration (1979b) *Criminal Victimization in the United States, 1977.* Washington, DC: U.S. Government Printing Office.

Lawton, M. Powell (1980) *Environment and Aging.* Monterey, CA: Brooks/Cole.

Lawton, M Powell (1981) Crime, victimization, and the fortitude of the aged. *Aged Care and Services Review* 2(1):1,20-31.

Lawton, M. Powell and Lucille Nahemow (1973) Ecology and the aging process. In C. Eisdorfer and M. Powell Lawton's (Eds.) *Psychology of Adult Development and Aging.* Washington, DC: American Psychological Association.

Lawton, M. Powell, Lucille Nahemow, Silvia Yaffe, and Steven Feldman (1976) Psychological aspects of crime and fear of crime. In Jack Goldsmith and Sharon S. Goldsmith's (Eds.) *Crime and the Elderly*. Lexington, MA: Lexington.

Lawton, M. Powell and Silvia Yaffe (1980) Victimization and fear of crime in elderly public housing tenants. *Journal of Gerontology* 35(5):768-779.

Lebowitz, Barry D. (1975) Age and fearfulness: Personal and situational factors. *Journal of Gerontology* 30(6):696-700.

Lee, Gary R. (1982a) Sex differences in fear of crime among older people. *Research on Aging* 4(3):284-298.

Lee, Gary R. (1982b) Residential location and fear of crime among the elderly. *Rural Sociology* 47(4):655-669.

Lee, Gary R. (1983) Social integration and fear of crime among older persons. *Journal of Gerontology* 38(6):745-750.

Lejeune, Robert and Nicholas Alex (1973) On being mugged: The event and its aftermath. *Urban Life and Culture* 2(3):259-287.

Levine, James P. (1976) The potential for crime overreporting in criminal victimization surveys. *Criminology* 14(3):307-330.

Lewin, Kurt (1951) *Field Theory in Social Science*. New York: Harper & Row.

Lewis, Dan A. and Michael G. Maxfield (180) Fear in the neighborhoods: An investigation of the impact of crime. *Journal of Research in Crime and Delinquency* 17:160-189.

Liang, Jersey and Mary C. Sengstock (1981) The risk of personal victimization among the aged. *Journal of Gerontology* 36(4):463-471.

Lindquist, John H. and Janice M. Duke (1982) The elderly victim at risk: Explaining the fear-victimization paradox. *Criminology* 20(1):115-126.

Liska, Allen E., Joseph J. Lawrence, and Andrew Sanchirico (1982) Fear of crime as a social fact. *Social Forces* 60(3):760-770.

Lizotte, Alan J. and David Bordua (1980) Firearms ownership for sport and protection: Two divergent models. *American Sociological Review* 45(2): 229-244.

Lotz, Roy (1979) Public anxiety about crime. *Pacific Sociological Review* 22(2): 241-254.

Lowenberg, David A. (1981) An integrated victim services model. In Burt Galaway and Joe Hudson's (Eds.) *Perspectives on Crime Victims*. St. Louis: C. V. Mosby.

Lowenthal, Marjorie F. and Deetze Boler (1965) Voluntary vs. involuntary social withdrawal. *Journal of Gerontology* 20(3):363-371.

Lowenthal, Marjorie F. and Robinson, Betsy (1977) Social networks and isolation. In Robert H. Binstock and Ethel Shanas' (Eds.) *Handbook of Aging and the Social Sciences*. New York: Van Norstrand Reinhold.

Lynch, Richard P. (1976) Improving the treatment of victims: Some guides for action. In William F. McDonald's (Ed.) *Criminal Justice and the Victim*. Beverly Hills: Sage.

McDonald, William F. (1976) Criminal justice and the victim: An introduction. In William F. McDonald's (Ed.) *Criminal Justice and the Victim*. Beverly Hills: Sage.

McPherson, Marlys (1979) Realities and perceptions of crime at the neighborhood level. *Victimology* 3(3-4):319-328.

Mechanic, David (1962) *Student Under Stress*. New York: Free Press.

Medical News (1980) The elderly: Newest victims of familial abuse. *Journal of the American Medical Association* 243(12):1221, 1225.

Merry, Sally E. (1981) *Urban Danger: LIfe in a Neighborhood of Strangers.* Philadelphia: Temple University Press.

Morello, Frank P. (1982) *Juvenile Crimes Against the Elderly.* Springfield, IL: Charles C Thomas.

National Council on the Aging (1977) *Myths and Realities of Aging.* Washington, DC.

National Council on the Aging (1978) *Fact Book on Aging: A profile on America's older population.* Washington, DC.

Neugarten, Bernice and associates (1966) *Personality in Middle and Late Life.* New York: Atherton.

Nettler, Gwynn (1982) *Lying, Cheating, Stealing.* Cincinnati: Anderson.

Newman, Oscar and Karen A. Franck (1982) The effects of building size on personal crime and fear of crime. *Population and Environment* 5(4):203-220.

Newman, Stephen A. and Karin L. Straus (1977) The elderly consumer and fraud schemes. In Jonathan A. Weiss's (Ed.) *Law of the Elderly.* New York: Practising Law Institute.

Norton, Lee and Michael Courlander (1982) Fear of crime among the elderly: The role of crime prevention programs. *The Gerontologist* 22(4):388-393.

O'Brien, Robert M. (1983) Metropolitan structure and violent crime: Which measure of crime? *American Sociological Review* 48(3):434-437.

Ollenburger, Jane C. (1981) Criminal victimization and fear of crime. *Research on Aging* 3(1):101-118.

Palmer, John W. (1975) The night prosecutor: Columbus finds extrajudicial solutions to interpersonal disputes. *Judicature* 59(1):23-27.

Patterson, Arthur (1977) Territorial behavior and fear of crime of the elderly. *Police Chief* February:42-45.

Patterson, Arthur (1979) Training the elderly in mastery of the environment. In Arnold P. Goldstein, William J. Hoyer, and Phillip J. Monti's (Eds.) *Police and the Elderly.* New York: Pergamon.

Pedrick-Cornell, Claire and Richard J. Gelles (1982) Elder abuse: The status of current knowledge. *Family Relations* 31(3):457-465.

Pleck, E., J. Pleck, M. Grossman and P. Bart (1977) The battered data syndrome: A comment on Steinmetz's article. *Victimology.* 2(3/4):680-683.

Pollack, Lance M. and Arthur H. Patterson (1980) Territoriality and fear of crime in elderly and nonelderly homeowners. *Journal of Social Psychology* 111:119-129.

Poveda, Tony G. (1972) The fear of crime in a small town. *Criminology and Delinquency* 18(2):147-153.

President's Commission on Law Enforcement and Administration of Justice (1967) *Task Force Report: Crime and Its Impact—An Assessment.* Washington, DC: U.S. Government Printing Office.

Ragan, Pauline K. (1977) Crimes against the elderly: Findings from interviews with Blacks, Mexican Americans, and Whites. In Marlene A. Rifai's (Ed.) *Justice and Older Americans.* Lexington, MA: Lexington.

Rainwater, Lee (1966) Fear and the house as haven in the lower class. *Journal of the American Institute of Planners* 32:23-33.

Rathbone-McCuan, Eloise (1980) Elderly victims of family violence and neglect. *Social Casework* 61(5):296-304.

Rathbone-McCuan, Eloise and Barbara Voyles (1982) Case detection of abused elderly parents. *American Journal of Psychiatry* 139(2):189-192.

Reid, Sue T. (1982) *Crime and Criminology.* New York: Holt, Rinehart and Winston.

Reiman, Jeffrey H. (1976) Aging as victimization: Reflections on the American way of (ending) life. In Jack Goldsmith and Sharon S. Goldsmith's (Eds.) *Crime and the Elderly.* Lexington, MA: Lexington.

Reiss, Albert (1967) *Studies in Crime and Law Enforcement in Major Metropolitan Areas.* Washington, DC: U.S. Government Printing Office.

Reiss, Albert (1971) *The Police and the Public.* New Haven: Yale University Press.

Reppetto, Thomas (1974) *Residential Crime.* Cambridge, MA: Ballinger.

Rifai, Marlene A. (1977) Perspectives on justice and older Americans. In Marlene A. Rifai's (Ed.) *Justice and Older Americans.* Lexington, MA: Lexington.

Rifai, Marlene A. Young (1977) The response of the older adult to criminal victimization. *Police Chief* February:48-50.

Rifai, Marlene A. Young and Sheila A. Ames (1977) Social victimization of older people: A process of social exchange. In Marlene A. Rifai's (Ed.) *Justice and Older Americans.* Lexington, MA: Lexington.

Riger, Stephanie, Margaret T. Gordon, and Robert Le Bailly (1979) Women's fear of crime: From blaming to restricting the victim. *Victimology* 3(3-4): 274-284.

Riley, Matilda W., Marilyn Johnson, and Anne Foner (1972) *Aging and Society. Volume 3: A Sociology of Age Stratification.* New York: Russell Sage Foundation.

Rollin, Boyd C. and Kenneth L. Cannon (1974) Marital satisfaction over the family life cycle: A re-evaluation. *Journal of Marriage and the Family* 35(May):271-284.

Rotter, Julian B. (1966) Generalized expectancies for internal versus external control of reinforcement. *Psychological Monographs* 80(1 whole no. 609).

Russell, Harold F. (1977) *Foozles & Frauds.* Altamonte Springs, FL: Institute of Internal Auditors.

Ryan, William (1972) *Blaming the Victim.* New York: Vintage Books.

Sacco, Vincent F. (1982) The effects of mass media on perceptions of crime: A reanalysis of the issues. *Pacific Sociological Review* 25(4):475-493.

Salend, Elyse, Rosalie Kane, Maureen Satz, and John Pynoos (1974) Elder abuse reporting: Limitation of statutes. *The Gerontologist* 24(1):61-69.

Schafer, Stephen (1976) The victim and correctional theory: Integrating victim reparation with offender rehabilitation. In William F. McDonald's (Ed.) *Criminal Justice and the Victim.* Beverly Hills: Sage.

Schafer, Stephen (1977) *Victimology: The Victim and His Criminal.* Reston, VA: Prentice-Hall.

Schneider, Anne L., Janie M. Curcart, and L. A. Wilson II (1976) The role of attitudes in the decision to report crimes to the police. In William F. McDonald's (Ed.) *Criminal Justice and the Victim.* Beverly Hills: Sage.

Schneider, Anne L. and Peter R. Schneider (1981) Victim assistance programs: An overview. In Burt Galaway and Joe Hudson's (Eds.) *Perspectives on Crime Victims.* St. Louis: C. V. Mosby.

Sellin, Thorsten (1980) *The Penalty of Death.* Beverly Hills: Sage.

Shanas, Ethel (1970) Aging and life space in Poland and the U.S. *Journal of Health and Social Behavior* 11(3):183-190.

Sherman, Edmund A., Evelyn S. Newman, and Anne D. Nelson (1977) Patterns of age integration in public housing and the incidence and fears of crime among elderly tenants. In Jack Goldsmith and Sharon S. Goldsmith's (Eds.) *Crime and the Elderly.* Lexington, MA: Lexington.

Shotland, R. Lance, Scott C. Hayward, Carlotta Young, Margaret L. Signorella, Kenneth Mindingall, John K. Kennedy, Michael J. Rovine, Edward F. Danowitz (1979) Fear of crime in residential communities. *Criminology* 17(1):34-45.

Skogan, Wesley G. (1976) Sample surveys of the victims of crime. *Review of Public Data Use* 4(1):   .

Skogan, Wesley G. (1977) Public policy and the fear of crime in large American cities. In John A. Gardiner's (Ed.) *Public Law and Public Policy.* New York: Praeger.

Skogan, Wesley G. and Michael G. Maxfield (1981) *Coping with Crime: Individual and Neighborhood Reactions.* Beverly Hills: Sage.

Smith, A. Emerson and Dal Maness, Jr. (1976) The decision to call the police: Reactions to burglary. In William F. McDonald's (Ed.) *Criminal Justice and the Victim.* Beverly Hills: Sage.

Stannard, Charles I. (1973) Old folks and dirty work: The social conditions for patient abuse in a nursing home. Social Problems 20(3):329-342.

Steinmetz, Suzanne (1977) The battered husband syndrome. *Victimology* 2(3/4): 499-509.

Steinmetz, Suzanne (1978) Battered parents. *Society* :54-55.

Steinmetz, Suzanne (1983) Dependency, stress, and violence between middle-aged caregivers and their elderly parents. In Jordan I. Kosberg's (Ed.) *Abuse and Maltreatment of the Elderly.* Boston: John Wright.

Stookey, John A. (1981) A cost theory of victim justice. In Burt Galaway and Joe Hudson's (Eds.) *Perspectives on Crime Victims.* St. Louis: C. V. Mosby.

Strauss, Murray A., Richard J. Gelles, Suzanne K. Steinmetz (1980) *Behind Closed Doors.* Garden City, NY: Anchor.

Sundeen, Richard (1977) The fear of crime and urban elderly. In Marlene A. Young Rifai's (Ed.) *Justice and Older Americans.* Lexington, MA: Lexington.

Sundeen, Richard A. and James T. Mathieu (1976) The fear of crime and its consequences among elderly in three urban communities. *The Gerontologist* 16(3):211-219.

Sundeen, Richard A. and James T. Mathieu (1977) The urban elderly: Environments of fear. In Jack Goldsmith and Sharon S. Goldsmith's (Eds.) *Crime and the Elderly.* Lexington, MA: Lexington.

Sutherland, Edwin H. and Donald R. Cressey (1970) *Criminology.* 8th edition. Philadelphia: J. B. Lippincott.

Sykes, Richard E. (1976) The urban police function in regard to the elderly: A special case of police community relations. In Jack Goldsmith and Sharon S. Goldsmith's (Eds.) *Crime and the Elderly*. Lexington, MA: D. C. Heath and Company.

Tallmer, Margot and Bernard Kutner (1970) Disengagement and Morale. *The Gerontologist* 10(4):317-320.

Thomas, Charles W. and Jeffrey M. Hyman (1977) Perceptions of crime, fear of victimization, and public perceptions of police performance. *Journal of Police Science and Administration* 5(3):305-317.

Thomas, William I. and Dorothy S. Thomas (1970) Situations defined as real are real in their consequences. In Gregory P. Stone and Harvey A. Farberman's (Eds.) *Social Psychology Through Symbolic Interactionism*. Waltham, MA: Ginn Blaisdell.

U. S. Congress: House of Representatives (1977) *In Search of Security: A National Perspective on Elderly Crime Victimization*. Select Committee on Aging. 95th Congress, 1st session. Washington, DC: U.S. Government Printing Office.

Time (1981) The curse of violent crime. 3/23:16-21.

Viano, Emilio (1983) Victimology: An overview. In Jordan I. Kosberg's (Ed.) *Abuse and Maltreatment of the Elderly*. Boston: John Wright.

Viano, Emilio (1976) Crimes, victims, and justice. In Jack Goldsmith and Sharon S. Goldsmith's (Eds.) *Crime and the Elderly*. Lexington, MA: D. C. Heath and Company.

Ward, Russell (1979) *The Aging Experience: An Introduction to Social Gerontology*. New York: J. B. Lippincott.

Warr, Mark (1980) The accuracy of public beliefs about crime. *Social Forces* 59(2):456-470.

Warr, Mark (1982) The accuracy of public beliefs about crime: Further evidence. *Criminology* 20(2):185-204.

Warr, Mark and Mark Stafford (1982) Fear of victimization: A look at the proximate causes. *Social Forces* 61(4):1033-1043.

Wilbanks, William (1982) Trends in violent death among the elderly. *International Journal of Aging and Human Development* 14(3):167-175.

Williams, Kristen M. (1976) The effects of victim characteristics on the disposition of violent crimes. In William F. McDonald's (Ed.) *Criminal Justice and the Victim*. Beverly Hills: Sage.

Wilson, James Q. (1968) *Varieties of Police Behavior*. Cambridge, MA: Harvard University Press.

Wilson, James Q. (1977) *Thinking about Crime*. New York: Vintage Books.

Wolfgang, Marvin E. (1972) Making the criminal justice system accountable. *Crime and Delinquency* :15-22.

Yin, Peter (1980) Fear of crime among the elderly: Some issues and suggestions. *Social Problems* 27(4):492-504.

Yin, Peter (1982) Fear of crime as a problem for the elderly. *Social Problems* 30(2):240-245.

Yunker, James (1982) Testing the deterrent effect of capital punishment: A reduced form approach. *Criminology* 19(4):626-649.

Ziegenhagen, Eduard A. (1976) Toward a theory of victim-criminal justice system interactions. In William F. McDonald's (Ed.) *Criminal Justice and the Victim*. Beverly Hills: Sage.

Ziegenhagen, Eduard A. and John Benyi (1981) Victim interests, victim services, and social control. In Burt Galaway and Joe Hudson's (Eds.) *Perspectives on Crime Victims*. St. Louis: C. V. Mosby.

APPENDIXES

APPENDIX 1

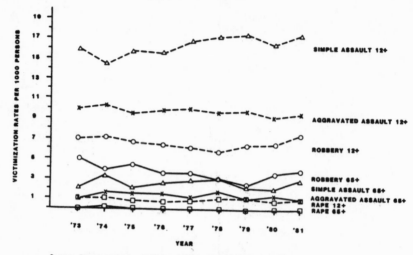

Source: Bureau of Justice Statistics (1980c), (1981a), (1981b), (1982a), (1983). Law Enforcement Assistance Administration (1976c), (1977d), (1977f), (1979a), (1979b).

Appendix 1.1. Trends in crimes of violence: 1973-1981. Source: Bureau of Justice Statistics (1980c), (1981a), (1981b), (1982a), (1983). Law Enforcement Assistance Administration (1976c), (1977d), (1977f), (1979a), (1979b).

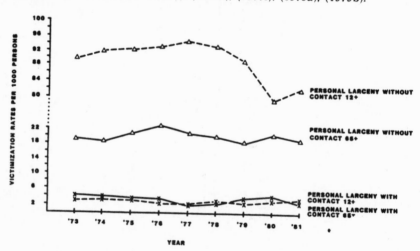

Source: Bureau of Justice Statistics (1980c), (1981a), (1981b), (1982a), (1983). Law Enforcement Assistance Administration (1976c), (1977d), (1977f), (1979a), (1979b).

Appendix 1.2. Trends in personal crimes of theft: 1973-1981. Source: Bureau of Justice Statistics (1980c), (1981a), (1981b), (1982a), (1983). Law Enforcement Assistance Administration (1976c), (1977d), (1977f), (1979a), (1979b).

190

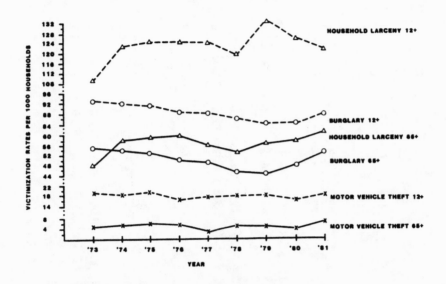

Source: Bureau of Justice Statistics (1980c), (1981a), (1981b), (1982a), (1983).   Law Enforcement Assistance Administration (1976c), (1977d), (1977f), (1979a), (1979b).

Appendix 1.3. Trends in household crimes: 1973–1981. Source: Bureau of Justice Statistics (1980c), (1981a), (1981b), (1982a), (1983). Law Enforcement Assistance Administration (1976c), (1977d), (1977f), (1979a), (1979b).

APPENDIX 2

		Atlanta	Baltimore	Boston	Buffalo	Chicago	Cincinnati	Cleveland	Dallas	Denver	Detroit	Houston	Los Angeles	Miami
Rape	12+	2.4	2.5	2.0	2.0	2.4	2.0	2.2	1.7	2.5	1.8	3.0	2.2	1.0
	65+	*0	*0	0	0	*.3	0	*.7	*0	*0	*.3	0	*0	0
Robbery	12+	17.6	34.7	31.0	16.0	28.8	15.0	27.0	12.3	19.0	36.9	17.0	17.7	10.0
	65+	14.0	21.2	21.0	8.0	17.3	8.0	18.8	7.1	11.2	28.5	7.0	12.3	7.0
Aggravated Assault	12+	12.3	20.5	17.0	14.0	15.7	22.0	20.2	17.5	22.5	21.0	17.0	16.5	7.0
	65+	*8	*1.9	*3.0	*2.0	2.0	*3.0	5.0	*1.7	3.8	4.4	*3.0	*3.0	2.0
Simple Assault	12+	11.4	20.5	18.0	17.0	13.8	25.0	17.4	16.9	27.2	17.7	16.0	22.2	5.0
	65+	*1.7	3.2	*2.0	4.0	3.7	4.0	5.3	*3.8	4.9	5.5	*2.0	6.8	3.0
Larceny with contact	12+	9.3	18.5	26.0	7.0	16.7	7.0	9.4	6.3	5.8	8.2	6.0	7.9	5.0
	65+	8.7	28.5	32.0	7.0	23.6	10.0	13.8	5.5	9.5	11.9	9.0	16.2	7.0
Larceny without contact	12+	83.7	86.1	93.0	67.0	74.2	104.0	75.6	110.1	128.1	82.6	116.0	115.5	39.0
	65+	21.3	27.5	30.0	14.0	27.1	24.0	27.1	26.5	31.5	23.2	32.0	27.9	11.0

*Estimate, based on 10 or fewer sample cases, is statistically unreliable.

Source: Law Enforcement Assistance Administration (1975) (1976a) (1976b).

Appendix 2.1. Personal victimization rates by Age in twenty-six cities. Source: Law Enforcement Assistance Administration (1975), (1976a), (1976b).

	Milwaukee	Minneapolis	New Orleans	Newark	New York	Oakland	Philadelphia	Pittsburgh	Portland	St. Louis	San Diego	San Francisco	Washington, D.C.	National Sample
Rape	2.0	4.0	3.0	1.5	.7	3.0	1.3	2.0	3.7	1.0	2.0	3.0	1.0	1.0
	*2	0	*2	*0	*.3	0	*0	0	*.9	*0	0	*2	0	.2
Robbery	18.0	21.0	25.0	23.1	23.9	22.0	20.7	15.0	15.7	19.0	11.0	29.0	17.0	7.1
	14.0	10.0	11.0	21.0	19.6	24.0	14.0	8.0	6.2	13.9	6.0	24.0	10.0	3.9
Aggravated Assault	17.0	18.0	13.0	7.6	8.6	16.0	13.5	13.0	21.7	14.3	16.0	14.0	6.0	10.3
	*3.0	*3.0	*2.0	*.9	2.9	5.0	3.9	*1.0	3.8	2.6	6.0	*2.0	*3.0	1.6
Simple Assault	24.0	28.0	13.0	5.7	9.7	18.0	13.4	17.0	29.6	13.9	24.0	25.0	7.0	14.4
	6.0	6.0	*3.0	5.0	*2.5	7.0	4.5	4.0	*2.5	*2.3	*3.0	6.0	*2	3.4
Larceny with contact	7.0	6.0	14.0	10.5	14.8	10.0	12.4	7.0	5.7	9.1	5.0	23.0	12.0	3.1
	9.0	9.0	20.0	9.6	19.5	14.0	21.0	6.0	7.7	14.1	4.0	43.0	21.0	3.4
Larceny without contact	96.0	113.0	80.0	34.5	50.6	92.0	72.3	76.0	136.8	82.9	136.0	106.0	53.0	91.8
	15.0	21.0	21.0	16.1	21.2	28.0	24.6	17.0	34.1	26.5	28.0	38.0	23.0	18.5

Appendix 2.1. Personal victimization rates by Age in twenty-six cities (continued).

		Atlanta	Baltimore	Boston	Buffalo	Chicago	Cincinnati	Cleveland	Dallas	Denver	Detroit	Houston	Los Angeles	Miami
Burglary	12+	158.2	117.9	149.0	97.0	121.7	143.0	136.8	160.5	165.8	153.6	164.0	149.1	85.0
	65+	69.5	43.0	74.0	43.0	43.7	71.0	71.9	82.8	93.7	83.5	85.0	93.8	46.0
Household Larceny	12+	116.8	124.0	87.0	92.0	85.6	103.0	105.6	178.0	186.8	106.8	167.0	144.6	66.0
	65+	60.5	53.0	29.0	29.0	34.7	41.0	41.0	100.3	75.6	44.5	78.0	79.6	31.0
Motor Vehicle Theft	12+	24.0	42.1	86.0	30.0	37.9	25.0	73.4	23.4	39.8	69.8	32.0	38.6	18.0
	65+	8.8	16.4	35.0	15.0	13.8	10.0	22.9	*6.2	9.9	24.7	8.0	10.3	*5.0

*Estimate, based on 10 or fewer sample cases, is statistically unreliable.

Source: Law Enforcement Assistance Administration (1975) (1976a) (1976b).

Appendix 2.2. Household victimization rates by Age in twenty-six cities. Source: Law Enforcement Assistance Administration (1975), (1976a), (1976b).

194

	Milwaukee	Minneapolis	New Orleans	Newark	New York	Oakland	Philadelphia	Pittsburgh	Portland	St. Louis	San Diego	San Francisco	Washington,D.C.	National Sample
Burglary	152.0	177.0	112.0	97.6	77.4	174.0	91.0	93.0	174.4	134.7	138.0	115.0	75.0	92.6
	70.0	85.0	58.0	45.2	39.7	111.0	50.2	53.0	71.7	65.1	68.0	49.0	42.0	54.4
Household Larceny	128.0	164.0	116.0	49.1	46.2	108.0	82.5	90.0	188.5	94.4	190.0	85.0	51.0	123.4
	47.0	62.0	55.0	19.2	18.3	59.0	38.2	37.0	76.4	43.4	72.0	33.0	21.0	57.9
Motor Vehicle Theft	29.0	41.0	32.0	40.0	27.5	36.0	35.6	43.0	37.0	46.3	25.0	38.0	15.0	18.7
	7.0	5.0	14.0	14.5	8.1	14.0	13.0	13.0	8.1	17.8	*5.0	11.0	7.0	5.7

Appendix 2.2. Household victimization rates by Age in twenty-six cities (continued).

crime prevention programs, 81-82 (*See also* Crime prevention programs)
defined, 81
evaluation of, 83
home protection programs (*See* Home protection programs)
household protection (*See* Home protection programs)
household victimization (*See* Home victimization)
individual responses, 81
insurance, 82
loss reduction, 82, 93
mobilization, 81
of the elderly, 85
personal precaution, 82
pioneer work on, 80
problems of research on, 86-87
reactions to crime, 82-83
self-defense courses, 85
street crime prevention, 84
street victimization loss reduction, 84
street victimization prevention, 87-89
surveillance, 82
target hardening (*See* Target hardening)
types of, 84
typologies of, 81-82
    table, 85
Corporate fraud, 98
Counterfeiting, 95
Crime, ordinary (*See* Ordinary crime)
Crime education programs, 163
Crime index, 165-166
Crime prevention programs
    crime education program, 163
    private-minded, 81-82
    public-minded, 81-82
Crime statistics, 12-15
    crimes unreported to police, 13
    problems with, 12-13
    sources of data, 12
    victimization survey, 13 (*See also* Victimization survey)
Crimes of theft (*See* Theft)
Criminal justice system (*See also* Justice system)
    goal of, 142-143
    victim as gate-keeper to, 130-133, 153
        police as reactive, 130, 153
        rate unreported crimes, 131-133

study reporting/nonreporting of crimes, 131-133
Crisis center, 151, 154

E

Elder abuse
    by family members, 106, 127, 161
    causal factors, 118-119, 127
        cycle of violence, 119
        psychological traits, 119
        stress as, 119
        sub-culture of violence, 119
        types research, 118-119
    child abuse reporting similarities, 114, 170
    definition, 108-111, 127
    determinants of, 118, 126, 127, 161, 164
    family transitional theory of (*See* Family transitional theory)
    financial abuse, 108, 110, 121-122, 127
    in homes of the aged, 107-127
        case illustrations, 107
        roots of, 107
    in nursing homes, 106, 126, 127
    intimate perpetrator, 105, 126
    mandatory reporting of, 170
        concerns regarding, 170-172
    physical abuse and neglect (*See* Physical abuse and neglect)
    prevalence of, 112-117, 127
        Conflict tactics scale (*See* Conflict tactics scale)
        husband battering, 115-116
        lack reports violence, 115
        studies of, 112-115, 127
        use volunteered information on, 115
    psychological abuse of aged, 108, 127
    recommendations to reduce
        at individual level, 161-162
        at neighborhood level, 164-165
        at the societal level, 169-172
    self-abuse, 109, 127, 170-171
    summary, 126-128
    types of, 108, 127
    use of respite care, 164-165
    violation of individual rights, 109, 127
Embezzlement, 95
Environmental peril, 37, 38-40, 42-51, 60, 160
    age-homogeneity and, 45

composition neighboring residents as, 44-46, 60

elderly people as reducing, 45

largely federally-assisted moderate income housing as, 45, 60

non-white race and, 43-44, 60

physical nature of environment, 43, 60

predictive powers of, 48

relationship reace and socioeconomic status to, 42-43

reputation of neighborhoods as, 46-47

scale of incivility, 42-43

diminsions of, 43

size of community as, 46

social dimension of environment, 43-44, 60

F

Family transitional theory of elder abuse degrees of dependence and, 124-125

family development basis, 121-122, 127-128

predictors, illustrated, 123

previous parent-child relationship, 125-126

Resource theory of intrafamily violence, 124-125

Schedule of recent events, 123

stress as basis, 122

use of, 128

predictors, 122, 128

Fear of crime, 31-61

age effect, 57-59

and community size, 41

and the aged

avoidance of street due to, 23, 159-160

comparison to younger people, 55-56

discripancy perceived risk and likelihood, 55

factors in four of and rate of crime, 55-56

perceived risk and victimization, 55-57, 59-61

as an attitude, 33, 59

components of, 33

association vicarious victimization, 50

beginning studies of, 34

cohort effect, 57-59, 61

and life experience, 58

cognitive approach to, 33

merits of, 33-34

conditions necessary for, 33

decrease annually after victimization experience, 54

definition, 31-34

behavioral approach to, 32

emotional approach to, 32-33

dimensions of, 31-32

effects of victimization and (*See* Victimization effects)

experience with victimization, 48-51 (*See also* Victimization effects)

fear of irrational, 53, 54, 169

fear as rational, 53-54, 169

fear of strangers as, 44

blacks vs. Chinese, 44

females more fearful than men, 40

illustration, 53

impacts of (*See* Fear of crime, impacts on aged)

manifestations of fear response, 32

mass media effect on, 50, 160-161, 168-169

measurement of, 33-36, 38, 59

approaches to, 34-36

concern for crime, 38

conditions measured, 33

methods of, table, 35

weaknesses of, 36

person-environment theory of (*See* Person-environment theory)

personal vulnerability (*See* Personal vulnerability)

provocation of, 32

recommendations to reduce

at individual level, 160-161

at neighborhood level, 163-164

at the societal level, 168-169

summary, 173-174

relationship sense of personal control to, 155

relationship to external control, 42

summary, 59-61

trend of, 168

table, 169

use of term, 31

Fear of crime impacts on aged, 69-80

as a social problem, 69

indications of, 69-70

assessment of, 71
feelings of anxiety, mistrust, and aliena-
    tion
  case illustration, 74-75
  "house arrest," 74
  prisoners of fear, 74
  limiting social activity, 74 (*See also*
      Social activities of aged)
  morals and, 73, 92
  neighborhood satisfaction and, 73-74, 92
  problems with studies of, 75-76, 92
  roots of, 69, 92
  social activities (*See* Social activities of
      aged)
  study of by NCOA, 70, 71-73
    results of, table, 72
  summary, 80
Financial abuse of aged, 108, 110 (*See also*
    Elder abuse)
Fraud, 94-104
  against organizations, 95
    counterfeiting, 95
    embezzlement, 95
    insurance fraud, 95
    medicare/medicaid/social security fraud,
        95
  bunco (*See* Bunco)
  consumer fraud (*See* Consumer fraud)
  definition, 94, 95, 103
  determinants of, 100-103
    comments of con-artists, 102
    components of, 100
    methods research, 101-102
    research issues on, table, 101
    type person approached, 101
    vulnerability of older people, 103
  predator characteristics, 94
  prevalence of, 100
  problems of, 100
  recommendations to reduce
    at individual level, 162
    at neighborhood level, 165
    at the societal level, 172
  types of, 95-100
    against organizations, 95
    bunco (*See* Bunco)
    consumer fraud (*See* Consumer fraud)

G

Gallup Poll of 1965, use of term unsafe, 35
Guardian Angels, 163

H

Home protection programs, 81, 82, 84, 93
Homicide
  arrest rate for 136
  analysis rates of, 166-167
  changes in rates of, 166-167
Household crimes
  burglary, 16 (*See also* Burglary)
  definitions, table, 17
  household larceny
    classification, 16
    definition, 17
    of aged, 27
  motor vechicle theft, 16 (*See also* Motor
      vehicle theft)
  trends in rates of by age groups, 19-20
    table, 191, 194
  victimization (*See* Household victimiza-
      tion)
Household victimization
  burglary (*See* Burglary)
  characteristics participants, 89
  loss reduction, 82, 84, 91-92, 93, 158
  prevention of, 84, 89-91, 93, 158
  rates by age groups, 18
    table, 18
  target hardening (*See* Target hardening)

I

Insurance fraud, 95

J

Justice system (*See also* Criminal justice
    system)
  arrest and trial proceedings, 136-138, 153
    grand jury, 137
    plea bargaining, 138
    preliminary hearing, 137
    sequence of events, 137
    trial, 137
  case disposition, 143-144
  compensation (*See* Compensation)
  cost of being a victim-witness, 144-146
    extent of cost, 145
    inconveniences for victim, 144-145
    remedies for, 145-146
  crime, defined, 142
  dissatisfaction of victims toward, 141
  distinction torts and crime, 142
  feelings of powerlessness of victim, 141
    case illustration, 140-141

interaction between victim and, 133-146
arrest and trial proceedings, 136-138
cost of being a victim-witness, 144-146
police, 133-135 (*See also* Police)
victim's characteristic and case outcomes, 138-139
victim's input and case outcomes, 139-144
investigation of crimes, 136-137
overprotection of offenders, 140
relationship between victim and, 129-130
restitution (*See* Restitution)
restoring the victim, 146-153
compensation (*See* Compensation)
restitution (*See* Restitution)
social services (*See* Social services)
right prosecutor system, 143
social services (*See* Social services)
study without referral to age, 129, 153
summary, 153-154
torts defined, 142
unreported crimes, 131-133, 153
analysis determinants to, 131-132
methods of study, 131
reasons given for, 132
study of, 132
summary study, 132-133
victim advocacies, 143, 154
victim's characteristics and case outcomes, 153-154
studies of, 138-139
victim's input and case outcomes, 153
right to file civil suit, 144
systems proposed, 142-144, 154
victim as a witness only, 139-140
work as independent of victim, 140
case illustration, 140-141

L

Larceny
definition, 94
household (*See* Household larceny)
personal with contact (*See* Larceny with contact)
personal without contact (*See* Larceny without contact)
Law Enforcement Assistance Administration (*See also* Victimization survey)
analysis cost crime compensation program, 151

public vs. private-minded crime prevention, 81-82
role in National Crime Survey, 14-15
social activities of aged and fear of crime study, 78-79
factors inhibiting, table, 78
results of, 79
victimization surveys conducted by, 15, 27-28
victim-witness assistance programs of, 146
Loss reduction measures, 82

M

Mail-order fraud, 99
Mass media, influence on fear of crime, 50, 160-161, 168-169
Medical fraud, 98
Medicare/Medicaid fraud, 95
Motor vehicle theft
classification, 16
definition, 17
Mugging, study of victims, 28-29
Murder (*See* Homicide)

N

National Council on Aging
method use, 71
results of, 71-73
table, 72
study crime and the aged, 70, 71
National Crime Survey
analyses data of, 27
arrest rates of ordinary crimes, 136
table, 136
comparison Uniform Crime Report to, 165-266
computation dollar losses of crimes, 148
contributions to, 28
definition, 14-15
division of crimes by, 16
household crimes, 16 (*See also* Household crimes)
personal crimes, 16 (*See also* Personal crimes)
drawbacks of, 28
elderly as least victimized age group, 16, 18-20, 24, 30
questions raised by, 20
verification of, 19
lacking reporting of crimes, 131

non-stranger victimization, 105
origin of, 14, 19, 30
problems with, 166
summary findings, 24-25, 30
techniques used, 15
use of, 165-166
victimization rate changes, 166
National Opinion Research Center, 34-35
study of fear of crime, 168
use of term "unsafe," 34-35
Neighborhood crime less due to, 44
Neighborhood watch to deter crime
attitude burglary toward, table 162
rationale, 162

O

Older or old, definition of terms, 5
Ordinary crime victimization (*See also* Victimization and victimization of the aged)
deterrants to, 162-163
feelings of fear of (*See* Fear of crime in aged)
image of over-victimized aged, 11, 157
neighborhood watch programs, 81, 162, 164
older vs. younger victim of, 11, 157
principle of homophily, 21, 22, 23, 24
recommendations to reduce
at individual level, 157-160
at neighborhood level, 162-163
at the societal level, 165-168
summary, 30
use of term, 11
victimization aged (*See* Victimization)

P

Personal crime
by teenage offenders, table, 25
characteristics offenders of aged, 21, 23-24
characteristics of victim, 21-22
components of, 20-21
crimes of theft, 16 (*See also* Theft)
definitions, table 17
life-style theory of, 21-22
setting of, 20-21
time of occurrence, 21
trends in rates by age groups, 19-20
table, 190, 192-193

violent crimes, 16 (*See also* Violent crimes)
Personal larceny with contract
classification, 16
definition, 17
household larceny (*See* Household larceny)
occurrence in public places, 21
rates for, 27
victimization rates, 16-18, 19
table, 18
Personal larceny without contact
classification, 16
definition, 17
household larceny (*See* Household larceny)
rates for, 27
victimization rates by age groups, 18
table, 18
Personal victimization (*See* Personal crime)
Personal vulnerabilities
demonstration of, table, 39
due to age, 40-41, 60
due to health, 41, 52, 60
due to sex, 40, 52, 60
external control and, 41-42, 160
factors in, 38, 40, 60
fear of crime due to, 56
internal control and, 41-42, 160
physical vulnerability variables, 41, 60
predictive powers of, 48, 52
psychological traits associated with, 41-42
variables of, 40, 60
Person-environment theory of fear of crime, 36-40 (*See also* Fear of crime)
basis of, 37
conceptualization two variables, 53
definition, 37
determination intercorrelation among variables, 47-48
determinants of fear, 160
dimensions of, 37, 60
empirical generalizations, 37
questions regarding, 60
environmental dimension (*See* Environmental peril)
modes of analyses, 47-48
personal dimension (*See also* Personal vulnerabilities)
predictive powers of variables, 48

variables in a fear of crime, 55-57
victimization experience (*See* Victimization experience)
Physical abuse and neglect of aged, 108, 127
  (*See also* Elder abuse)
  aspects of, 110-111
  definition, 110, 112-113
Pick-pocketing (*See* Personal larceny with contact)
Pigeon drop, description, 96
Police, 133-135, 153
  as source social service referrals, 134-135
  expectations of victim, 133
  response police to victim, 133
  study victim-police interaction, 134
Police protection of elderly, recommendation in 1971, 3
Police statistics, problems with, 12-13
President's Commission on Crime
  fear of strangers as fear of crime, 44
  work on coping with crime, 80
Price-fixing, as a form of fraud, 98
Psychological abuse of aged, 108, 109
Purse-snatching (*See* Personal larceny with contact)
Pyramid game, 99

R

Rape
  arrest rate for forcible rape, 136
  as a violent crime, 16
  definition, 17
  occurrence in public places, 21
  rate of for elderly, 16
    table, 18
  time of occurrence, 21
Rape center, 151, 154
Real estate fraud, 98-99
Restitution
  definition, 147, 154
  in Middle Ages, 147
  rationale of, 147
  use of, 148, 154
Robbery
  arrest rate for, 136
  as a violent crime, 16
  definition, 17, 94
  factors in victims surprise, 28-29
  occurrence in public places, 21
  of older victims by teenage offenders, 24

  rate of for elderly, 16
    table, 18
  time of occurrence, 21

S

Short con (*See* Bunco)
Simple assault
  as a violent crime, 16
  definition, 17
  rate of for elderly, 16
    table, 18
Social activity of aged
  conclusion studies of, 79-80
  factors inhibiting, table, 78
  involuntary isolation, 76-77
  limitations of due fear of crime, 159-160
  lonely-alone distinction, 74, 76, 77
  measurement of, 75-76
    types of, 75
  problems with studies of, 75-76
  studies fear of crime, 77-78, 89-79
Social Security fraud, 95
Social services to crime victims, 151-153
  cost per victim, 153
  early empirical data from, 152-153
  follow-up assistance, 152
    case illustration, 152
  history of, 151
  services provided, 151
  use of, 151
Street con (*See* Bunco)
Street victimization
  avoidance behavior, 87-89, 93
  conspicious protection, 87
  loss reduction, 91
  prevention of, 87-89
Surveillance, characteristics people regarding, 90-91
Switch bunco, 97

T

Target-hardening
  definition, 82
  devices for, 83, 89, 90, 93, 158
Tax-evasion, as fraud, 98
Television, cultivation hypothesis, 50-51
Theft, crimes of
  burglary (*See* Burglary)
  definitions, table 17

household larceny (*See* Household larceny)
motor vehicle (*See* Motor vehicle)
personal larceny with contact (*See* Personal larceny with contact)
personal larceny without contact (*See* Personal larceny without contact

U

Uniform Crime Report of F.D.I., 12
  as source of data, 165
  comparison National Crime Survey to, 165–166
  Crime index, 165
    changes in, 165–166
  use by mass media, 58
Unsafe
  origin of term, 34
  use of term, 34

V

Victimization
  antistreet victimization measures, 158–159
  as a process of aging, 4–5
  as a social problem, 4
  characteristics of older victims, 25, 157
    broad approach to, 4–5
    creation of, 9
    narrow approach to, 5–6
    of concepts, 9
  determinants of rates personal crimes for aged, 27
  effects of and fear of crime (*See* Victimization effects)
  examples of, 5
  household (*See* Household victimization)
  issues in, 25–29
    characteristics older victims, 25
    relative prevalence crimes, 25
    victimization in urban areas, 25–29
  life-style theory of support for, 24, 26, 157
  malleable variables in, 155–156, 172–174
  national study of, 80
    problems with, 80
  of the ages (*See* Victimization of the ages)
  older vs. younger victims, 5–6, 157
    empirical approach, 6
    normative approach, 6

ordinary crimes (*See* Ordinary crimes)
  pattern of, 27
  personal crime rates and sex of victim, 25–26, 157
  race and personal crimes, 26, 157
  rates by age groups, 16
    table, 18
  rates by types crime and age victim, table, 18
  rates for aged, 27–28
  rates for personal crimes, table, 26
  rates of by type crime, 27
  recommendations regarding, 157–162, 173–174
    elder abuse (*See* Elder abuse)
    fear of crime (*See* Fear of crime)
    fraud (*See* Fraud)
    need for society to change, 156–157
    ordinary crime victimization (*See* Ordinary crime)
    summary, 172–174
    undesirable site effects of, 156
    victim and blame, 156–157
  results of, 7
  theory of, 20–25 (*See also* Victimization theory)
  unethical acts as, 5 (*See also* Fraud)
  use of term, 31
  variance rates of among different cities, 28
  verification results studies of, 19
Victimization effects and fear of crime, 62–93
  coping and (*See* Coping with crime)
  household victimization prevention, 89–91
  impact of victimization on aged (*See* Victimization impact on aged)
  impacts fear of crime (*See* Fear on crime impacts on aged)
  street victimization prevention, 87–89, 93
  summary, 92–93
Victimization experience, 48–51
  and fear of crime, 56–57, 160
  personal experience, 48, 49, 52, 60
  types of, 48
  vicarious experience, 48, 49–50, 52, 60
    association fear of crime and, 50
    effects television programming, 50–51
    influence mass media, 50

rippling effect, 49
  victim as "star," 49-50
Victimization impact on aged, 63-69
  concepts regarding, 65-66
  conclusion of, 69
  definition, 63
  diminution of well-being, 64, 67-68
    definition, 64
  facets of well-being, 64
  financial loss, 64-65
    definition, 64
  physical injury, 64, 65
    definition, 64
  problem of, 63
  seriousness of, 66-67, 92
  studies on, 64-65
  study elderly residents in public housing,
    68-69
  sufferings of victim, 66, 67, 92
  types of, 64, 92
Victimization of the aged
  beginning interest in, 3-4
  by teenage offenders, 24
  elderly as least victimized age group, 16
  exposure to crimes and rate of, 22
  impact of victimization (*See* Victimiza-
    tion impact on aged)
  ordinary crimes (*See* Ordinary crime)
  principle of homophily and, 24
  selective victimization, 23, 24
  victimization (*See* Victimization)
Victimization rates, purpose complication,
  54
Victimization statistics, 16-20
  elderly as least victimized age group,
  16

Victimization studies (*See* Crime statistics)
Victimization survey
  analysis findings of, 23-24
  by Bureau of the Census, 13-14
  by Law Enforcement Assistance Admin-
    istration, 15
    cities surveyed, 15
    procedure used, 15
  definition, 13
  introduction of, 13
  non-reporting of crime, 13-14
  problems of, 13-14
  use interview guide, 14
  use semi-panel design, 14
  victimization statistics, 16-20
Victimization theory and the aged, 20-25
  definition, 20
  selective victimization, 23, 24
  use of, 20
Victimology
  development of, 129-130
  early emphasis of, 129
Violent crimes
  aggravated assault (*See* Aggravated as-
    sault)
  definitions, table 17
  rape (*See* Rape)
  robbery (*See* Robbery)
  simple assault (*See* Simple assault)
  trends in rates, 19-20
    table, 190

W

Work-at-home fraud, 99

AUTHOR INDEX

A

Aldous, Joan, 121, 125, 175
Alex, Nicholas, 29, 49, 52, 183
Ames, Sheila A., 4, 185
Antonovsky, Aaron, 122, 175
Antunes, George E., 23, 64, 65, 66, 67, 175, 177
Arcuri, Alan F., 133, 175
Ashton, Nancy, 149, 150, 175

B

Balkin, Steven, 20, 175
Barnett, Randy E., 147, 175
Bart, P., 115, 184
Baumer, Terry L., 40, 49, 175
Becker, Theodore M., 140, 142, 143, 178
Bell, Sharon L., 108, 112, 118, 119, 120, 176
Benyi, John, 142, 143, 149, 151, 188
Biderman, Albert D., 13, 14, 49, 54, 80, 81, 83, 175, 178
Binstock, Robert H., 76, 183
Block, Richard L., 35, 175
Blum, Richard H., 100, 102, 175
Boler, Deetze, 76, 183
Bordua, David, 44, 91, 183
Bragg, David F., 170, 176
Braungart, Margaret M., 40, 41, 42, 70, 74, 176
Braungart, Richard G., 40, 41, 42, 70, 74, 176
Brock, Anna, 108, 112, 170, 176
Brooks, James, 70, 176
Brostoff, Phyllis M., 11, 63, 134, 135, 176
Brown, Roberta B., 11, 63, 176
Butler, Robert N., 11, 20, 40, 63, 70, 74, 98, 99, 103, 176

C

Callahan, James J., Jr., 106, 109, 176
Calvin, Mary L., 143, 145, 147, 177
Cannon, Kenneth L., 121, 185
Carey, Mary, 96, 176
Carrington, Frank, 144, 176

Champlin, Leslie, 108, 109, 161, 176
Chappell, Duncan, 140, 145, 151, 179
Chen, Pei N., 108, 112, 118, 119, 120, 176
Chesney, Steve, 151, 152, 177
Christensen, Harold T., 121, 177, 180
Clarke, Alan H., 40, 75, 177
Clemente, Frank, 40, 41, 42, 46, 55, 70, 177
Clotfelter, Charles T., 86, 177
Cohen, Lawrence E., 20, 44, 177
Cohn, Ellen S., 177
Comer, Michael J., 98, 177
Conklin, John E., 12, 13, 22, 69, 81, 83, 85, 98, 177
Cook, Fay L., 3, 19, 23, 24, 64, 65, 66, 67, 175, 177
Cook, Thomas D., 19, 23, 24, 64, 65, 66, 67, 175, 177
Courlander, Michael, 36, 40, 49, 164, 184
Cramer, James A., 138, 178
Cressey, Donald R., 149, 186
Culp, Marilyn W., 143, 145, 147, 177
Cunningham, Carl L., 11, 63, 177
Curcart, Janie M., 131, 132, 185
Cutler, Stephen J., 177

D

Danowitz, Edward F., 36, 186
David, Deborah S., 36, 181
Davis, James S., 169, 177
DeFronzo, James, 91, 178
Demo, Deborah, 138, 178
Doerner, William G., 134, 141, 145, 149, 178, 181
Doob, Anthony N., 51, 178
Douglass, Richard L., 108, 112, 118, 119, 120, 180
Doyle, John, 108, 112, 118, 119, 120, 176
Droegemueller, W., 107, 181
Dubow, Frederic L., 80, 82, 83, 85, 86, 89, 91, 140, 142, 143, 178
Ducovny, Amram, 94, 98, 99, 103, 178
Duke, Janice M., 20, 183
Dunn, Moira, 108, 112, 118, 119, 120, 176
Dussick, John P. J., 151, 178

E

Ehrlich, I., 167, 168, 178
Eisdorfer, C., 182
Elley, Michael, 50, 51, 179
Elmore, Elizabeth, 96, 98, 99, 178
Ennis, Philip H., 13, 14, 49, 80, 131, 178
Erskine, Hazel, 34, 35, 40, 41, 42, 46, 178
Eustis, Nancy N., 178

F

Fairchild, Thomas, 181
Farberman, Harvey A., 187
Faulkner, Lawrence R., 109, 119, 170, 171, 172, 178
Feldman, Steven, 41, 42, 70, 182
Felton, Barbara, 181
Foner, Anne, 57, 59, 185
Fontana, Andrea, 106, 178
Franck, Karen A., 44, 184
Friedman, David M., 152, 178
Furstenberg, Frank F., Jr., 34, 35, 38, 46, 81, 83, 178

G

Galaway, Burt, 4, 130, 140, 143, 144, 145, 146, 147, 148, 149, 150, 151, 152, 153, 160, 177, 178, 180, 181, 183, 186, 188
Gaquin, Deirdre A., 15, 179
Garafalo, James, 20, 21, 22, 23, 24, 26, 37, 41, 43, 44, 46, 49, 88, 157, 179, 180
Gardiner, John A., 46, 186
Geis, Gilbert, 6, 140, 145, 150, 151, 152, 172, 179
Gelles, Richard, 107, 109, 111, 114, 115, 116, 117, 119, 120, 127, 179, 184, 186
George, Linda, 122, 123, 179
Gerbner, George, 50, 51, 179
Gil, David G., 110, 111, 114, 115, 127, 179
Glick, Rush G., 95, 96, 97, 98, 99, 179
Goldsmith, Jack, 4, 11, 40, 45, 63, 69, 70, 129, 134, 135, 152, 172, 176, 177, 178, 179, 182, 185, 186, 187
Goldsmith, Sharon S., 4, 11, 40, 45, 63, 69, 70, 129, 134, 135, 152, 172, 176, 177, 178, 179, 183, 185, 186, 187
Goldstein, Arnold P., 70, 74, 133, 145, 146, 149, 150, 176, 179, 180, 184
Goode, William, 124, 180

Gordon, Margaret T., 40, 180, 185
Gottfredson, Michael, 20, 21, 22, 23, 24, 26, 88, 130, 132, 157, 180
Gray, 162, 163
Greenberg, Jay, 178
Grieken, R. R., 122, 180
Gross, Larry, 50, 51, 179
Grossman, M., 115, 184
Gubrium, Jaber F., 32, 180

H

Hacker, George A., 4, 106, 180
Hahn, Paul H., 96, 180
Hamel, Robert, 145, 146, 149, 150, 180
Harbin, Henry T., 113, 118, 180
Harel, Zev, 181
Harland, Alan T., 149, 150, 180
Harris, Louis, 71
Hartnagel, Timothy F., 73, 75, 76, 180
Harvey, Joan, 44, 177
Haskell, Martin R., 97, 99, 180
Hayward, Scott C., 36, 186
Heath, Linda, 40, 180
Henig, Jefrey, 53, 69, 180
Hickey, Tom, 108, 112, 118, 119, 120, 180
Hill, Reuben, 121, 180
Hindeland, Michael J., 20, 21, 22, 23, 24, 26, 88, 130, 132, 157, 180
Hirsch, Paul, 51, 181
Hochschild, Arlie R., 76, 181
Holmes, T. H., 123, 181
Hooyman, Nancy R., 119, 181
House, J. S., 181
Hoyer, William J., 40, 41, 42, 70, 74, 133, 145, 146, 149, 150, 176, 179, 180, 184
Hudson, Joe, 4, 130, 140, 143, 144, 145, 146, 149, 150, 151, 152, 153, 163, 177, 178, 180, 181, 183, 186, 188
Hyman, Jeffrey M., 36, 187

J

Jackson-Beeck, Marilyn, 50, 51, 179
Janson, Philip, 46, 53, 181
Jaycox, Victoria, 46, 53, 181
Jeffries-Fox, Suzanne, 50, 51, 179
Johnson, Kirk A., 181
Johnson, Louise A., 13, 14, 49, 54, 80, 175
Johnson, Marilyn, 14, 57, 59, 185

K

Kahana, Eva, 181
Kane, Rosalie, 170, 171, 185
Kaplan, Gail, 80, 82, 83, 85, 86, 89, 91, 178
Katz, Katheryn D., 109, 119, 120, 164, 170, 171, 181
Kempe, C. Henry, 107, 181
Kennedy, John F., 36, 186
Kennedy, Leslie W., 181
Kidder, Louise H., 44, 177
Kimsey, Larry R., 170, 176
Kleiman, Michael B., 40, 41, 42, 46, 55, 70, 177
Kleinman, Paula H., 36, 181
Klingbeil, Karil, 119, 181
Kluegel, James R., 20, 177
Knudten, Mary S., 134, 141, 145, 181
Knudten, Richard D., 134, 141, 145, 181
Kosberg, Jordan I., 108, 109, 113, 114, 115, 116, 118, 119, 129, 181, 186, 187
Kutner, Bernard, 76, 187

L

Lamborn, LeRoy L., 150, 181
Land, Kenneth C., 20, 177
Lau, Elizabeth E., 108, 109, 113, 118, 181
Laub, John, 41, 43, 44, 46, 49, 179
Lavrakas, Paul J., 81, 82, 83, 85, 86, 89, 182
Lawrence, Joseph J., 43, 44, 46, 74, 183
Lawton, M. Powell, 34, 35, 37, 41, 42, 45, 46, 49, 50, 64, 68, 69, 70, 73, 75, 76, 106, 182, 183
Le Bailly, Robert K., 40, 180, 185
Lebowitz, Barry D., 41, 55, 70, 183
Lee, Gary R., 36, 40, 46, 49, 50, 183
Lejeune, Robert, 29, 49, 52, 183
Lester, David, 96, 98, 99, 133, 149, 150, 175, 178
Levine, James P., 14, 183
Lewin, Kurt, 37, 183
Lewis, Dan A., 35, 81, 82, 83, 85, 86, 89, 177, 182, 183
Lewis, Margaret J., 40, 75, 177
Liang, Jersey, 27, 157, 181, 183
Lindquist, John H., 20, 183
Liska, Allen E., 43, 44, 46, 74, 183
Lizotte, Alan J., 44, 91, 183
Lotz, Roy, 49, 50, 183

Lowenberg, David A., 146, 152, 183
Lowenthal, Marjorie F., 76, 183
Lynch, Richard P., 144, 145, 152, 183

M

Madden, Denis J., 113, 118, 180
Maness, Dal, Jr., 132, 186
Mathieu, James T., 45, 186
Maxfield, Michael G., 32, 33, 35, 42, 43, 45, 46, 49, 50, 51, 53, 54, 69, 74, 81, 82, 83, 85, 86, 88, 89, 90, 180, 183, 186
McCabe, Edward, 80, 82, 83, 85, 86, 89, 91, 178
McDonald, William F., 51, 131, 132, 134, 138, 139, 140, 141, 142, 143, 144, 145, 149, 150, 152, 178, 179, 180, 181, 183, 185, 186, 187, 188
McIntyre, Jennie, 13, 14, 49, 54, 80, 175
McPherson, Marlys, 46, 183
Meade, Anthony, 134, 141, 145, 181
Mechanic, David, 122, 183
Merry, Sally E., 31, 33, 44, 184
Mindingall, Kenneth, 36, 186
Monahan, John, 179
Monohan, 140, 145, 151
Monti, Phillip J., 70, 74, 133, 145, 146, 149, 150, 176, 179, 180, 184
Morello, Frank P., 23, 184

N

Nahemow, Lucille, 37, 41, 42, 70, 182
Nelson, Anne D., 186
Nettler, Gwynn, 94, 184
Neugarten, Bernice, 41, 184
Newman, Evelyn S., 186
Newman, Oscar, 44, 98, 99, 184
Newman, Stephen A., 184
Newsom, Robert S., 95, 96, 97, 98, 99, 179
Norton, Lee, 36, 40, 49, 164, 184

O

O'Brien, Robert M., 14, 28, 184
Ollenburger, Jane C., 40, 41, 49, 184

P

Palmer, John W., 143, 184
Patten, Sharon, 178
Patterson, Arthur H., 35, 40, 41, 42, 70, 160, 184

Pedrick-Cornell, Claire, 107, 109, 119, 184
Pleck, E., 115, 184
Pleck, J., 115, 184
Pollack, Lance M., 35, 40, 41, 42, 70, 184
Poveda, Tony G., 46, 184
Pynoos, John, 170, 171, 185

R

Ragan, Pauline K., 36, 184
Rahe, R. H., 123, 181
Rainwater, Lee, 74, 184
Rathbone-McCuan, Eloise, 107, 113, 118, 119, 120, 181, 185
Reid, Sue T., 13, 108, 130, 136, 137, 138, 142, 147, 185
Reiman, Jeffrey H., 4, 185
Reiss, Albert J., Jr., 13, 80, 130, 175, 185
Reppetto, Thomas, 22, 158, 159, 162, 185
Rifai, Marlene A. Young, 4, 6, 36, 81, 106, 177, 179, 180, 184, 185, 186
Riger, Stephanie, 40, 180, 185
Riley, Matilda W., 57, 59, 185
Robinson, Betsy, 76, 183
Rodgers, Roy H., 121, 180
Rollin, Boyd C., 121, 185
Rotter, Julian B., 41, 185
Rovine, Michael J., 36, 186
Russell, Harold F., 98, 185
Ryan, William, 156, 185
Ryder, Louise L., 46, 53, 181

S

Sacco, Vincent F., 50, 185
Salend, Elyse, 170, 171, 185
Sanchirico, Andrew, 43, 44, 46, 74, 183
Satz, Maureen, 170, 171, 185
Schafer, Stephen, 129, 140, 147, 149, 185
Schneider, Anne L., 131, 132, 140, 143, 145, 146, 151, 153, 163, 185, 186
Schneider, Carole E., 151, 152, 177
Schneider, Peter R., 140, 143, 145, 146, 151, 153, 163, 186
Sellin, Thorsten, 168, 186
Sengstock, Mary C., 27, 157, 183
Shanas, Ethel, 76, 183, 186
Sherman, Edmund A., 186
Sherman, George, 96, 176
Shotland, R. Lance, 36, 186
Signorella, Margaret L., 36, 186

Signorielli, Nancy, 50, 51, 179
Silver, H. K., 107, 181
Silverman, F. N., 107, 181
Silverman, Robert A., 107, 181
Skogan, Wesley G., 23, 32, 33, 35, 42, 43, 45, 46, 49, 50, 51, 54, 64, 65, 66, 67, 74, 82, 83, 85, 86, 89, 90, 131, 132, 175, 177, 186
Smith, A. Emerson, 132, 186
Smith, Tom W., 169, 177
Spiegel, J. P., 122, 180
Stafford, Mark, 33, 36, 40, 169, 187
Stannard, Charles I., 106, 186
Steele, B. F., 107, 181
Steinmetz, Suzanne K., 107, 111, 113, 114, 115, 116, 117, 119, 127, 164, 170, 186
Stone, Gregory P., 187
Stookey, John A., 149, 186
Straus, Karin L., 98, 99, 184
Strauss, Murray A., 111, 114, 115, 116, 117, 127, 186
Sundeen, Richard, 45, 186
Sutherland, Edwin H., 149, 186
Sykes, Richard E., 134, 135, 187

T

Tallmer, Margot, 76, 187
Tarbox, Arthur R., 170, 176
Thomas, Charles W., 36, 187
Thomas, Dorothy S., 71, 187
Thomas, Noel, 11, 63, 179
Thomas, William I., 71, 187

V

Viano, Emilio, 129, 187
Voyles, Barbara, 185

W

Ward, Russell, 56, 187
Warr, Mark, 33, 36, 40, 51, 169, 187
Wasielewski, Patricia L., 14, 181
Weir, Adrianne W., 13, 14, 49, 54, 80, 175
Weiss, Jonathan A., 98, 99, 184
Wilbanks, William, 16, 187
Williams, Kristen M., 138, 139, 187
Wilson, James Q., 187
Wilson, L. A., II, 131, 132, 134, 163, 185
Wolf, Elizabeth L., 133, 179, 180
Wolfgang, Marvin E., 140, 187

Y

Yablonsky, Lewis, 97, 99, 180
Yaffe, Silvia, 35, 41, 42, 45, 46, 49, 64, 68, 69,
    70, 73, 75, 76, 182, 183
Yin, Peter, 33, 34, 50, 53, 55, 69, 70, 71, 72,
    73, 76, 77, 78, 79, 80, 187

Young, Carlotta, 36, 186
Yunker, James, 58, 166, 167, 168, 187

Z

Ziegenhagen, Eduard A., 140, 142, 143, 149,
    150, 151, 188